20
CUSTOM DESIGNED
TRACK PLANS

BY JOHN ARMSTRONG

Editor: George Drury
Copy Editor: Mary Algozin
Art Director: Sabine Beaupré
Cover photo: Jim Forbes

KALMBACH BOOKS

Library of Congress Cataloging-in-Publication Data

Armstrong, John H.
    20 custom designed track plans / by John H. Armstrong
    p. cm. — (Model railroad handbook ; no. 44)
    Includes index
    ISBN 0-89024-191-0

    1. Railroads—Models. I. Title. II. Title: Twenty custom designed track plans.
  III. Title: Custom designed track plans. IV. Series.

TF197.A69 1994   625.1'9
                                      QBI94-799

INTRODUCTION

THE 20 TRACK PLANS in this book have been selected from a much larger number, each custom-designed to match specific spaces and prioritized model railroading goals. It may appear as though I've made up some of the room sizes and shapes to illustrate a point—or just to make you feel better about your space—but they're all real situations faced by real people.

Constraints and desires governing the development of each plan are summarized in its "Givens & Druthers" box. In selecting plans for this book I gave some preference to those that in my experience could fit within a space typical of those encountered by many would-be empire builders.

In general, these are not starter railroads, built primarily for the construction experience, operation, and enjoyment they provide en route to something bigger and better. These layouts are more in the lifetime class. They may not take a modeling lifetime to complete, but they are aimed at providing such a variety of operating pleasures and scenicking possibilities that running trains on them and embellishing them with details will be fun for a long time.

The most ambitious plans—large or complex enough that the ceremony of driving the golden spike may well be a decade or so in the future—are generally compatible with cranking up and maintaining worthwhile, enjoyable operations through several stages of construction.

Springboard custom plans

None of the railroads here are of the free-standing or island configuration appropriate for a pike planned for an undefined space or intended to be moved once or more during its lifetime. The proportion of the available space lost to the surrounding aisles with island layouts is simply so great that there is not much call for their custom design.

Since there's no such thing as a standard basement, bedroom, attic, or family room, you won't find a plan that precisely fits you. I hope, however, that these plans can serve as springboards to get you on the way to construction. Perhaps you'll adapt a basic design that fits your goals; more likely, you'll combine segments and ideas from several plans into your own dream plan.

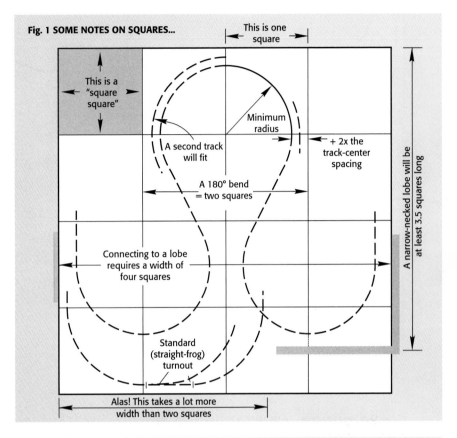

Fig. 1 SOME NOTES ON SQUARES...

This is one square

This is a "square square"

Minimum radius

A second track will fit

+ 2x the track-center spacing

A 180° bend = two squares

Connecting to a lobe requires a width of four squares

A narrow-necked lobe will be at least 3.5 squares long

Standard (straight-frog) turnout

Alas! This takes a lot more width than two squares

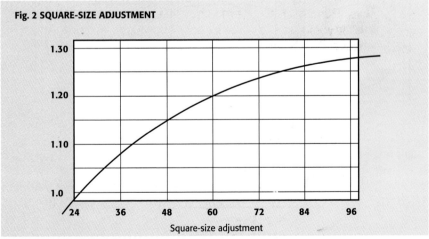

Fig. 2 SQUARE-SIZE ADJUSTMENT

Square-size adjustment

What league am I in?

Where do you look first? These plans are a mixed bag—in scales from N to O, standard and narrow gauge, short-line to transcontinental, Southern California to the Maritimes, basement to attic. They have been arbitrarily arranged in ascending order of size as measured in "adjusted square squares." Since you probably have some idea of the boundaries of the available space, the scale and gauge in which you expect to concentrate, and the minimum radius you would like to maintain, this number can be a fairly good indicator of what will fit. Rate your situation (the simple process is discussed below), and then

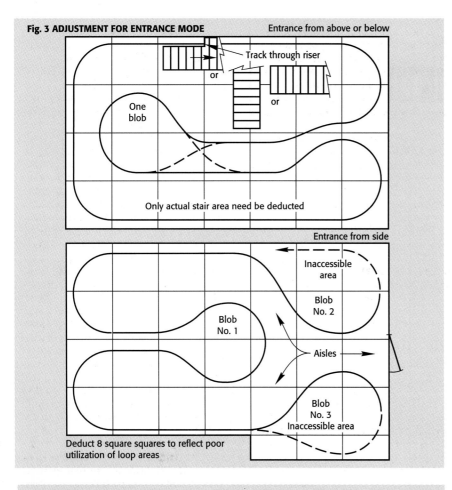

Fig. 3 ADJUSTMENT FOR ENTRANCE MODE

Entrance from above or below

Track through riser

or

or

One blob

Only actual stair area need be deducted

Entrance from side

Inaccessible area

Blob No. 2

Blob No. 1

Aisles

Blob No. 3 Inaccessible area

Deduct 8 square squares to reflect poor utilization of loop areas

Fig. 4 THESE ARE BLOBS...

"Turnback" loop

Helix

Reversing loop

...BUT THIS IS NOT...

View block

Aisle

Two separate loops of main line – all track accessible

---

pick out the plans that are in the same league for first consideration.

The basis of this arbitrary rating is the size of a "square"—the minimum radius for main-line trackage plus twice the track-center spacing, the minimum distance between adjacent tracks. This figure represents the most critical factor—the space required for the track to make a 90-degree turn. Thus, a 180-degree return bend will fit in a space two squares wide, as shown in Figure 1. Since the track-center spacing (typically 2 inches for HO, 3 inches for S scale, for example) reflects not only the scale but the gauge and the length of the governing rolling stock (the largest and least flexible equipment to be used on the layout); narrow gauge track spacing is closer than standard (though not in the same ratio as the track width), and articulated locomotives need extra room on curves. Those inches added for track-center spacing mean that a second track can make the turn within a square and that trains will not overhang the edge of the layout.

Adjusting for people and loopiness

Area can be measured in square squares—it sounds redundant, but the term is unavoidable, since our "square" is a linear dimension. What you're really interested in when you assess a particular space is its usability in comfortably accommodating railroad operations. Two adjustments to the figure turn out to be worthwhile.

The first recognizes that it is desirable to have aisleway access throughout the layout. Since people who choose to model in larger scales don't necessarily have larger waistlines, the number of square squares to be set aside for aisleways is smaller if the squares are larger. A 30-inch aisle represents more than a square for an N-scale plan with 20-inch curves, whereas the same aisle is only a half square wide if the plan is based on a typical 52-inch radius in O scale. The curve in Figure 2 is not strictly correct for radically different aisle arrangements, but it is valid for relatively conventional layout configurations. Find the size of your square along the bottom, go up to the curve, then left to the adjustment factor, and multiply the area you have measured by that factor.

A second adjustment reflects the desirability of using the entire perimeter of the area for mainline trackage that can be reached comfortably. The ultimate in efficiency would be attained if you and others could simply materialize within the wonderland. That being unlikely, at least in this millennium, next best is entry from above or below by a stairway located so that accessible trackage can run all the way around the room. Some room is occupied by the stairs, but along-the-wall space—the most valuable of all—is fully usable.

Unfortunately the most common situation is entry from the side. The political boundary between family and railroad space typically confines the tracks to one end of the basement, or entry is by way of a door—or, worse, two doors between which a passageway must be maintained. For entry from above or below, make the adjustment to the total of square squares by subtracting the actual area ruined for railroad purposes by the stairway (Figure 3). Since tracks can run under the upper part of the staircase, this adjustment is usually a matter of 2 square squares or so. For entry from the side the adjustment is an 8 square square penalty! Why this big a hit? As the sketch shows, providing walk-in access to the layout means that you must use a "blob" of space to turn back the tracks at each side of the entryway.

What is a blob and why is it bad?

Since even the biggest room is not nearly as long as you would like your main line to be, sooner or later the trains must somehow reverse direction if they are to continue their journeys. Attaining the elevations you need to reach a second deck or span a walk-under with a reasonable grade may require a loop or a multi-turn helix. Return bends, loops, and helixes have a common characteristic—they require a roughly circular chunk of real estate that we can call a "blob," to use a vague but understandable term.

Blobs are costly or otherwise undesirable for two reasons. First, they take up 4 square squares of precious space. Second, if they are located against a wall, they create an access problem; except in the tightest-radius model railroading, much of the center and rear of this area is beyond arm's length, reachable only by way of a duck-under and some sort of opening or hatch.

So if you must be able to walk into a layout from the side but you still want to drape a nice long main line around the area, there must be two blobs of track—hence an 8-square-squares penalty. A point-to-point plan can avoid the need for these turnbacks, but only larger pikes are likely to have a long enough run to make turning the trains after each trip acceptable—in which case there is probably so much space that adjusting the square-square count is purely academic.

A side entry thus appears to knock off almost a quarter of a space measuring 5 × 7 squares or so—but there may be an out. Assuming the railroad isn't strictly in the flatlands, there may be enough mainline run for the track to rise to "walk-under" height (roughly defined as an elevation where you don't have to stoop more than 6 inches or so to enter) or even "walk-in" altitude (no stooping at all). If doing so requires a helix of track, you eliminate only one of the two blobs, but you should still get back 4 square squares of the penalty.

Without a helix, a 4 × 6 square side-entry space ends up with an adjusted rating of 16 square squares, suggesting that accepting a duck-under or drawbridge entrance to the railroad is the best compromise. What is the point of this crude fine-tuning of the square-square numbers? Basically it's a way of helping you determine which plans fit within spaces that are in the same class as yours.

What space counts, anyway?

Real-world spaces often are anything but regular oblongs—they have notches and projections and even non-right-angle corners. The key factor in whether an irregular area should be counted or not is whether it is likely to be usable. As the sketch indicates, an alcove 2 squares or more wide will probably allow you to lengthen your main line and should be added to the total. A panhandle won't do anything for the main line but will be extremely useful as a site for a stub terminal and staging trackage, provided it's at least 36 inches wide—enough to accommodate a worthwhile shelf beside a railroader-width aisle. This is one place where the actual dimension rather than its equivalent in terms of squares is meaningful and should be used.

What do you do if you don't like the answer? Suppose your adjusted space comes out to 25 square squares and there's an attractive plan rated at 28? Remember that the square is basically a planning tool rather than a strait-jacket. It's a good idea to start planning with a somewhat generous radius—26 inches for an HO railroad to accommodate equipment that's at home on conventional curves (24-inch radius). In this situation, going back to 24 inches shouldn't jeopardize operations and will more than make up the difference between 25 and 28 square squares. Similarly, if your trial radius makes a long alcove come out to be 1.8 squares wide, consider rethinking the standards, if you haven't already strained the limits by using a tight radius.

Getting into the middle

Once you have a track running all the way around the area and have found your way inside the loop, it's apparent that there's territory in there that needs rail service. This brings up another critical dimension—width. Any line that curves into the center will have to start from a point at least one square from a corner. Getting it pointed into the promised land in the center will consume another square of width. If the main line is now to head back out, it will have to go around a turnback loop, unavoidably introducing a blob. Returning to the periphery of the area and continuing in the same direction will take another 2 squares of width. As Figure 6 shows, 4 squares is a critical width unless the tracks overlap. If the main line isn't to cross over itself unrealistically, one segment will have to be hidden somehow. That runs counter to the desire to have as much of the line as possible in the open where the trains can be seen and appreciated. So 4 squares is an important dimension. If a space works out to be 3.6 squares wide, for example, reconsider the minimum radius if possible.

In many track plans a simple loop into the middle and back doesn't exploit the potential of the real estate. Over the years there have been two contrasting approaches to filling such a void. In one, a series of lobes takes the main line in and out in a ribbon-candy configuration. In the other, a single spiraling peninsula leads the line around a return bend somewhere in the middle and then back out on the other side of a double-side backdrop or other view-block. The second approach provides a lot more of that desirable along-the-aisle territory because it does the job with a single blob, no matter how many turns of the spiraling peninsula makes. Since layouts almost always have an unrealistically high proportion of curved track, the great reduction in total curvature for the same length of line is another important plus. The spiral scheme also provides the longer straightaways so useful in yard design.

There are a couple of possible objections to the peninsula that spirals into the center. A train traversing the line first makes a number of turns in the same direction before going around the bend and doing the same thing in the other direction. However crooked they may be, real railroads can't do that if they're ever going to get somewhere. In practice, however, even nit-pickers seem to be oblivious to this flaw. A second matter is the amount of walking involved in moving from one side of

Fig. 5 RATING THE SPACE

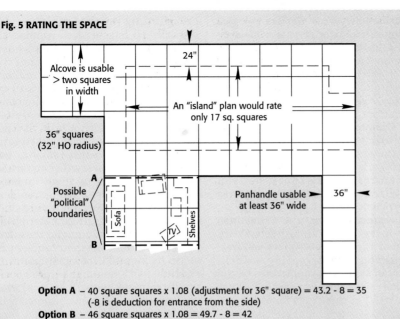

24"

Alcove is usable > two squares in width

An "island" plan would rate only 17 sq. squares

36" squares (32" HO radius)

Possible "political" boundaries

A

B

Sofa

TV

Shelves

Panhandle usable ≥ 36" wide

36"

Option A – 40 square squares x 1.08 (adjustment for 36" square) = 43.2 - 8 = 35
(-8 is deduction for entrance from the side)
Option B – 46 square squares x 1.08 = 49.7 - 8 = 42

Fig. 6 FILLING UP THE MIDDLE

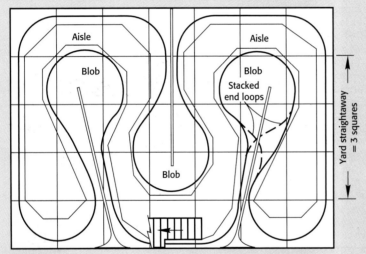

Aisle

Blob

Aisle

Blob

Stacked end loops

Blob

Yard straightaway = 3 squares

MULTI-LOBE SCHEME
Three blobs = 12 square squares (34% of overall area)
1880 degrees of curvature (5+ complete circles)

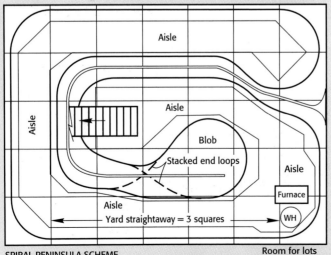

Aisle

Aisle

Aisle

Aisle

Blob

Stacked end loops

Aisle

Yard straightaway = 3 squares

Furnace

WH

Room for lots more impediments

SPIRAL PENINSULA SCHEME
One blob = 4 square squares (11% of overall area)
1330 degrees of curvature (3.5 complete circles)

the peninsula near its root to the opposite side when the objective is to retrieve a tool or whatever rather than to follow a train on its run. Including "step saver" duck-unders that provide as much headroom as possible in the benchwork planning eases this situation, which becomes more of a factor as you get older.

Reversing the consists

Real trains reach the end of the line and come back, even if their loads don't. To be practical you need an easy way to turn consists at the ends of the main line. Reversing loops are the most obvious choice; they also automatically require a blob of space. Fortunately, it is usually possible to locate one or both of them under a reverse bend so that little extra space is consumed. Some of the very longest and most scenically impressive model railroad main lines are found on plans that actually do the job with only one blob.

Layout planners have gradually become aware that one of the most important factors determining how gracefully a pike maintains its operating fascination is the capacity of its staging trackage. Birth control just doesn't work on rolling stock, and the most satisfactory way to keep varied consists rolling along the main line is to provide as much off-line, out-of-sight roosting space as possible. For greatest realism, locate as much of this as possible just beyond the points where the visible main line ends. Efficiently combining the reversing and staging function is important; a good measure of efficiency is the number of blobs it takes.

Five "end-game" candidates are shown in Figure 7. Most of them occur more than once in the plans that follow. All things considered, the reverted loop is hard to beat, especially if you can configure it so that the back-up movement is downhill and therefore can be executed reliably.

Aiming at the ultimate

Layout design is largely a matter of looking for clever and practical compromises between conflicting goals. Running the main line two or three times around the room enhances the length of the run, bringing a sense of accomplishment to the engineer and the dispatcher who cleared his way past train after train on the single track. However, the train watcher who sees No. 25 go through the same area twice in the same direction may enjoy the sight each time but will find it hard to think he's watching a railroad that goes somewhere. Putting the second lap on an upper deck can help, particularly if the layers are well separated vertically, but constructing suitable benchwork and arranging things so that both laps can be viewed comfortably is a challenge. In general, the bigger the scale, the more impressive the trains—except perhaps in number of cars. Also, the larger the layout, the easier the compromises. Notice that as the size of the track plans increases, the arrow on the "Givens & Druthers" scale that rates track and operation against scenic realism moves closer to the middle. There is no longer much reason not to have both.

How big is big enough? This isn't always the theoretical matter it seems to be when the space is already rigidly determined. Some pikes are to be built in rooms or buildings designed and built for the purpose; dimensions become a financial consideration. In many more cases, though, the room already exists and the amount of space available for the layout is to be determined in negotiations with another party. There is definite, if anecdotal, evidence that the probability of divorce is directly related to the portion of the home swallowed up by the railroad. It's important to know when further attempts to push back the political boundaries may not really be necessary for satisfying model railroading and may actually prove hazardous.

Goals

Here's a list of desirable factors (subject to some disagreement).

• It should be possible to walk along with a train throughout its run—the layout should be a walk-around railroad. All important or critical trackage (turnouts), facilities, and scenic features should be within arm's length of an aisle (no more than 27 inches). Everything topside should be within reach of some point of easy access. Popping up through a removable scenicked hatch is not considered "easy"—where do you set down the cover without mashing something?

Following a run from start to finish should not require backtracking—walking around a peninsula to catch up with the train, for example. A train should thus appear to be headed in the same direction throughout its journey. Preferably, as viewed from the aisle, eastbound trains should be going from left to right (assuming the railroad is located in the northern hemisphere), since railfans will generally want to chase the trains on the sunlit side and we are all used to maps with west to the left, east to the right.

• Trains should not pass through a scene more than once (switchbacks,

Tehachapi loops, and the like excepted, of course). Trackage on a separately scenicked deck meets this goal if the decks are far enough apart vertically to be visually separate, considering the size of the trains and the normal viewing distance—typically, 12 to 20 inches.

• Trains should be at a good viewing height for the owner—within a scenically effective range above or below the owner's eye level—standing or seated, as appropriate. Floor levels can be varied in places to help attain this goal. Multi-deck plans generally do not meet this criterion unless they are arranged (as in the mushroom scheme) so the decks are viewable from different platforms.

• The main line should be long enough to convey the impression that the railroad is going from somewhere to someplace else. Although at best highly compressed, the length of run should bear some reasonable relationship to the segment of the prototype being represented, whether scene, branch, district, or division. Most of the main line should be out in the open where it can be seen and appreciated.

• Lengths of yard, station, and passing tracks should be compatible with the train lengths to be operated, allowing (or necessitating) the doubling and saw-by maneuvers that would be used by the prototype railroad to the extent that they are fun, not tedious. Trackage and facilities for creating trains (staging tracks, turn-around loops, terminal yards) should

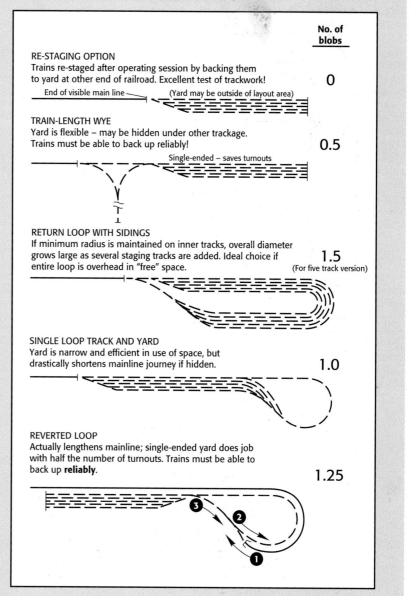

Fig. 7 "END-GAME" OPTIONS – with staging area rated by blobs

No. of blobs

RE-STAGING OPTION
Trains re-staged after operating session by backing them to yard at other end of railroad. Excellent test of trackwork!

End of visible main line

(Yard may be outside of layout area)

0

TRAIN-LENGTH WYE
Yard is flexible – may be hidden under other trackage.
Trains must be able to back up reliably!

Single-ended – saves turnouts

0.5

RETURN LOOP WITH SIDINGS
If minimum radius is maintained on inner tracks, overall diameter grows large as several staging tracks are added. Ideal choice if entire loop is overhead in "free" space.

1.5
(For five track version)

SINGLE LOOP TRACK AND YARD
Yard is narrow and efficient in use of space, but drastically shortens mainline journey if hidden.

1.0

REVERTED LOOP
Actually lengthens mainline; single-ended yard does job with half the number of turnouts. Trains must be able to back up **reliably**.

1.25

have capabilities and capacities compatible with the desired density and character of mainline traffic.

• If open-top traffic is important in the prototype, there should be a provision for continuous running so trains of loads can readily be kept moving in one direction, empties in the other.

• Branch lines and connecting railroads should be of respectable length and take a route well separated from the main line—vertically if roughly paralleling it, horizontally if heading off in a new direction.

• It should be possible to enter your railroad world comfortably, preferably without stooping at all, certainly without ducking, positively without crawling. Access should not interrupt or endanger railroad operations. In other words, a no-stoop walk-in pike is the ideal, especially as you get older; walk-under (slight-stoop) entry is a second choice; entry by duck-under or a drawbridge of some sort is a distant third choice.

Now, working within a "space budget" of adjusted square squares, how many of these goals can you expect to meet? Which layout will come closest to satisfying your desires? Some characteristics of the plans have been listed in a single (and rather formidable) table at the back of the book. The layouts are listed in ascending order of size. The columns of the table are related to those generally desirable goals that we have been kicking around; the characteristics are in yes/no form or in descriptive or numerical terms.

Access, yes!

With one exception (one of the four routes on the Santa Fe West Texas Lines layout involves a duck-under), all these plans, including the smallest, are walk-around affairs in which the engineer or railfan can follow a train from one end of its run to the other without ducking under the layout. In a few—all of them smaller than 30 adjusted square squares—lengthening the main route has meant accepting some backtracking. In all others—including several smaller than 25 square squares—the trip is uninterrupted.

Thanks to the general acceptance of double-faced backdrops and other view-blocks, all but five of the plans, including many of the smallest, are fully "sincere" in that a train passes through each scene in its journey only once per trip.

In the matter of getting into the railroad in the first place, an entry lower than about 60 inches was necessary only in two of the smallest plans (15 square squares or less) and in one larger pike with a peculiar but overriding tradeoff. All the other plans need nothing worse than a walk-under.

Compression ratio

"Compression ratio" is a fuzzy number obtained by dividing the length of the prototype railroad segment being modeled by the length of the main route in the track plan in scale miles. In general it indicates the degree to which individual features—sidings, stations, bridges, mountains—can be faithfully represented. A compression ratio of 10 or lower means the layout concentrates on a single locality, with the rest of the railroad consisting of staging trackage. In the case of completely free-lance railroads, which have no prototypes, this number is not applicable, of course. Though the compression ratio varies all over the lot from plan to plan, it doesn't have any relationship to the size of the model railroad. If twice as much space is available, it may be used to plan a closer-to-scale representation of the same piece of railroad or a condensed version of a longer territory.

How long is long?

The extent of the main route is expressed in train lengths, since that fairly well describes how long an end-to-end run will seem. The train length has been arbitrarily derived from the length of most of the sidings or yard tracks on the layout, with the assumption that train consists will be tailored to fit the railroad. Like compression ratio, this number doesn't change directly with layout size; larger pikes tend to be designed to accommodate longer trains.

The number of intermediate passing points (sidings, or on a double-track line, segments between pairs of crossovers) is some measure of the complexity (and fun) of running or dispatching a trip over the railroad. This also tends to increase only slowly as the railroad gets bigger and its trains get longer—rather than increasing the number of passing sidings, model railroaders prefer to lengthen the absurdly short distances between stations.

Staging

Having several trains offstage ready to enter the visible trackage on cue is important. Not only are operations enhanced, but having space to accommodate more rolling stock is a prime factor in lengthening the enjoyable life-span of any layout. As the table illustrates, the amount of staging trackage varies greatly from plan to plan. The good news is that even the smallest layouts can incorporate a good amount of rolling stock—in some cases two or three times the number of trains and cars that would clog all visible yards and sidings.

Gimmicks

A layout more than 12 square squares in area can meet most of the important requirements for a satisfying railroad. As the size gets up into the 20s things ease up somewhat—walk-in becomes the norm, there is room for more and better branches, and a heavy-duty, single-track line becomes more practical as the number and length of passing points increases. Layouts this size depend on including two unprototypical features of a gimmicky nature: helixes and double-decking. As is discussed in more detail in connection with Pennsylvania Railroad—Ohio River & Western plan, multi-level plans (those in which there is a second scenicked area stacked above another) not only involve some tricky engineering but ordinarily make watching the trains less comfortable and less satisfyingly realistic.

There's nothing like helixes for lifting the main line up over a doorway or getting trains from one deck to another in a minimum of space, but they do keep a lot of good track out of sight. There are ways to make helixes do triple duty by providing staging and meeting-point flexibility as well as elevation in virtually the same space. As the table indicates, the need for helixes peaks in the low 20s and tails off, except in special circumstances, as railroad size approaches 30 square squares.

By the time your space reaches 35 square squares there is little need for extensive double-decking. It is possible and practical to build a single-deck, walk-in, walk-around layout that provides a non-repetitive trip over a main line long enough to act like a railroad that goes somewhere and also provides ample staging area. Double-decking and a helix or two could make such a railroad even more extensive, but the additional enjoyment may not be proportional to the effort of adding a second deck.

CANADIAN NATIONAL AND CANADIAN PACIFIC IN NEW BRUNSWICK

Olive green, wine red, big steam, and 89-foot trilevels in a multiroute layout compressed into 13 square squares

Canadian National 4-6-2 5521, built in 1906 for Canadian Government Railways, leads the three cars of train 27 at South Devon, New Brunswick, on October 18, 1951. Photo by Kenneth S. MacDonald.

WHEN RUNNING THE longest, stiffest rolling stock is absolutely essential, but the available space puts the layout into the low teens in square squares, drastic measures are called for. True, the typical Canadian National and Canadian Pacific operations out of their joint station in Saint John*, New Brunswick, could be handled with the two railways' smaller power—nothing larger than Pacifics and Mikados. But this O scale pike must accommodate all units from the owner's

* New Brunswickers are punctilious about not abbreviating "Saint." Abbreviation is okay for St. John's, Newfoundland, but unthinkable for their largest city.

collection, including big Canadians from the West and the largest examples of big steam from south of the border. The result? A 68-inch minimum main-line radius—for planning purposes, 76-inch squares—which means there is no way two loops can fit side by side within the available width.

Scissoring the problem

The problem is that two lines must go their separate ways from a stub terminal representing the only major urban area in the province. The solution is the scissors wye, a width-saving configuration in which two legs of the wye cross each other, in this case at a comfortable 90 degrees. As shown in the schematic, the third leg of the wye not only allows consists to be turned around in one movement (at times when rearranging the cars and turning

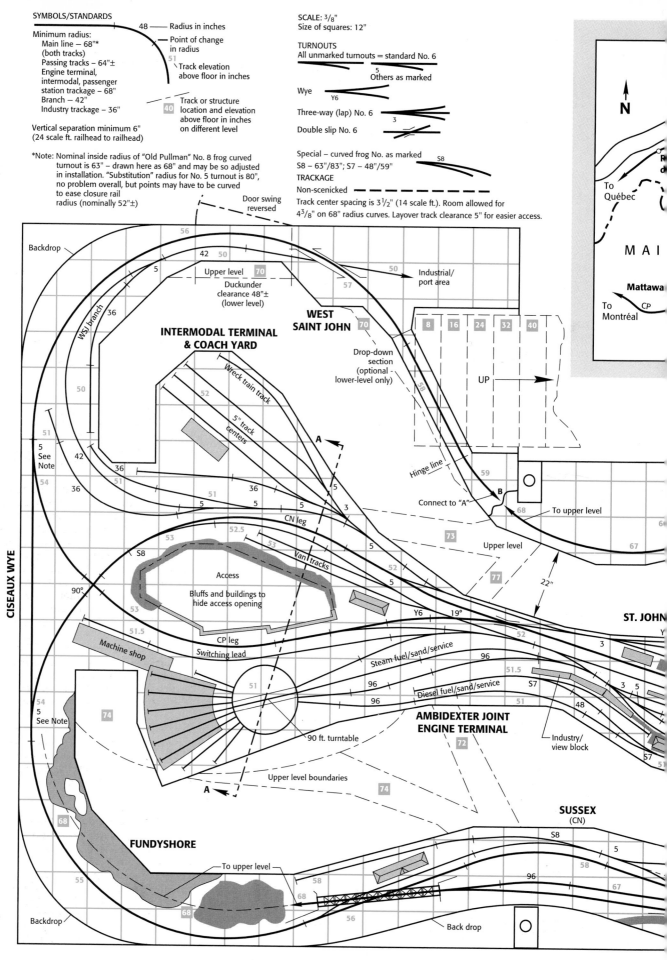

SYMBOLS/STANDARDS

Minimum radius:
Main line – 68"*
(both tracks)
Passing tracks – 64"±
Engine terminal,
intermodal, passenger
station trackage – 68"
Branch – 42"
Industry trackage – 36"

Vertical separation minimum 6"
(24 scale ft. railhead to railhead)

48 — Radius in inches
— Point of change
in radius
51 — Track elevation
above floor in inches

40 — Track or structure
location and elevation
above floor in inches
on different level

*Note: Nominal inside radius of "Old Pullman" No. 8 frog curved turnout is 63" – drawn here as 68" and may be so adjusted in installation. "Substitution" radius for No. 5 turnout is 80", no problem overall, but points may have to be curved to ease closure rail radius (nominally 52"±)

SCALE: 3/8"
Size of squares: 12"

TURNOUTS
All unmarked turnouts = standard No. 6
5 — Others as marked
Wye — Y6
Three-way (lap) No. 6 — 3
Double slip No. 6

Special – curved frog No. as marked — S8
S8 – 63"/83"; S7 – 48"/59"

TRACKAGE
Non-scenicked – – – – –
Track center spacing is 3½" (14 scale ft.). Room allowed for 4⅜" on 68" radius curves. Layover track clearance 5" for easier access.

N

MAI

To Québec

Mattawa

To Montréal   CP

Backdrop

56

42 50

Upper level 70
Duckunder
clearance 48"±
(lower level)

5

WSJ branch   36

INTERMODAL TERMINAL
& COACH YARD

Wreck train track

5" track centers

52

WEST SAINT JOHN 70

Industrial/ port area

50

57

Drop-down section (optional - lower-level only)

8 16 24 32 40

UP

50

51

See Note

54

50

42

36 36

51

36

5 5

5

CN leg

53

52.5

53

Van tracks

S8

90°

Access

Bluffs and buildings to hide access opening

A

5

3

Connect to "A"

Hinge line

59

B

68 To upper level

Upper level

73

5

52

5

77

Y6 19°

22"

ST. JOHN

Y

51.5

Machine shop

51.5

CP leg

Switching lead

Steam fuel/sand/service

96

96

Diesel fuel/sand/service

96

AMBIDEXTER JOINT ENGINE TERMINAL

96

51.5

S7

51

48

3

5

S7

Industry/ view block

72

74

51

90 ft. turntable

54

5

See Note

74

A

Upper level boundaries

68

FUNDYSHORE

55

To upper level

58

68

56

Backdrop

Back drop

74

SUSSEX (CN)

S8

5

58

96

58

67

CISEAUX WYE

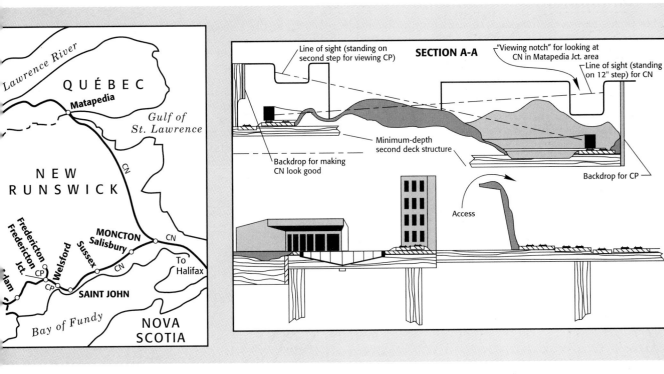

SECTION A-A

Line of sight (standing on second step for viewing CP)

"Viewing notch" for looking at CN in Matapedia Jct. area

Line of sight (standing on 12" step) for CN

Minimum-depth second deck structure

Backdrop for making CN look good

Backdrop for CP

Access

QUÉBEC

Lawrence River

Matapedia

Gulf of St. Lawrence

NEW BRUNSWICK

MONCTON
Salisbury

To Halifax

Fredericton
Fredericton Jct.
CP
Welsford
Sussex
CN
CN

CP
SAINT JOHN

Bay of Fundy

NOVA SCOTIA

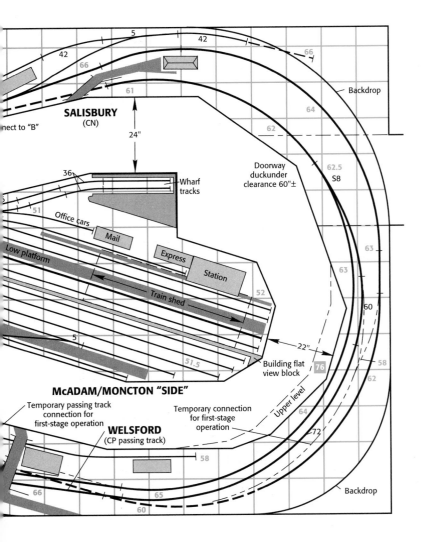

Backdrop

SALISBURY
(CN)

nect to "B"

24"

Wharf tracks

Office cars

Mail

Express

Station

Low platform

Train shed

Doorway duckunder clearance 60"±

S8

22"

Building flat view block

McADAM/MONCTON "SIDE"

Temporary passing track connection for first-stage operation

Temporary connection for first-stage operation

WELSFORD
(CP passing track)

Upper level

Backdrop

the locomotive separately is too much like work), but also serves as a bypass, providing for continuous running at some cost to realism because it involves running over both "CN" and "CP" trackage.

For the more normal out-and-back trips, an out-of-sight overhead loop with several staging tracks that can serve both roads represents a way-station layover point on purely one-railway routes. Returning to the urban area, a CN train, for example, after a run of some 300 feet from Saint John, can take the other route at the terminal throat and end up on the other side of a view-block at a small country station representing—in extremely condensed form—Moncton, the next division point on Canadian National's route to the rest of Canada. Small as it is, this "Moncton" can still turn around any reasonable consist, freight or passenger, thanks to the proximity of an engine terminal and run-around or wye trackage. If the incoming train had come over the Canadian Pacific route through Maine, the station would represent the border town of McAdam.

The duplicitous peninsula

The key to this duplicity is the extensive use of double-faced, almost zero-thickness buildings in the station area extending up above eye level (not unreasonable in O scale, where one story is about 4 inches). Why not a double-faced backdrop in the station area instead of the buildings? Well, in the throat area nearby it's desirable to

11

be able to see across the trackage to the engine terminal approaches. Working from one side, you can bring a train into Saint John, let its engine escape to the service area, and complete the arrival and rearrangement process. As cross-section A-A shows, as you get into the wye territory the access to the middle of this area—far wider than the "27-inch rule" for the maximum desirable reach from the aisle—becomes crucial. Bluffs on one side and buildings on the other can provide variety while doing the essential job of hiding the pop-up access without the nuisance of a hatch cover.

Is this a walk-in pike? Not quite. Entrance from the stairway is more of a duck-under proposition; but once inside, a continuous aisle system means no further hunching down. Is it a walk-around layout, then? Almost, but not quite. Following a CN train, for example, from the Saint John passenger platforms along its route involves walking around the peninsula to pick up the train as it swings across the CP leg of the wye and along the ocean on its way past some typical Bay of Fundy shoreline, sculpted to reflect the

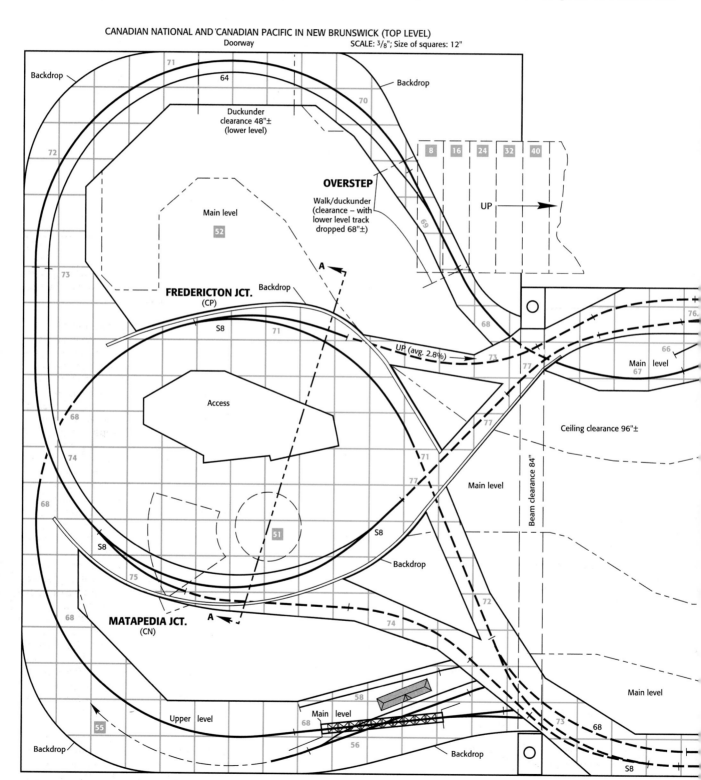

CANADIAN NATIONAL AND CANADIAN PACIFIC IN NEW BRUNSWICK (TOP LEVEL)

SCALE: 3/8"; Size of squares: 12"

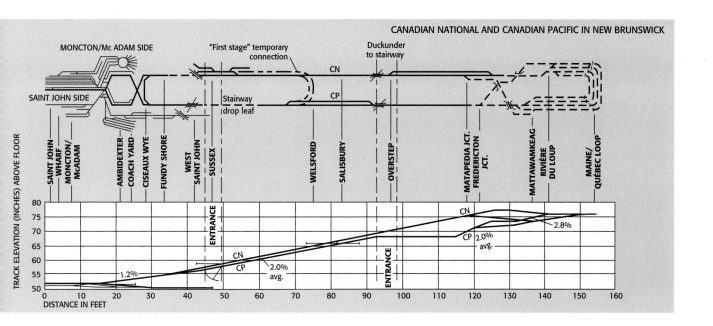

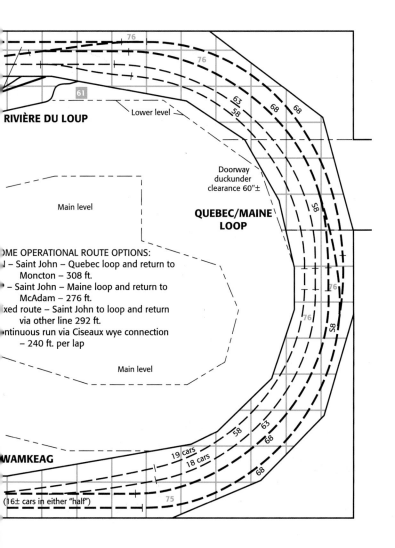

RIVIÈRE DU LOUP

Lower level

Doorway
duckunder
clearance 60"±

**QUEBEC/MAINE
LOOP**

Main level

Main level

[S]OME OPERATIONAL ROUTE OPTIONS:
[C]J – Saint John – Quebec loop and return to
Moncton – 308 ft.
[C]P – Saint John – Maine loop and return to
McAdam – 276 ft.
[Mi]xed route – Saint John to loop and return
via other line 292 ft.
[Co]ntinuous run via Ciseaux wye connection
– 240 ft. per lap

[MATTA]WAMKEAG

(16± cars in either "half")

19 cars
18 cars

world's highest tides. From there on
it's possible to follow the train's
progress up onto the upper deck
beyond Overstep until it disappears
behind a low backdrop on its way to
Matapedia Junction.

For once, a broad view

That isn't the last we see of it, however. As section A-A indicates, the
trackage through the junction is
scenicked. A carefully located viewing
notch in the backdrop completing the
companion CP scene near Fredericton
Junction provides an expansive vision
of the train as it sweeps around the
last curve before recrossing the aisle
into unscenicked, common-loop, overhead staging and layover country.

Most likely suspended from the
joists with tie rods, this trackage has
been arranged so all the turnouts are
accessible. The ruling grade (the average grade over a train-length or more
that determines the tonnage a given
locomotive can handle) getting into all
the tracks is not significantly greater
than the 2 percent required to reach
the upper deck in the first place.

Minimum vertical separation (measured railhead-to-railhead) has been
maintained at 24 scale feet (6 inches in
O scale) in deference to those high-
cubes and auto-rack cars. Stretching
the late steam era a few years to
encompass some of the most distinctive
latter-day freight equipment often
proves irresistible.

As a result, routings may not be
completely flexible. On some of the
tracks a CP train with high cars must
perforce return via the CN and vice

13

versa. Well, who says scheduling or dispatching should be a no-brainer? The fairly modest ruling grade has been selected to preclude the routine use of helper locomotives, since they are not typical in New Brunswick railroading.

How about that No. 3 priority for local-freight operations? It's a matter of taking advantage of sharper curve standards and the availability of curved turnouts to fit industry trackage into nooks and crannies wherever they are found. Doing so opens possibilities for a West Saint John branch to a wharf.

This plan fits a lot of railroading in just 13 square squares, which means that some of the construction is not simple. Several holiday seasons may go by before trains can run over all that trackage. Fortunately, a simple temporary connection makes out-and-back operation a practical first-stage proposition.

New Brunswick's summertime landscape east of Moncton is complemented by a matched set of Canadian National diesels, Montreal-built FA2 6752 and FB2 6852, and a train of baggage cars, sleepers, and a diner—train 2, the Montreal-to-Halifax Ocean Limited. CN photo.

Canadian Pacific D4g Ten-Wheeler 453 has a consist of mixed freight on its drawbar at Prince of Wales, N. B., on August 1, 1958. Photo by H. Bentley Crouch.

SANTA FE — WEST TEXAS LINES

Pullmans, doodlebugs, and mixed trains on a network of main, secondary, and branch lines compressed into an 11 × 12-foot bedroom

GP7s 2687 and 2863, wearing the black and silver they were delivered in, are ready to depart Presidio, Texas, with the biweekly freight train in April 1961. Photo by Everett L. DeGolyer, Jr.

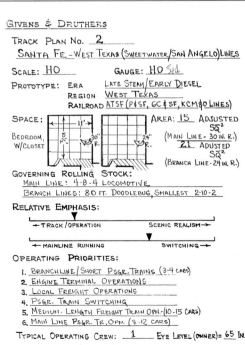

GIVENS & DRUTHERS

TRACK PLAN NO. __2__

SANTA FE - WEST TEXAS (SWEETWATER/SAN ANGELO)LINES

SCALE: HO   GAUGE: HO Std

PROTOTYPE: ERA   LATE STEAM/EARLY DIESEL
           REGION WEST TEXAS
           RAILROAD ATSF (P&SF, GC&SF, KCM&O LINES)

SPACE: AREA: 15 ADJUSTED
                                      SQ²
BEDROOM,   (MAIN LINE - 30 IN. R.)
W/CLOSET   21 ADJUSTED
                                      SQ²
                               (BRANCH LINE-24 IN. R.)

GOVERNING ROLLING STOCK:
  MAIN LINE: 4-8-4 LOCOMOTIVE
  BRANCH LINES: 80 FT. DOODLEBUG, SMALLEST 2-10-2

RELATIVE EMPHASIS:
  ←TRACK/OPERATION   SCENIC REALISM→
  ←MAINLINE RUNNING   SWITCHING→

OPERATING PRIORITIES:
  1. BRANCHLINE/SHORT PSGR. TRAINS (3-4 CARS)
  2. ENGINE TERMINAL OPERATIONS
  3. LOCAL FREIGHT OPERATIONS
  4. PSGR. TRAIN SWITCHING
  5. MEDIUM-LENGTH FREIGHT TRAIN OPN.-(10-15 CARS)
  6. MAIN LINE PSGR. TR. OPN. (8-12 CARS)

TYPICAL OPERATING CREW: __1__ EYE LEVEL (OWNER)= 65 IN.

I N THE DAYS before merg-ers brought into existence Burlington Northern, CSX, Norfolk Southern, and the enlarged Union Pacific (UP plus Missouri Pacific and Western Pacific), the Santa Fe's 13,000 miles of line was tops in the United States. It covered a big part of the West, of course, but several thousand of those miles represented an astonishing number and variety of branch lines blanketing Texas, Oklahoma, and Kansas. Thanks at least in part to state commerce commissions disinclined to allow discontinuance of even the most lightly patronized passenger-accommodating trains, motor trains (doodle-bugs) and mixed trains lasted well into the diesel era on the Santa Fe. What an opportunity for the model railroader interested in variety! Variety in rolling stock, variety in operations—and most of the consists will be authentic, even if of typical model length.

How much variety can be accommodated in a fairly small bedroom that must be entered from a hallway (of course), when the layout must also allow direct access to a closet? As the "Givens & Druthers" diagram shows, if we are talking about curves broad enough to handle mainline connecting trains with their irresistible 4-8-2s or bigger, we have only 15 square squares to work with. Adjusting this downward to see what could be done with a walk-in plan would be pointless. The best plan will be a doughnut, with a duck-under into an interior aisleway. The

Text continued on page 19.

15

SANTA FE WEST TEXAS LINES

SCALE: 1/2"
Size of squares: 12"

SYMBOLS/STANDARDS

22 ——— Radius in inches

Minimum radius:
Houston-Clovis
main line — 30"
GC&SF loop — 25"
San Angelo-Coleman — 21"
Sonora, Ft. Stockton
branches — 18"

——— Point of change
in radius

51 ——— Track elevation
above floor in inches

TURNOUTS

All unmarked turnouts = standard No. 6

Standard turnout angle as marked
5

Special turnout as marked
(Curved, curved-frog, etc.)
S 30
25

Wye (frog angle as marked)
Y4

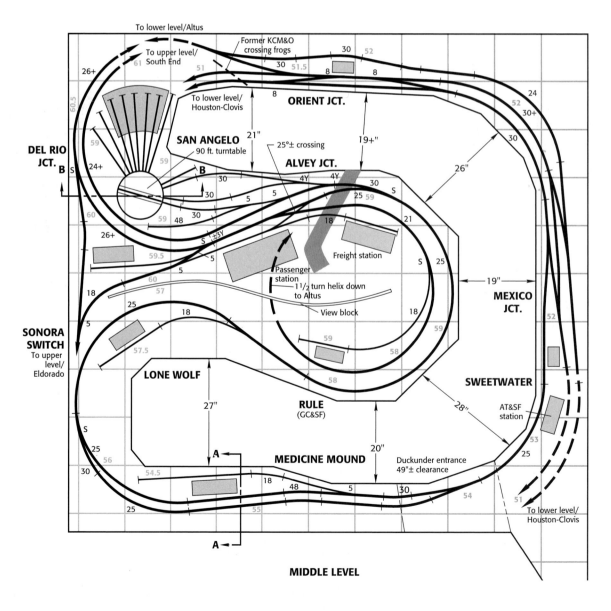

MIDDLE LEVEL

CROSS-SECTIONS

SECTION A-A

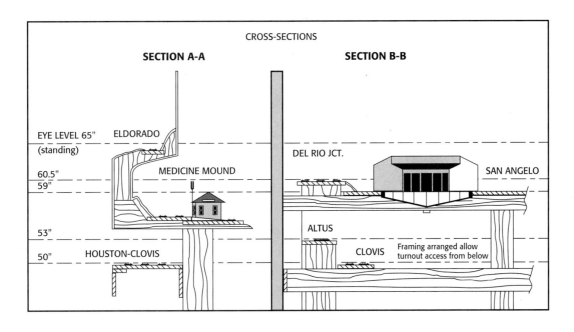

- EYE LEVEL 65" (standing) — ELDORADO
- 60.5"
- 59" — MEDICINE MOUND
- 53"
- 50" — HOUSTON-CLOVIS

SECTION B-B

- DEL RIO JCT.
- SAN ANGELO
- ALTUS
- CLOVIS — Framing arranged allow turnout access from below

SANTA FE WEST TEXAS LINES

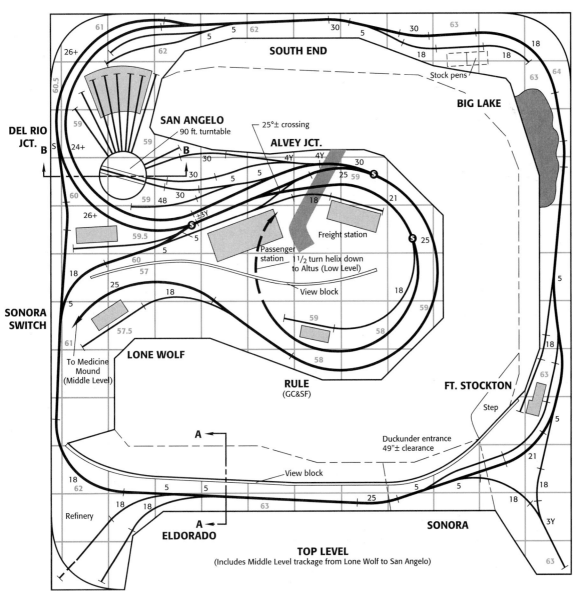

SOUTH END

61
26+
62
5 5 62 30 5 30 63
18 18 18

Stock pens

BIG LAKE
63 64

60.5

SAN ANGELO
90 ft. turntable

25°± crossing

ALVEY JCT.

DEL RIO JCT.
B S
59
24+
59
B
30
4Y 4Y
30
25 59 S
30 5 5
21
S 25

60
59 48 30
±3Y
S
5
18
Freight station

26+
59.5

Passenger station

1½ turn helix down to Altus (Low Level)

60
57
18
25
18
5

View block

59
59

SONORA SWITCH
57.5
18
58

61
To Medicine Mound (Middle Level)

LONE WOLF

58

RULE
(GC&SF)

FT. STOCKTON
Step

18
63
5

5
18
63

18
62
5 5
View block

25
5 5
21
18

18
18 18
63
Refinery

A
A
ELDORADO

25

SONORA

3Y
63

TOP LEVEL
(Includes Middle Level trackage from Lone Wolf to San Angelo)

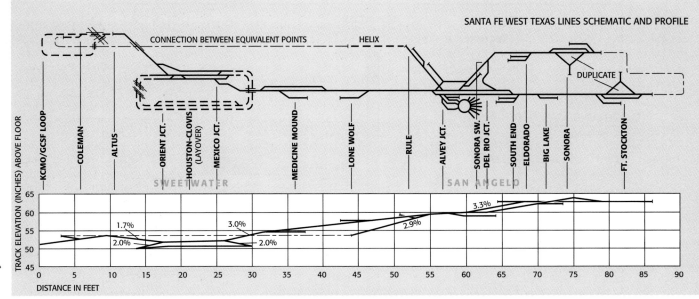

SANTA FE WEST TEXAS LINES SCHEMATIC AND PROFILE

CONNECTION BETWEEN EQUIVALENT POINTS   HELIX   DUPLICATE

KCMO/GCSF LOOP | COLEMAN | ALTUS | ORIENT JCT. | HOUSTON-CLOVIS (LAYOVER) | MEXICO JCT. | MEDICINE MOUND | LONE WOLF | RULE | ALVEY JCT. | SONORA SW. DEL RIO JCT. | SOUTH END ELDORADO | BIG LAKE | SONORA | FT. STOCKTON

SWEETWATER   SAN ANGELO

TRACK ELEVATION (INCHES) ABOVE FLOOR

1.7%   3.0%   3.3%
2.0%   2.0%   2.9%

DISTANCE IN FEET

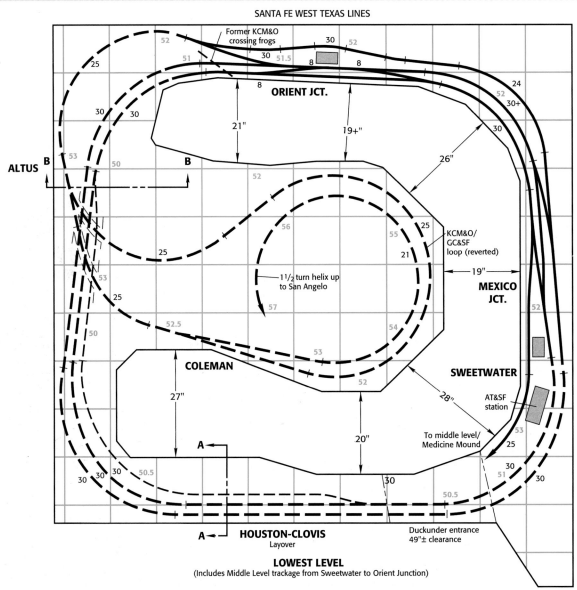

SANTA FE WEST TEXAS LINES

Former KCM&O crossing frogs

ORIENT JCT.

21"   19+"   26"

ALTUS

KCM&O/ GC&SF loop (reverted)

1½ turn helix up to San Angelo

19"

MEXICO JCT.

SWEETWATER

AT&SF station

COLEMAN

27"   20"

28"

To middle level/ Medicine Mound

A

HOUSTON-CLOVIS
Layover

Duckunder entrance
49"± clearance

LOWEST LEVEL
(Includes Middle Level trackage from Sweetwater to Orient Junction)

18

branch lines can be of smaller radius, swelling the space to about 21 square squares. That's better, but not enough to make a double-deck plan feasible, even if this railroad were in the mountains—and in the Texas panhandle it definitely isn't.

Double-duty trackage

The principal ploy in representing the operations on several Santa Fe lines in West Texas is multiple-use secluded trackage. It allows trains typical of the various lines in the Sweetwater-San Angelo area to do the right thing where they're visible, then somehow disappear and reappear in due course at the appropriate point, facing in the right direction. The result is too complicated a mess to be intelligible on any one diagram. Hence, the three separate layers are shown in three separate drawings, with some trackage shown more than once.

At the bottom is a 30-inch radius oval representing the main line from Houston, Texas, to Clovis, New Mexico. The visible station and accompanying junctions represent Sweetwater, where AT&SF subsidiaries Panhandle & Santa Fe and Gulf, Colorado & Santa Fe connect. Texas law stipulated that only companies chartered in the Lone Star State could operate railroads within its borders. Because its lines had originated at different times and places, the Santa Fe ended up with two such corporations.

In this case the distinction between Santa Fe proper and the Texas subsidiaries is imperceptible as the nightly trains pause only for a station stop (typically about 4 a.m.), and their plush Pullmans, lounges, diners, and chair cars are en route between such distant points as New Orleans and San Francisco. So no rolling stock, however modern or ponderous, is ruled out. If some locomotives positively won't negotiate 26-inch curves, they will find themselves running in the same direction for a long time. Less picky consists can be reversed by a trip around the hidden loop connecting at Orient Junction and labeled KCM&O-GC&SF.

Crossing at Sweetwater (on the middle layer of the plan) is the exotically named Kansas City, Mexico & Orient, a chronically insolvent road taken over by the Santa Fe in 1928 and represented in this era by some crossing frogs left in place after the KCM&O line toward San Angelo was integrated with Santa Fe trackage. The secondary main line to San Angelo makes its conventional-curvature way through Medicine Mound, Rule, and Alvey Junction. This is freight, motor-train, and mixed-train territory. San Angelo is the principal operating base, with a roundhouse and a 90-foot turntable but, for space reasons, only minimal yard trackage.

Hey! a Pullman!

Surprisingly, every morning a genuine passenger train hauled by a locomotive comes into San Angelo via Alvey Junction. Carrying the markers is the overnight Pullman from Houston via Brownwood. We represent this GC&SF route by a 21-inch radius, one-turn helix connected (in reverted form) with the same lowest-level loop that represents the KCM&O north of Sweetwater.

Opposite the San Angelo engine terminal is Del Rio Junction, from which a busy branch extends south (past an 18-inch-radius wye connection at Sonora Switch) through oil country at Eldorado to its terminal (with run-around siding and wye) at Sonora.

The old KCM&O line extends out the south end of San Angelo uphill past Big Lake to Fort Stockton. The fact that the wye and the run-around siding also serve as the end-of-line trackage for the Sonora branch is not as obvious as it might be because a double-faced backdrop insures that the turn-around switching must take place from opposite sides of the scene.

None of the five distinct routings represented can boast a long run, but the switching involved in making up, operating, and terminating the trains can make for a considerably more varied (and longer) "day" than you might expect in 15 or 20 square squares. For times when running and watching trains would be welcome relief from those switching chores, the fact that the two branchline terminals are the same place means that loop-to-loop operation over the longer route is a built-in possibility.

Santa Fe motor car M.186, the entire consist of San Angelo, Texas-Kiowa, Kansas, train 46, pauses at Rule, Texas, for mail on August 24, 1957. Photo by Joe R. Thompson.

BOSTON & ALBANY IN THE BERKSHIRES

Important in the history of motive power development, the scenic main line through Pittsfield provides the grades and tunnels needed to fit a lot of O-scale railroading into a 16 × 30-foot room.

WHEN THE PRIMARY objective is to represent faithfully the operations of a prototype railroad within a practical space budget, the compression ratio—the relationship between the length of a selected segment of the real thing and the scale mileage of the model main line—takes prominence.

What are reasonable, real-world compression ratios? Well, except in the case of switching or terminal pikes, they are a lot greater than 1! The longest main line in any of the plans in this book measures a little less than 8 scale miles, and such a plan represents at least 200 miles of busy Class 1 railroading, for a compression ratio of about 25—far from those 5000-to-1 ratios in the cartoons (New York to Chicago on a 4 × 8 sheet of plywood). Capturing the look and feel of a particular piece of a railroad is a lot more effective with a compression ratio in the low-double-digit range. It requires restraint in selecting the line segment to be modeled. Keeping things attrac-

tive and fun then becomes a matter of picking a chunk of the prototype where there is a lot of concentrated action and scenery as well.

In the case of the Boston & Albany—already a nice choice because its whole busy main line is only 195 miles long—this plan zeroes in on its crossing of the main ridge of the Berkshires. From the State Line tunnels (what a handy way to let the trains emerge onto the scene in 100 percent prototypical fashion) east through Pittsfield, Massachusetts, over Washington summit, and well into the Connecticut River watershed is about 25 miles. A visible stretch of O-scale main line a mile and a half or so in length certainly can't aspire to a literal, milepost-by-milepost, station-by-station depiction of the route, but it can accommodate recognizable freight and passenger consists of better-than-average length (for models), passing through equally recognizable Berkshire scenes.

Now come the mechanical details of fitting this much railroad into a converted carport measuring 16 × 30 feet. The minimum comfortable radius for an O-scale B&A Berkshire is about 48 inches; the relatively long cab-end overhang makes its appearance a bit awkward on any tighter curve. If you pick a 58-inch square as a trial figure (50-inch radius plus twice the 4-inch track centers appropriate for such curves and rolling stock), the area comes out to be only 3.3 squares wide. Bad news! No way for an around-the-wall main line to curve into the middle area and get back out again, since that takes four squares. Going to a tighter radius isn't a solution; 40 inches is just too sharp.

Third-dimension rescue

The terrain saves the situation. We're crossing the Berkshires, so part of the line can well be high enough for a second, overlapping deck. After adjustment for square size and the fact

The Berkshire on the head end is already in the rock cut at Washington, Massachusetts, but it and the pusher barely visible behind the caboose are still working hard to get their westbound Boston & Albany freight over the summit of the line. NYC photo by Ed Nowak.

GIVENS & DRUTHERS

Track Plan No. __3__

Boston & Albany R.R. - In The Berkshires

SCALE: __O__   GAUGE: Standard

PROTOTYPE: ERA Late Steam (1948)
REGION Western Massachusetts
RAILROAD Boston & Albany/New Haven

SPACE:
Converted
Car-Port
(9'6" Ceiling)

AREA: 15½ Adjusted Sq²
(50" Min. Radius)

GOVERNING ROLLING STOCK:
2-8-4, 4-8-2 Steam; 85 Ft. Passenger Cars;
Schnabel-Car Dimensional Loads

RELATIVE EMPHASIS:

← Track/Operation   Scenic Realism →

← Mainline Running   Switching →

OPERATING PRIORITIES:
1. Main-Line Psgr. Train Op'n (8-9 cars)
2. Medium-Length Fgt. Train Op'n (12-18 cars)
3. Helper-District Operations
4. Local Fgt. Operations
5. Psgr. Train Switching
6. Branch-Line Psgr. Train Op'ns

TYPICAL OPERATING CREW: __1-6*__ Eye Level (Owner) = __62 In.__
* Including 2 or 3 "Supervisory" Types

that entrance to the layout must be from a side door, the area amounts to 15½ square squares—an indication that a duck-under entrance to a walk-around aisle is the best approach, and that a helix is necessary to attain sufficient altitude for a scenically separate upper deck.

The resulting schematic shows a double-track continuous main line some 200 feet long (1.8 scale miles in O scale). Of that, 70 feet must be hidden, but elongating the helix slightly to accommodate alternating facing-point and trailing-point crossovers makes this segment ideal staging and layover space for two long trains. Thirty-car freights—heavy enough that helper service is a genuine necessity—can hide here without impeding other traffic in either direction. Though it probably won't be a critical matter, the crossovers have been arranged so a train that is comfortable only on a 54-inch curve can be routed to the outer track at all points.

Another crucial operating objective of this 1948 B&A is to accommodate representative examples of its passenger trains, including Boston sections of New York Central's "Great Steel Fleet" to the Midwest as well as milk, mail, and express peddlers in both directions. At least one more set of staging and layover tracks is necessary, along with full out-of-sight train-reversing capability, eastbound-to-westbound and vice versa.

This is where the flexibility of the reverted loop comes into play. From a single connection to the main line dipping below the helix, three single-end staging tracks tucked under Pittsfield and as long as could be desired are

accessible to all westbound trains. The trains can subsequently exit in any desired order to pass through Pittsfield and face the eastward Berkshire climb. Eastbound trains can turn into westbounds as if they had been to Boston and back via a connection sneaking off from the topside entrance to the helix. This link itself is 12 boxcars long, enough to stage a local freight or a short but respectable passenger train. More importantly, all these staging tracks are accessible from the aisles alongside, even though they are secluded and their entrances and exits are inconspicuous. (The tunnels at State Line are the only ones on B&A's main line.)

Compact complications

Railroading in the Berkshires, as shown on the map sketch, was not confined to B&A's fairly dense and varied mainline traffic. Trains from New York Central's Harlem Division came onto the B&A at Chatham, New York, stopped in Pittsfield, then branched off to North Adams, on the Boston & Maine just west of the historic Hoosac Tunnel. (The spelling on the map is correct—the line to North Adams follows the Hoosic River alongside Hoosac Mountain; a few miles northwest is the town of Hoosick Falls, New York.) Coming up the Housatonic valley through Connecticut is a New Haven line to Pittsfield important enough to rate daily diner-lounges and Friday-and-Sunday parlor-car service on its best trains.

How close can we come to providing routes that can accommodate the branch to North Adams and the New Haven line while copying actual track

arrangements and terrain? Within the segment we model is North Adams Junction, a wye connection about two miles east of Pittsfield Union Station. A small freight yard serves the branch. Nearby is the sprawling General Electric plant, source of many outsize transformer loads, some rating special "dimensional extra" handling.

Staying within arm's reach (27 inches) in O scale means you can't have a respectably tracked passenger station and a freight yard side by side. By the time a scaled-down GE plant is tucked into a corner there isn't room for more than a couple of team tracks in Pittsfield, and the junction has to go somewhere else. Since simulating operations is more important than maintaining specific track locations, the North Adams Junction wye is moved to the upper deck, where there is room for a 48-inch-radius curve that should accommodate any locomotive likely to be in pusher service. There is also room for a small stub yard, and it's possible to work in a North Adams branch that takes off over the aisle to reach an upper-level end-of-line area after a 45-foot journey without impairing the walkaround aisleway. As a feeble gesture toward the prototype, that yard near the junction is named "Pittsfield."

The North Adams branch strains reality in a couple of ways: it goes up instead of down—by virtue of the 22 years of agony spent digging Hoosac Tunnel, the Boston & Maine gets through the Berkshires at an elevation some 600 feet lower than the B&A's Washington summit—and it joins the B&M line headed east rather than west. Raising the floor two steps in this

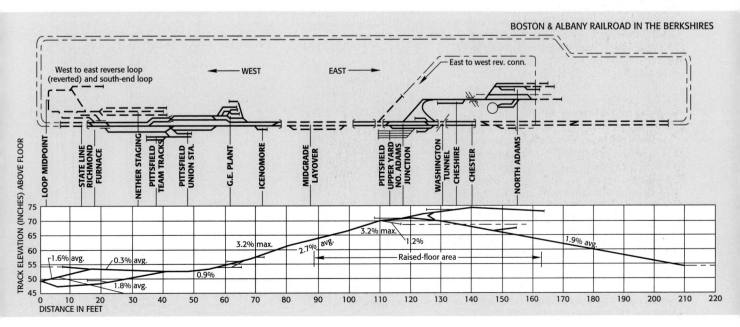

BOSTON & ALBANY RAILROAD IN THE BERKSHIRES

West to east reverse loop (reverted) and south-end loop

◄— WEST   EAST —►

East to west rev. conn.

LOOP MIDPOINT / STATE LINE / RICHMOND FURNACE / NETHER STAGING / PITTSFIELD TEAM TRACKS / PITTSFIELD UNION STA. / G.E. PLANT / ICENOMORE / MIDGRADE LAYOVER / PITTSFIELD UPPER YARD NO. ADAMS JUNCTION / WASHINGTON TUNNEL / CHESHIRE / CHESTER / NORTH ADAMS

TRACK ELEVATION (INCHES) ABOVE FLOOR

1.6% avg.   0.3% avg.   1.8% avg.   0.9%   3.2% max.   2.7% avg.   3.2% max.   2%   Raised-floor area   1.9% avg.

DISTANCE IN FEET

area mitigates the elevation problem somewhat, since this end of the aisle serves only top-level trackage. North Adams will simply have to remain backwards, as well as vastly reduced in scale, but the essential capabilities for turning passenger trains and interchanging freight remain. The B&M eliminated electrified operation through the tunnel in 1946, so our 1948 B&A must pass up the opportunity for more clearly identifying the neighbor railroad's line by hanging some catenary overhead.

The raised-floor aisleway secures the overlapping-deck advantage of complete visual separation between the upper and lower levels in the central layout area. The main line beneath North Adams is too close (7 to 12 inches) for effective scenicking. Use a few more tunnel portals to let trains sneak in and out of the dark, and add another secluded but accessible 14-boxcar-length staging track. You can never have too many!

Union Station, for real

If you drop down to 42-inch curvature and accept the presence of two dams in the Housatonic to go with a 1.8 percent railroad grade, a simple second connection from the reverted loop representing the New Haven can pop out from underneath the B&A at Richmond Furnace and enter a Pittsfield platform track in proper fashion, making it the Union Station it was in this pre-Amtrak era. Ultimately a small engine terminal with turntable will be necessary for steam operation. Fortunately, there is room in the aisle, but the engine facilities must be kept small and carefully located to retain access to the vital trackage in the rear.

The trains can now replicate the spectrum of operations in the area, including interchange between branches and main lines and the three railroads. Although part of the New York Central System, the B&A still considered itself very much its own line, with its 75-inch-drivered J-2 Hudsons sporting the full Boston & Albany name on their tenders.

How well can the model catch the flavor of its prototype? State Line tunnels are a case in point. Actually some distance west of the New York-Massachusetts state line and the settlement and junction so named, the tunnels are unique. There are two, both short. For once, the model can outdo reality. In 1948 the south (eastbound) bore still had two tracks, the outer one more a siding than a main track; the westbound hole was single track. To simulate this often-photographed situation, you can add a

BOSTON & ALBANY RAILROAD
IN THE BERKSHIRES – MAIN LEVEL

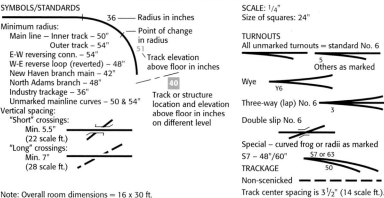

SYMBOLS/STANDARDS

36 —— Radius in inches

Minimum radius:
Main line – Inner track – 50"
Outer track – 54"
E-W reversing conn. – 54"
W-E reverse loop (reverted) – 48"
New Haven branch main – 42"
North Adams branch – 48"
Industry trackage – 36"
Unmarked mainline curves – 50 & 54"

Point of change in radius

51 — Track elevation above floor in inches

Vertical spacing:
"Short" crossings:
Min. 5.5"
(22 scale ft.)
"Long" crossings:
Min. 7"
(28 scale ft.)

40 — Track or structure location and elevation above floor in inches on different level

SCALE: ¼"
Size of squares: 24"

TURNOUTS
All unmarked turnouts = standard No. 6
Others as marked — 5
Wye — Y6
Three-way (lap) No. 6 — 3
Double slip No. 6
Special – curved frog or radii as marked
S7 – 48"/60" — S7 or 63
TRACKAGE — 50
Non-scenicked – – – – – – –
Track center spacing is 3½" (14 scale ft.).
Curves 4", to be confirmed by test.

Note: Overall room dimensions = 16 x 30 ft.

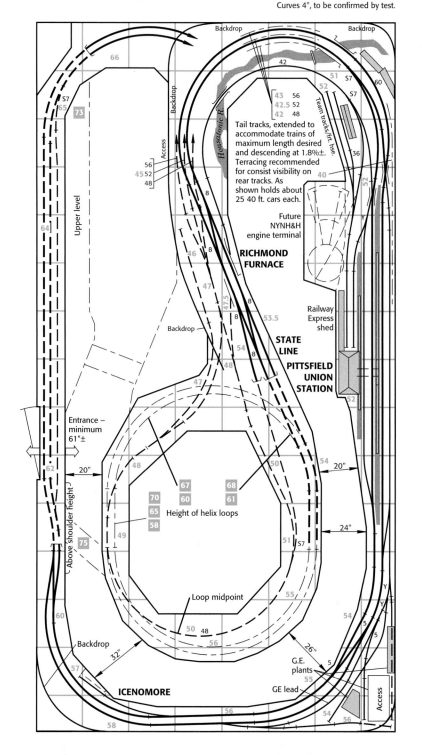

Backdrop

Backdrop

66

Backdrop

42

51

52

S7

60

Housatonic R.

S7

65

73

Access

56
45 52
48

43 56
42.5 52
42 48

Tail tracks, extended to accommodate trains of maximum length desired and descending at 1.8%±. Terracing recommended for consist visibility on rear tracks. As shown holds about 25 40 ft. cars each.

Team tracks/frt. hse.

36

Upper level

64

8

40

46   8

Future NYNH&H engine terminal

RICHMOND FURNACE

47

47.5

8

Railway Express shed

53.5

Backdrop

54

8

STATE LINE

48

PITTSFIELD UNION STATION

52

47

Entrance – minimum 61"±

62

20"

48

50

54

20"

24"

Above shoulder height

67 68
60 61

70
65
58

49

75

Height of helix loops

51   S7

Loop midpoint

55

60

50 48

56

54

54

5

Backdrop

57

32"

ICENOMORE

26"

G.E. plants

GE lead

5

5

Access

58

56

54 56

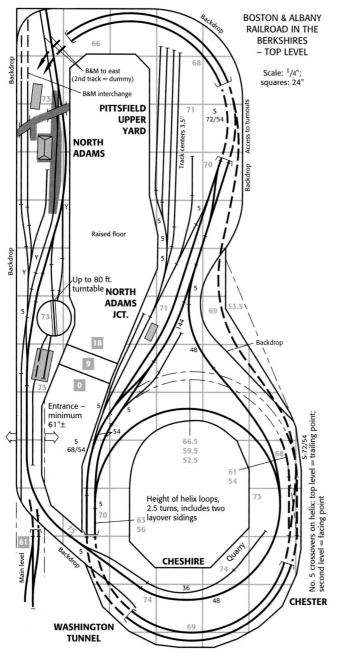

BOSTON & ALBANY
RAILROAD IN THE
BERKSHIRES
– TOP LEVEL

Scale: 1/4";
squares: 24"

redundant crossover between the two main tracks. The right-hand bore then becomes the spurious connection to the subterranean reverted loop. The deception is revealed by the actual routing of the trains, with westbounds taking the correct route only when they're en route to the turnaround loop, but is perhaps worthwhile.

Richmond Furnace was an active place in the past, with sidings and an iron works, derelict by now. There is room for a spur, but it should probably slope upward from the main track to provide extra clearance below for easy access to the key trackage at the throat of the reverted loop and its staging tracks.

To stay at comfortable elevations, there is a slight downgrade eastward from State Line rather than a continued upgrade. The exaggerated river slope should be able to disguise this. Pittsfield Union Station is on the correct side of the tracks, and there's room for a station that, though still selectively condensed, can be an impressive, larger-than-average model.

The eastbound grade must start immediately, but that's appropriate. The Pittsfield switcher gave heavy eastbound passenger trains a boost out of the station.

Icenomore is only the site of the structure that used to store ice cut from nearby ponds, though the spur is still there. Though misplaced, North Adams Junction has room for a selection of representative New England industrial, village, and yard structures while fulfilling its railroad functions. A short tunnel on the main line behind the yard provides accessible but surreptitious exit from the east-to-west reversing connection. It also conveniently fills up an area that's beyond arm's reach.

At Washington summit where the tracks start downward, another incorrect but appropriate tunnel lets the North Adams branch slip overhead after passing a quarry and milk-car siding on the other side of a slope. Least sincere are those parallel branch and main lines in the Chester/Cheshire area. They're above eye level and well separated vertically, however, and a hillock separating a pair of artfully placed groups of buildings in the space between the two lines can give the impression of two villages. The other 170 miles of the Boston & Albany are offstage—but from this sampling of the line that need never be apparent.

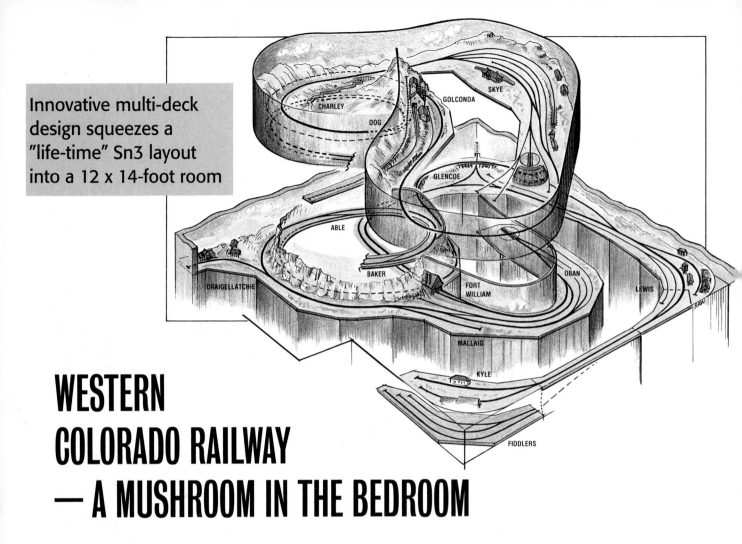

WESTERN COLORADO RAILWAY — A MUSHROOM IN THE BEDROOM

WHAT'S THE NICEST PLACE to build a model railroad? Not the usual basement, garage, or attic! The bedroom or other civilized spare room is it. With a high, finished ceiling that won't shed dirt, a temperate climate summer or winter, and a minimum of layout-height obstacles like ducts and drainpipes, it's just more comfortable. Even the floor is easier on your arches.

Assuming the family situation is such that the lease on this idyllic space won't be revoked in the foreseeable future, what's the rub? Space. The typical bedroom is on the small side for a "lifetime" layout, one that will provide detailing and operating challenges and opportunities over a substantial model railroading career. Also there's almost always a closet as far as possible from the entrance, and crawl-under access to this closet isn't acceptable.

Space utilization: 125 percent

In mitigating these difficulties, the plan for the Western Colorado Railway fits 196 square feet of top-level, "scenickable" model railroad into a room with a total floor area of 158 square feet (12 × 12 feet plus a 2 × 7-foot entryway), while maintaining a 24-inch aisle to a closet in the far corner and walkaround access to all mainline points.

The key is double-decking. With that 8-foot ceiling there's height aplenty for two decks, maintaining good headroom above the top layer and the 15- to 20-inch separation between levels desirable for independent appreciation of the separate scenes. That's nice, but how can you look at the trains from a desirable eye level on both decks? The answer is a raised floor beside the upper deck—not just a short step up, but 21 inches to match the vertical separation of the two realms. Now, if from any one point you could see only a single deck of the layout . . .

That's where the "mushroom"

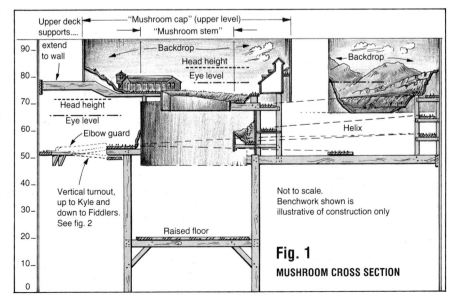

Fig. 1
MUSHROOM CROSS SECTION

Upper deck supports....

"Mushroom cap" (upper level)

"Mushroom stem"

extend to wall

Backdrop

Head height

Eye level

Backdrop

Head height

Eye level

Elbow guard

Helix

Vertical turnout, up to Kyle and down to Fiddlers. See fig. 2

Raised floor

Not to scale.
Benchwork shown is illustrative of construction only

In a setting that could inspire the West Park scene on the Sn3 Western Colorado Railway, the Denver & Rio Grande Western's *San Juan* climbs the west slope of Cumbres Pass in 1948. Photo by C. W. Hauck.

comes in. As shown in the cross-section, the raised platform in the fat "stem" of the mushroom opens up vistas of an irregular doughnut of upper-level railroad extending over the track, scenery, and aisles below. These expansive views are inside an irregular loop of freestanding backdrop—an upturned rim on the mushroom cap, if you will—that blocks any awareness of something extraneous below.

Down below is a conventional walk-in layout, equally isolated from the sights and goings-on topside—the "ground" around the mushroom stem. With the upper-deck structure just above head height and the lower-level at near-optimum viewing and comfort elevations, the mushroom averts the double-deck irritation of scrooching down for a look at the lower-deck scene and knocking your head on the upper deck when you straighten up.

But how does the railroad get from down below to up above? With a helix, of course, though that's not without drawbacks. We can minimize the drawbacks later; now we need to know more about the Western Colorado.

Laid out for modeling

Like the Western Maryland, Colorado Midland, and Clinchfield, the Western Colorado was surveyed and built with the model railroader in mind. Traversing largely vertical terrain, its steep grades, sharp curves, and heavy mineral traffic called for a lot of powerful but compact locomotives

to pull and shove fairly short trains amid almost fanciful scenery.

Kyle, the junction with the Rio Grande, was in such a confined canyon that the WC had to locate its engine terminal, main yard, and headquarters at Skye instead. It may seem an unlikely division point because it's near the summit of the main line—but so was Bluefield, West Virginia, on the Norfolk & Western, come to think of it.

Like the Uintah Railway a couple of hundred miles to the northwest, the WC connected two points at about the same elevation, but in different watersheds separated by a horrendous mountain ridge. The far end of the WC is at Oban. (Since there were no previous communities worthy of names, the determined Scottish entrepreneur who threaded the WC through some of the Western Slope's most inaccessible territory during the narrow gauge boom of the late 1800s took the liberty of tagging points on the line with appellations borrowed from Scotland.) Coal mined around Oban was of such low quality that it wasn't worth transporting over the line to outside consumers. However, it made nearby Fort William a logical place for a coal-fueled smelter to convert ore from the Castle Drum Mine at Glencoe into a refined product well worth the trip back to the Rio Grande connection at Kyle.

De-horning the helix

Now, what about minimizing those unsavory characteristics of the helix

connecting the lowland ends of the point-to-point main line with the alpine crossing of the mountain range? A helix takes considerable space: Its diameter must be a bit more than twice the minimum radius. A good part of every train's journey—at best shorter than you'd like—is out of sight and therefore uninteresting. Construction, though not as challenging as scratch-building a double-slip switch in Z scale, is something you'll enjoy more in retrospect than in the process.

As shown in the schematic and profile of the Western Colorado, you can combine several approaches to reduce the magnitude of Project Helix and to make every inch of space and foot of track give its all:

• The same helix takes the main line up the mountain and down.

• The lowest and highest turns of the helix are mostly in the open.

• Trains get off to a flying start in both directions, gaining considerable elevation before entering the corkscrew. With the 4 percent grade appropriate for this line, just two turns out of sight provide the 15 inches of additional rise necessary for comfortable separation between the decks. With a 30-inch minimum radius, the spacing between turns is a very comfortable 7½ inches. (Incidentally, the steeper the grade on a helix, the better the access for maintenance and rerailing.)

• The helix is double-tracked, not to carry dense traffic but to let it serve as a layover and staging track that

Text continued on page 28.

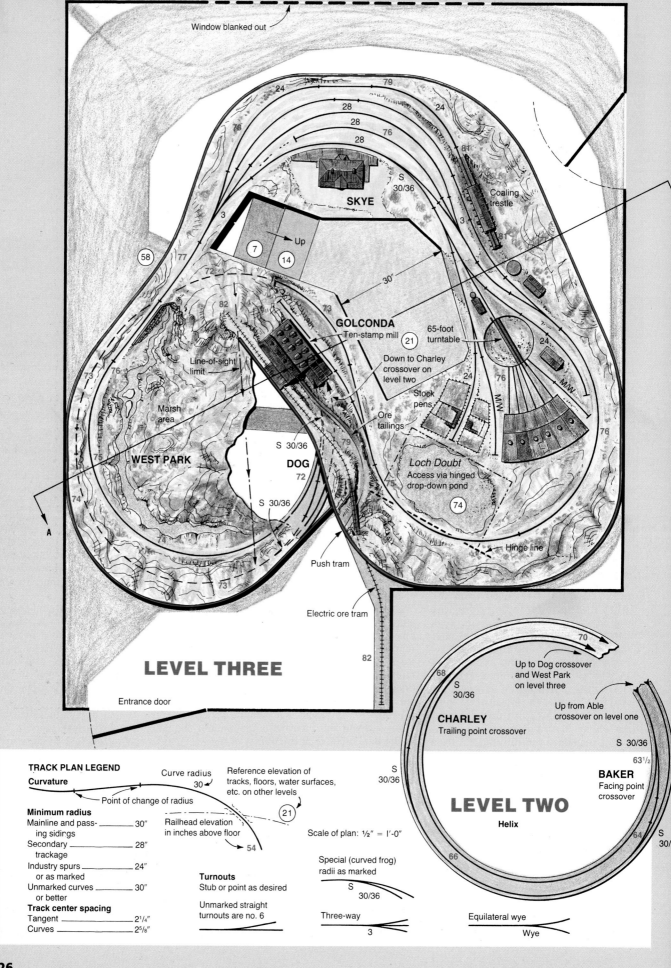

Window blanked out

24   79
28
28   24
28   76

SKYE

S
30/36

81   Coaling trestle

81

3

58   77

72

7   Up

14

30"

73   GOLCONDA
Ten-stamp mill   65-foot turntable

21   24

82   Down to Charley crossover on level two   76

Line-of-sight limit

73   76   Stock pens   24   MW   76

75   Ore tailings   MW

Marsh area

WEST PARK   S 30/36   Loch Doubt   76
Access via hinged drop-down pond

74   DOG   79   75
72

S 30/36   74

73   Hinge line

A

Push tram

Electric ore tram   82

LEVEL THREE

Entrance door

TRACK PLAN LEGEND

Curvature   Curve radius   Reference elevation of tracks, floors, water surfaces, etc. on other levels
30

Point of change of radius

21

Minimum radius
Mainline and pass-_____30"   Railhead elevation in inches above floor
  ing sidings
Secondary _____28"   Scale of plan: ½" = 1'-0"
  trackage   54
Industry spurs _____24"
  or as marked   Special (curved frog) radii as marked
Unmarked curves _____30"   **Turnouts**
  or better   Stub or point as desired   S
Track center spacing   30/36
Tangent _____2¼"   Unmarked straight turnouts are no. 6   Three-way
Curves _____2⅝"   3

70

68
S
30/36

Up to Dog crossover and West Park on level three

Up from Able crossover on level one

CHARLEY
Trailing point crossover   S 30/36

63½

S
30/36   **BAKER**
Facing point crossover

LEVEL TWO

Helix

64   S
30/3

66

Equilateral wye
Wye

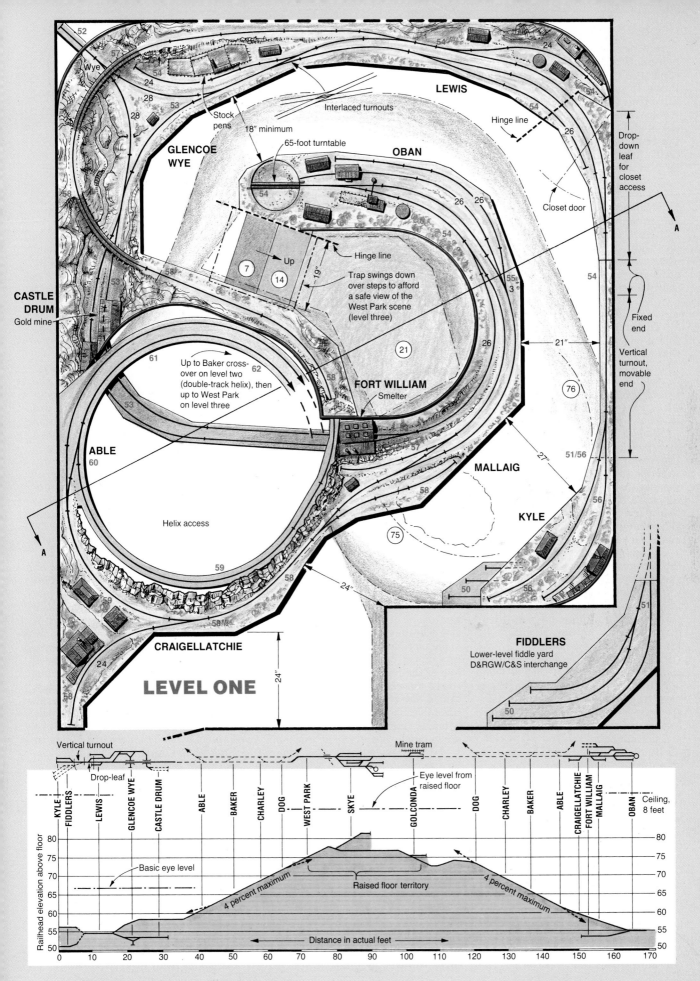

52

57

Wye

24

28

28

53

58

Stock pens

18" minimum

Interlaced turnouts

LEWIS

54

24

Hinge line

26

54

Drop-down leaf for closet access

GLENCOE WYE

65-foot turntable

OBAN

54

Closet door

26   **26**

54

CASTLE DRUM

Gold mine

53

7   Up   14

19"

Hinge line

Trap swings down over steps to afford a safe view of the West Park scene (level three)

55
3

54

Fixed end

58

61

62

Up to Baker cross-over on level two (double-track helix), then up to West Park on level three

58

21

26

21"

76

Vertical turnout, movable end

53

ABLE

60

Helix access

58

FORT WILLIAM

Smelter

57

MALLAIG

27"

51/56

KYLE

56

A

59

58

59

75

50

56

51

59

58

24"

FIDDLERS

Lower-level fiddle yard
D&RGW/C&S interchange

58 1/4

CRAIGELLATCHIE

24

24"

LEVEL ONE

50

58

Vertical turnout

Drop-leaf

Mine tram

Eye level from raised floor

Ceiling, 8 feet

Basic eye level

Raised floor territory

4 percent maximum

4 percent maximum

Distance in actual feet

Railhead elevation above floor

KYLE · FIDDLERS · LEWIS · GLENCOE WYE · CASTLE DRUM · ABLE · BAKER · CHARLEY · DOG · WEST PARK · SKYE · GOLCONDA · DOG · CHARLEY · BAKER · ABLE · CRAIGELLATCHIE · FORT WILLIAM · MALLAIG · OBAN

80 75 70 65 60 55 50

80 75 70 65 60 55 50

0 10 20 30 40 50 60 70 80 90 100 110 120 130 140 150 160 170

represents about half of the railroad's capacity for absorbing rolling stock. Properly parked behind crossovers, three trains with a total of 30 of those stubby freight cars can be in various out-of-sight stages of progress along the route without blocking mainline traffic in either direction. Trains may have to follow a wiggly route through alternating facing and trailing-point crossovers, but they can get through.

Double-tracking the helix is a bargain in terms of space. For typical radii and track centers, the extra width is less than 10 percent. Curved crossovers can make the helix a dispatching asset in only 20 percent more space than a single-track spiral.

Riding the line

To appreciate the extent to which this prosperous little road maintains Class 1 pretensions, let's take a trip on "The Limited." This train is the only first-class run on the timetable. Its twice-a-week schedule is primarily justified by traffic from the mountain resort at Oban.

Daily passenger service is provided by mixed trains. Their second-class timetable status still makes them superior to the third-class and extra freights that haul most of the ore and timber, and the WC runs the mixeds closely enough to schedule to serve the significant local passenger, express, mail, and package-freight traffic.

A well-maintained C-16 2-8-0 hauls the Limited's three cars at speeds as smart as its saucer-sized drivers and the curvature of the equally well-maintained track will permit. Like most of the Western Colorado's mainline motive power, the Consolidation is a Rio Grande hand-me-down.

Readying the train for departure is complicated by the fact that at Oban only the last couple of car-lengths of yard track and the turntable itself—the only runaround connection—are level. Everything else tilts up or down at 2 percent or worse.

By the time the Limited passes the spurs at Mallaig, the grade has stiffened to 4 percent. The passenger train, of course, needs no helper. Add a car, though, and one of the K-28 Mikados would have to be assigned.

The ascending train remains in the open, though in the shadow of the near-vertical cliffs, as it passes another spur at Craigellatchie and disappears around the bend. Like other Colorado narrow gauge lines of its era, the WC squeezes through the mountains with a minimum of tunneling. Our miniature version manages to sneak in and out of the hidden helix four times with only one exposed tunnel portal.

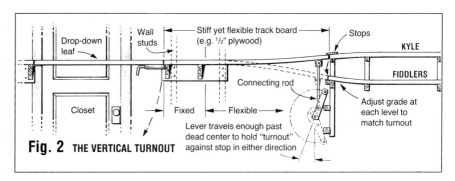

Fig. 2 THE VERTICAL TURNOUT

Drop-down leaf · Wall studs · Stiff yet flexible track board (e.g. 1/2" plywood) · Stops · KYLE · FIDDLERS · Closet · Fixed · Flexible · Connecting rod · Adjust grade at each level to match turnout · Lever travels enough past dead center to hold "turnout" against stop in either direction

Inside the helix, the Limited passes the morning mixed (which left Oban an hour earlier) and meets a train of ore from Castle Drum bound for Fort William via Oban. Out in the sunshine again but still climbing, the little train enters West Park—one of those surprisingly level spots amid the Rockies like its counterparts Estes, Middle, and South Parks east of the Divide.

West Park is beautiful, with a meandering stream below the curving track and the majestic mountain range in the distance looking almost like a painted backdrop. It's a pity the terrain is such that pioneering railfans (this is the late 1940s) found that only distant photos of the trains were practical. Rather than slog across the intervening marshland, the smart ones learned to appreciate an occasional view emphasizing the diminutiveness of the whole train dwarfed by the mountain majesties.

A lofty hub

Cresting the summit after one last stream crossing, the Limited makes its only intermediate stop at Skye, the metropolis of this lofty, remote country. The passenger station there is made more imposing by the WC corporate offices upstairs. As the operating hub of the line, Skye features the railroad's only locomotive coaling trestle and a six-stall engine house with turntable. Two turntables are ordinarily one too many to maintain, but these are manually operated—no problem.

Skye's sprawling sidings mostly hold an assortment of that irresistible narrow gauge maintenance-of-way equipment: a rotary plow, a pile driver, and a derrick, each with its own tender, water car, or idler flat. During the stock season, when cattle and sheep that summered in the surrounding high pastures are shipped to lower altitudes, the railroad must find other roosts for its nonrevenue equipment to free tracks serving the stock pens.

Yard tracks elsewhere in Skye are adequate, but just barely. Only one through track is of mainline radius, so care is in order when a Mikado ventures toward the sharper curves. A

reminder of the WC's early days is the prevalence here of stub turnouts. Point switches have replaced stubs at other places along the line, but Skye's heavy snowfall is a good argument for keeping the rail-benders: They make snow-sweeping a lot easier. Just don't try throwing a stub switch while the lead truck of a locomotive is resting on it.

Down—not quite the same way

Already starting downward, the Limited circles picturesque Loch Doubt and sweeps past the most impressive structure in the area, the ten-stamp mill at Golconda, processing ore from a hard-rock mine. Far up the hillside is an electric tram that brings raw ore from the diggings to the top story of the mill. Gravity then moves the ore through the pulverizing and concentration process. A 2-foot gauge push tram suffices to explain how the mine tailings are dumped, out of sight and mind, behind the backdrop. Mine concentrate is shipped out in WC boxcars.

Ducking into a tunnel portal a bit taller than you might expect—that pile driver rides almost 17 feet above the rail even folded and locked down—Lewis-bound trains re-enter the same helix they ascended en route to Skye. The Limited passes a train of empties bound for Glencoe and Castle Drum between Charley and Baker, and crosses over at the latter point to emerge from the helix beyond Able on the right track (the left one, in this case) to take it into Lewis. The dispatcher has to think ahead on this railroad: A misrouting at Baker would send the train back to its origin at Oban.

The rest of the trip to Lewis is also scenic. Two trestles take us over the Castle Drum Mine tracks and the Glencoe wye tail, and alongside a canyon. With no tracks hiding below, that gorge can be a deep one!

Most of the passenger are headed for the Rio Grande connection, so the Limited chuffs into a stub track at Kyle to unload the connecting passengers, then backs to Lewis, where local passengers detrain. The C-16 backs around its train, turns on the Glencoe wye, and is ready for the return trip.

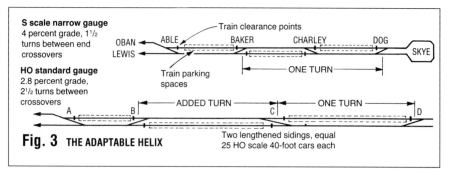

Fig. 3 THE ADAPTABLE HELIX

Lewis has no surplus of track, either, so the morning mixed that follows the Limited would have no place to disassemble itself if the Limited didn't immediately reverse to Kyle and park in the second stub track. Mixed-train patrons have plenty of time to get off at Lewis while the crew distributes its boxcars here and there, finally pushing the coach and baggage-mail car to Kyle.

What's a vertical turnout?

With relatively heavy on-line freight traffic such as the livestock and Castle Drum-Fort William ore movements, the Western Colorado isn't entirely dependent on the Rio Grande interchange. As a result of bad blood between the companies in the past, the interchange isn't at Lewis or Kyle, but an out-of-the-way set of spurs called Fiddlers. The many reefers, boxcars, and tank cars stored here could in no other way be accommodated on WC's visible tracks.

Connecting this den of mild iniquity to the main track at Lewis is a "vertical turnout"—simply a 48-inch plank (Figure 2) firmly attached to the wall at the left end and flexible enough to bend up or down to connect with either of two stacked levels. The generous vertical spacing allows hand room for fiddling with freight cars on the lower deck. There you can reconcile the size of the car roster with the capacity of

the railroad and, incidentally, convey the idea that the WC interchanged with the Colorado & Southern (during its narrow gauge existence) as well as with the Rio Grande.

It doesn't have to be Sn3

With no change to the track plan, the Western Colorado can be built as an Sn3½ railroad to make use of HO standard gauge track, wheelsets, locomotive mechanisms, and the like, with superstructures and roadbed in ³⁄₁₆-inch scale, 1:64 proportion. That would be appropriate for modeling the wilder parts of the 42-inch gauge railways found all over the world, from Newfoundland and Japan to Australia and South Africa.

What about an HO standard gauge version representing a similarly rugged route? The Colorado Midland was standard gauge and just as steep. If its financial situation had not been so precarious, and if during World War I the USRA had not first glutted it with traffic and then bypassed it altogether, it might have hung on into the more popular late-steam modeling era. Since HO standard gauge rolling stock is a half inch or so lower in height and a little narrower than Sn3 equipment, there's no question of its compatibility with the clearances and track centers.

Four percent grades are perhaps on the steep side for a more commonplace mountain short line. Adding one turn

to the helix results in a 2.8 percent grade. The 30-inch radius is luxurious in the smaller scale, and the turn-to-turn vertical separation in the helix is still 5½ inches—with reasonably shallow roadbed construction, enough for access between layers.

What about those crossovers that make the helix so useful? If this "stretch limo" helix has the same number and sequence of trailing-point and facing-point crossovers but their spacing is revised as in Figure 3, it will have the same three sidings, but two will be of double length, accommodating the longer trains that the lighter grades will encourage. Since a 30-foot Sn3 boxcar is almost the same length as a 40-foot standard gauge HO car, assembling longer trains at Oban and Lewis will test the ingenuity of the train crews.

S scalers of necessity are generally not fazed by building or commissioning those curved turnouts that make the versatile double-track helix fit the space available—straight-frog No. 5 crossovers would add 16 inches to its long axis. HO scale aficionados who want to take advantage of all the products available will realize that coming down to a 24-inch minimum radius allows the use of straight-frog No. 5s in the same length. Curved turnouts, available in HO with No. 7 frogs and 24-inch and 28-inch radii, will do the job in about 10 inches less. Those inches can be put to any number of good uses, including fitting the plan into an 11-foot room or relaxing the slopes of the often blatantly vertical scenery.

Stone-age control

How do you determine that a train has reached a parking place inside the helix when it has been out of sight for half a scale mile? This could be done with an elaborate system of optical sensors or detection circuits. There's a simpler way, however, if you're not allergic to caveman technology.

As shown in Figure 4, all it takes is a set of stopping sections at the strategic locations turned off by turnout position or (gasp!) toggle switch. Approach at something less than warp speed, and when the train stops, you know where it is. You must, of course, be sure that the train is shorter than the passing track. You could position reference markers along the right-of-way approaching the secluded tracks—again stone-age technology instead of an elegant computer program comparing the sum of the coupled lengths of each car and locomotive in the consist with the distance between clearance points—assuming no errors in keying in the engine and car numbers!

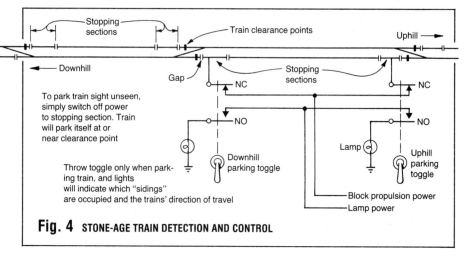

Fig. 4 STONE-AGE TRAIN DETECTION AND CONTROL

NICKEL PLATE ROAD — CONNEAUT TERMINAL

Concentration on Lake Erie terminal operations matches a variety of yard and mainline freight and passenger movements within a garage-size area ideally suited to double-decking

A high-drivered Nickel Plate Berkshire leads a fast freight west across the trestle at Conneaut, Ohio. Just beyond the left edge of the photo is Bessemer & Lake Erie's Conneaut Branch. Photo by Richard J. Cook.

REAL RAILROADS aren't double-deck—or are they? Along the south shore of Lake Erie is a mix of terrain and traffic that comes as close as you could ask to serving as a prototype for two-level model railroading! Over much of the distance between Erie, Pennsylvania, and the Cleveland-Lorain area there is an escarpment separating the narrow shore plain from higher plateau country inland. The New York Central and Nickel Plate main lines (now Conrail and Norfolk Southern) generally run along the top of this cliff. Lake ports such as Conneaut, Ohio, are located where north-flowing streams have carved their way down through the escarpment. The stream valleys provide routes for railroads such as the Bessemer & Lake Erie to approach the docks, passing under the impres-

sive trestles of the east-west main lines.

The more compact the segments of a prototype railroad represented in any layout, the less drastic the condensation it takes to cut, bend, and fit reality into the space available. The Conneaut Terminal track plan represents most of the Nickel Plate and Bessemer & Lake Erie operations in and around the port by reducing the main line trackage supporting this traffic to staging loops and out-of-sight connections.

Rampant deception below!

As detailed with great clarity in the standard reference on the subject, *The Bes-*

GIVENS & DRUTHERS

TRACK PLAN NO. _5_
NICKEL PLATE ROAD - CONNEAUT TERMINAL

SCALE: _HO_   GAUGE: STANDARD + 3 FT. TRAM

PROTOTYPE: ERA _1950-1956_
           REGION _LAKE ERIE_
           RAILROAD _NYC&STL, B&LE_

SPACE: _____   AREA _24_ ADJUSTED
2-CAR ____20'____ DOORWAY   SQ²
GARAGE ____   BLANKED   (MAIN LINE =33" R.)
(CONVERTED) ____   ____108"
           MODELING WORKSHOP CEILING
           GENERAL WORKSHOP AREA

GOVERNING ROLLING STOCK:
2-8-4, 2-10-4 LOCOMOTIVES
80' PASSENGER CARS

RELATIVE EMPHASIS:
├───────────────────▼──────────────┤
   ←TRACK/OPERATION   SCENIC REALISM→
├─────────────────────────────▼─────┤
  ←MAINLINE RUNNING   SWITCHING→

OPERATING PRIORITIES:
1. LOCAL FREIGHT (TERMINAL) OPERATIONS
2. MEDIUM-LENGTH FREIGHT TR. OPN'S (10-15 CARS)
3. ENGINE-TERMINAL OPERATIONS
4. BRANCHLINE OR SHORT PSGR. TRAINS (3-5 CARS)
5. PSGR. TRAIN SWITCHING
6. HELPER-DISTRICT OPERATIONS

TYPICAL OPERATING CREW: _1-2_ EYE LEVEL (OWNER) = 66 IN.

semer and Lake Erie Railroad, by Roy C. Beaver (Golden West Books, 1969), the Bessemer has separate coal, ore, and limestone dock facilities at Conneaut. Transshipment machinery and yards extend along a harbor dredged out from Conneaut Creek. They are similarly present—in highly condensed form, of course—in the lower-level trackage of the plan. Figuring out just how their operations mimic reality is a matter for study. But some background on B&LE traffic patterns and hints as to the subterfuges for modeling them will help you, if your curiosity should warrant trying to solve the puzzle.

Coal traffic to the boats is about equal in tonnage to iron ore coming off the lake. The hopper cars used in this ore service are of coal-carrying cubic capacity and are empty only during the brief trip from the coal dumper to the ore dock, where they are filled to the weight limit with a single skimpy pile of iron ore over each truck—because iron ore is so much denser than coal. Because real loading and unloading of all those cars is beyond the practicalities of HO model railroading, a complex pattern of routes through the receiving, coal dumper, and ore loading yards is arranged so that two sets of loaded cars—one coal, one ore—can be swapped in traditional empties-in–loads-out fashion.

Movements where cars should be empty and those where cars are moving the wrong class of load are kept out of sight with the aid of back-

Bessemer & Lake Erie's youngest 2-10-4, No. 647, built by Baldwin in 1944, starts up the 1 percent grade of the Conneaut Branch with a train of ore for the steel mills of Pittsburgh. Two more 2-10-4s are pushing on the rear of the train, down beyond the Nickel Plate viaduct. B&LE photo.

drops, ore stockpiles, buildings, and deep cuts hiding "wrong way" trackage. A third set of cars—empties—is pushed up to the coal dumper behind some hillocks. Ostensibly having been unloaded, they roll into the empties track via the kickback. From there they are moved to the ore yard, only to repeat the cycle via the "wrong way" and pull-back tracks.

In reality, B&LE traffic doesn't interchange with the Nickel Plate up above. To provide some main-line running for the ore and coal loads, however, a steep double-track helix connects the Bessemer with an NKP loop-to-

loop line via two fictitious junctions just east and west of Conneaut (Harbor Junction and Oreline Junction). Operationally, this isn't as unrealistic as it might seem. Southbound B&LE trains face a 12-mile grade to the edge of the plateau at Albion, so there is ample justification for dispatching the ore with 2-10-4s at both ends.

The accessible topside

Up above, the second deck is free to rise well above head height because of the 9-foot ceiling of the garage. It is about half division-point yard and half main line, including one of those spec-

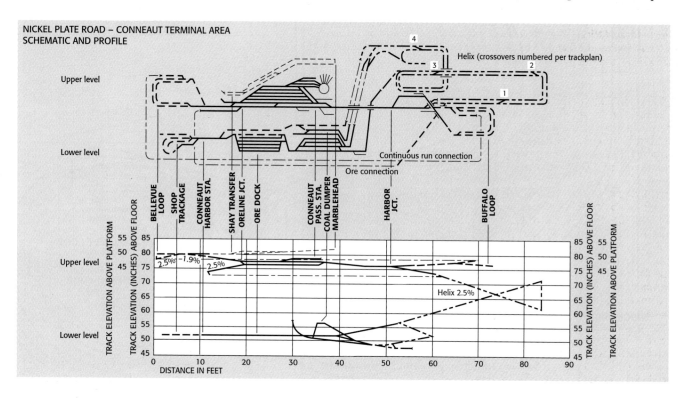

SYMBOLS/STANDARDS

Minimum radius:
- Main line – 33"
  (includes main yards)
  (S8 turnouts are approx. = 32"
  at some points)
- Restricted passing or layover tracks – 30"
- Ore & limestone dock tracks – 26"
- Industry trackage – 20"
- Unmarked curves are – 33"
- Narrow Gauge – 15"

Vertical spacing:
- "Short" crossings:
  Min. 3"
  (22 scale ft.)
- "Long" crossings:
  Min. 5.5"
  (40 scale ft.)

36 — Radius in inches
— Point of change in radius
51 ↗ Track elevation above floor in inches
40 Track or structure location and elevation above floor in inches on different level
51 Platform & elevation

SCALE: 3/8"
Size of squares: 12"

TURNOUTS
All unmarked turnouts = standard No. 6
Others as marked
Wye — Y4
Three-way (lap) No. 6 — 3
Special – curved frog No. as marked — S8
TRACKAGE
Non-scenicked – – –
Track center spacing is 2" (14.5 scale ft.).
Curves 2¹/₄", to be confirmed by test.
Helix layover trackage – 3"

tacular Nickel Plate trestles—the only area that is part of both decks scenically. Conneaut engine terminal is a busy place, since Hudsons typically handled passenger trains west to Chicago, and Pacifics east to Buffalo; NKP Berkshires and Mikados often were similarly exchanged in freight service. The 2-8-4s would fit on NKP's 90-foot turntables, but a 100-footer is specified here to accommodate the inevitable

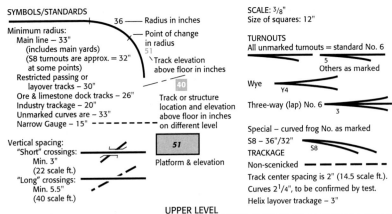

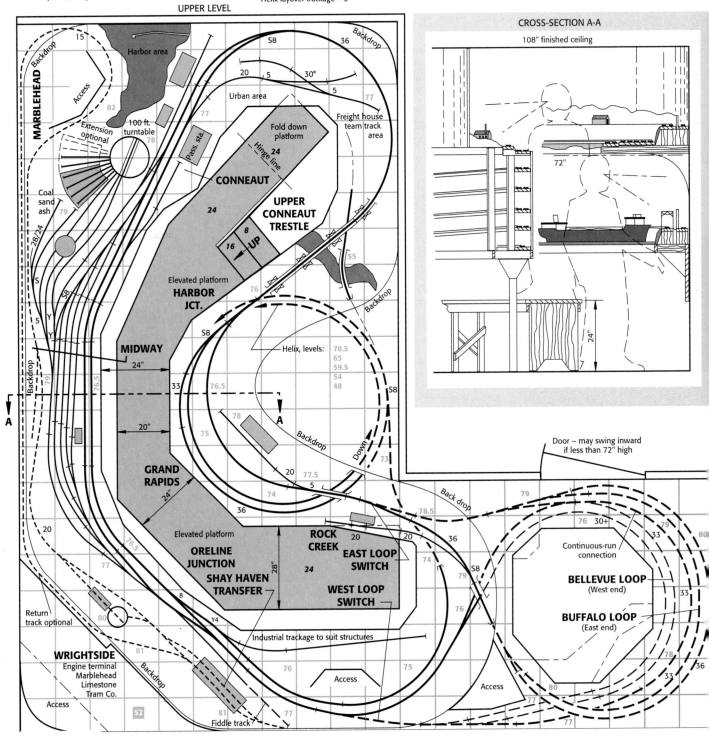

CROSS-SECTION A-A
108" finished ceiling
72"
24"

visits from Bessemer's Texas-type monsters. With the staging loops and continuous-run options provided upstairs there's no need to rotate motive power this way, but it would be a shame not to enjoy seeing both sides of the big engines as they turn on the table. B&LE passenger trains on the NKP are also logical; they reached Erie, Pennsylvania, by trackage rights on Nickel Plate's Buffalo Division.

What about that "accessibility" claim? As the cross section shows, with an upper deck above head height it is practical to have the lower-deck aisleway beneath the upper deck. This arrangement creates space for an elevated floor that provides walk-around viewing and operating for the upper level. The upper-deck structure must be shallow. Its aisle-side edge can be supported from the ceiling by steel rods, a scheme which has proven visually acceptable in practice no matter how fenced-in it may look on a drawing.

Big boats and little Shays

Ordinarily, HO scale ships are so long and high there simply isn't room for them on the layout. Here one or two waterline models, only slightly foreshortened from typical lakers of the era (450 feet instead of 600), pay their way by serving as part of the view-block you need to conceal the hopper-car exchanges on the docks.

Finally, the Marblehead Peninsula, which helps form Conneaut's sheltered harbor, was the site of limestone quarrying for many years. The rock was brought to a standard-gauge transfer by a Shay-powered narrow-gauge tram railroad. Need we say more? If the optional return track is added behind a low view-block—terrain, trees, or whatever—two circulating consists passing each other at Midway can provide the illusion of genuine transportation without the muss and fuss of actual loading and dumping. The interesting right-hand side of the locomotives can always be toward the aisle, too.

What about the New York Central, whose "Great Steel Fleet" passed through Conneaut on tracks between the Nickel Plate main and the lake shore? It is simply omitted—enough is enough. Two full decks over a 24 square square expanse can provide a lifetime of model railroading without introducing a third major railroad.

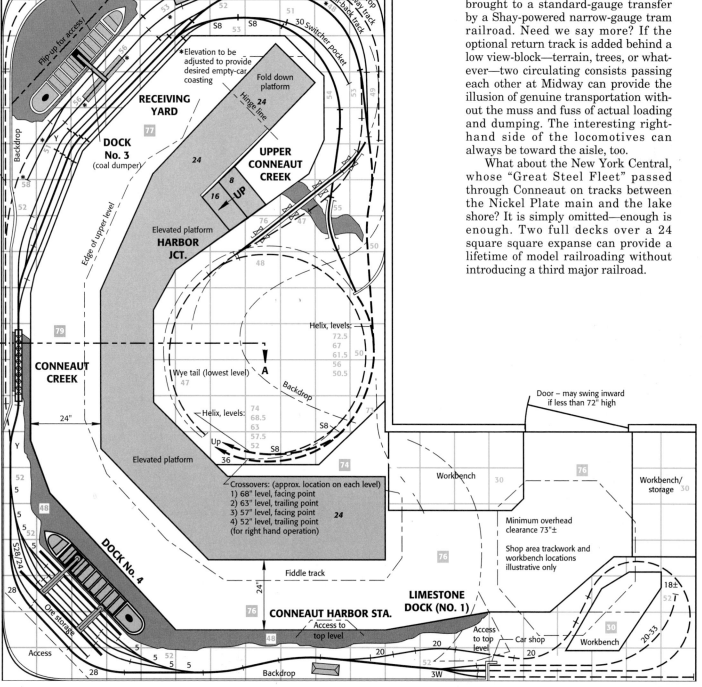

NICKEL PLATE ROAD
CONNEAUT TERMINAL AREA
LOWER LEVEL

WESTERN MARYLAND — THOMAS SUBDIVISION

Representing the grades, curves, and multi-engine coal trains of the "Wild Mary" as they connect with the main line of the "Fast Freight Line"

IF EVER A STANDARD-GAUGE railroad was an ideal prototype for model railroading, it had to be the Western Maryland. It had a variety of interesting locomotives that were kept polished, it ran a few neat local passenger trains to spice up the parade of individualistic red coal hoppers and "Alphabet Route" manifest freights, and the entire property was a paragon of maintenance.

This track plan aims at compressing the most representative WM operations and scenic features to fit an almost ideal attic room in O scale. The railroad is being built to Proto-48 standards—exact 1.177-inch track gauge matched to wheelsets maintaining the correct 5½-inch tread width and 1-inch flange depth. This does not affect the track plan directly, but it does serve as an incentive to develop a scheme displaying typical WM scenes and operations with a minimum of false notes.

The welcome spiral staircase

In evaluating the space in this specially finished attic room, it is unnecessary to deduct for an entrance from the side or even for a conventional stairway. The hole for a prefabricated steel spiral staircase to provide access will occupy only 2 square squares at most. A trapdoor large enough for sheets of plywood will be important during the construction phase (and quite possibly in emergencies later on), but it can be located so most of its area will be in an aisleway. One side of the ceiling slopes, but about 29 square squares are available within the area with at least 60-inch clearance so there should be no need to suffer the width-versus-height tradeoff that comes with trying to stretch attic layouts. With a ceiling height of 8 feet elsewhere, double-deck possibilities are rampant.

The Thomas Subdivision, extending down from Cumberland to the coal-marshaling capital of Elkins, West Virginia, had curves sharper than 20 degrees in several places. The largest locomotives permitted were the massive H-9 Consolidations. In O scale you can comfortably accommodate the big 2-8-0s on 42-inch main-track curves and squeeze them around 38-inch curves on some secondary trackage. The only locomotives with trailing trucks in this territory were small Pacifics hauling passenger trains of two and three cars. The freight trains were mostly long drags of 32-foot, 50-ton hoppers interspersed with 2-8-0s whose short cab overhang blended nicely with their 12-wheel tenders on any curve.

Grades to the rescue

To mitigate the problems of double-deck pikes (one deck is too low, the other is too high, and it takes a helix to get up there), this version of the WM locates top-of-the-divide Thomas, West Virginia, in the cap of the mushroom scheme. Around the stem down below are the yards of Cumberland, Maryland. Here a scissors wye connects with an around-the-room oval representing the railroad's main line between Hagerstown, Maryland, and Connellsville, Pennsylvania. As shown in the profile, there is enough mileage in the wrapped-around route to get

One of WM's enormous Decapods boosts a westbound freight around Helmstetter's Curve, a few miles west of Cumberland, Maryland. Photo by Stanwood K. Bolton.

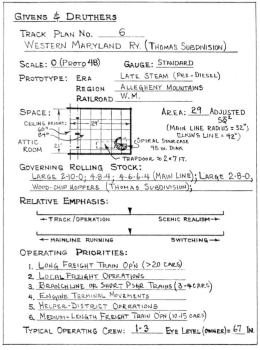

GIVENS & DRUTHERS

TRACK PLAN NO. 6
WESTERN MARYLAND RY. (THOMAS SUBDIVISION)

SCALE: O (PROTO 48)   GAUGE: STANDARD

PROTOTYPE: ERA   LATE STEAM (PRE-DIESEL)
           REGION   ALLEGHENY MOUNTAINS
           RAILROAD   W.M.

SPACE: AREA: 29 ADJUSTED
CEILING HEIGHT: 60", 84"   5 □²
          29'   (MAIN LINE RADIUS = 52";
ATTIC   ELKINS LINE = 42")
ROOM   21'   (SPIRAL STAIRCASE
                48 IN. DIAM.)
          TRAPDOOR ≈ 2×7 FT.

GOVERNING ROLLING STOCK:
LARGE 2-10-0; 4-8-4; 4-6-6-4 (MAIN LINE); LARGE 2-8-0;
WOOD-CHIP HOPPERS (THOMAS SUBDIVISION);

RELATIVE EMPHASIS:

←TRACK/OPERATION   SCENIC REALISM→

←MAINLINE RUNNING   SWITCHING→

OPERATING PRIORITIES:
1. LONG FREIGHT TRAIN OP'N (>20 CARS)
2. LOCAL FREIGHT OPERATIONS
3. BRANCHLINE OR SHORT PSGR TRAINS (3-4 CARS)
4. ENGINE TERMINAL MOVEMENTS
5. HELPER-DISTRICT OPERATIONS
6. MEDIUM-LENGTH FREIGHT TRAIN OP'N (10-15 CARS)

TYPICAL OPERATING CREW: 1-3   EYE LEVEL (OWNER) = 67 IN.

from Elkins up to Thomas with a 4 percent slope—not much of an exaggeration of the prototype's 3.05 percent Blackwater Fork grade. Coming back down, a single Tehachapi-style loop lets the line descend to Cumberland at 2.5 percent. This slope is considerably steeper than the long 1 percent grade that trains of WM empties climb back to the mines, but it is still gentle enough to let westbound trains do the job with far fewer helpers.

Scenically, however, the line from Fairfax down past the dam at William and on to Wolf Den is treated in entirely non-Tehachapi fashion, with a view-blocking ridge separating two scenes along the Potomac. Here and elsewhere, WM's profusion of tunnels makes such deception practical.

The mushroom design raises the floor level from which the upper deck is visible, thus keeping the viewer's eye-level in sync with the scene. On the theory that rural, out-on-the line scenes are best seen from a somewhat lower vantage point than yard trackage, the floor rises only about two-thirds as much as the main line does (12 inches vs. 18 to 20 inches). This theory is subject to revision on the basis of the way things actually look; in practice, revision means raising the platform higher than the suggested 12 inches. In any case, it's clear that the Thomas area is in a world of its own, far removed from both Elkins and Knobley Yard below.

Open-tops come first

In the interest of simulating as wide a variety of Western Maryland traffic patterns as is practical, the schematic is relatively complex—and confusing if only casually explored.

Since coal is definitely king on the Thomas subdivision and important on the main line as well, priority is given to loads-out–empties-back operations. The cars are not actually loaded and unloaded. Instead, cuts and trains of matching hopper cars with and without coal are shuttled over routings that conceal the return trip. Since the main line up Sand Patch toward Connellsville is also represented in the plan and there are plenty of mines up there as well, there are extensive possibilities for mineral traffic in addition to the basic Elkins-Knobmount-Hagerstown circulation. The Thomas area is a major source of loads to fill out trains that have made it up the hill from Elkins.

As did the WM, the layout has two yards in the "Queen City of the Alleghenies"—Knobmount, a cramped "rider" hump yard (it has no retarders; men ride the cars and control their speed with hand brakes) for classifying coal coming east from Elkins, and Ridgely, a flat yard primarily for main-line traffic. Both are served by a single engine terminal. The engine terminal at Maryland Junction is the heart of the operation, with almost every train changing motive power—giant 2-10-0s and 4-6-6-4s toward Connellsville and 4-8-4s for the east. There is a 120-foot turntable to handle any locomotive, including those for which the 48-inch curve of the third leg of the wye may be too sharp. Engine service trackage outside the roundhouse is limited; fortunately, helper-engine assignments will keep the large stable of 2-8-0s away from Cumberland most of the time.

Post-1930 mainline passenger service consisted of coach-only locals between Baltimore, Hagerstown, Cumberland, and Elkins. A backing maneuver is necessary to get Baltimore-Cumberland trains in and out of the impressive Cumberland station.

An eastbound bias

Past the north wye switch the Connellsville Extension is well represented by a double-track, 3.0 percent ascent (not seriously out of scale with the 1.8 percent of the prototype). It brings helper-assisted freights through the single-track bottleneck of Big Savage tunnel into capacious staging and layover trackage and a return loop. Comfortably overhead, this yard also serves as a concealed source of coal loads for the mine at Sand Run.

As is the case with the Black Fork Grade line, this trackage is not scenicked as a second, overlapping deck until it has risen far enough above the line below (14 inches or so) to assume a separate identity. Ultimate separation between decks is in a comfortable 18- to 22-inch range.

It wouldn't be WM's Sand Patch Grade without the photogenic, wide-sweeping arc of track known as Helmstetter's Curve. Since this track, unfortunately, must turn left instead of right, the model is named Stetterhelm's Curve.

Westbound mainline trains eventually round the Connellsville loop and come back down into Cumberland as eastbounds. A scenic trip past Ridgely Yard and through Knobley tunnel leads to a fair sampling of the twelve Potomac River crossings of the line east to Hagerstown; secluded trackage through the Baltimore & Ohio connection at Big Pool leads back to the north wye switch. With no equivalent loop to

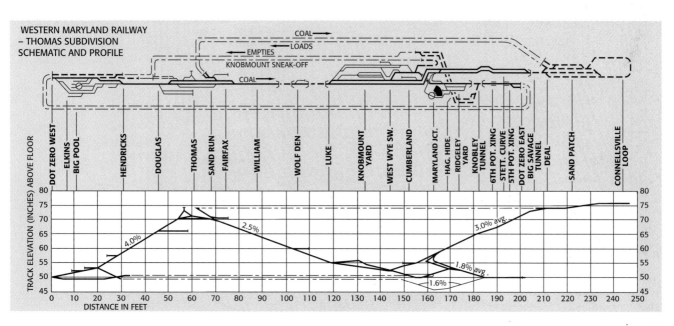

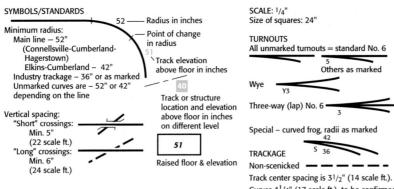

SYMBOLS/STANDARDS

Minimum radius:
Main line – 52"
(Connellsville-Cumberland-Hagerstown)
Elkins-Cumberland – 42"
Industry trackage – 36" or as marked
Unmarked curves are – 52" or 42" depending on the line

Vertical spacing:
"Short" crossings:
Min. 5"
(22 scale ft.)
"Long" crossings:
Min. 6"
(24 scale ft.)

52 — Radius in inches

Point of change in radius

51 — Track elevation above floor in inches

40 — Track or structure location and elevation above floor in inches on different level

51 — Raised floor & elevation

SCALE: 1/4"
Size of squares: 24"

TURNOUTS
All unmarked turnouts = standard No. 6
Others as marked 5
Wye Y3
Three-way (lap) No. 6 3
Special – curved frog, radii as marked 42
S 36

TRACKAGE
Non-scenicked – – – – –
Track center spacing is 3 1/2" (14 scale ft.).
Curves 4 1/4" (17 scale ft.), to be confirmed by test.

return a train to westbound status, balancing traffic is a matter of using the Hagerstown hideaway trackage to keep westbounds from going up Sand Patch prematurely and occasionally bringing orbiting eastbounds into Ridgely for dismemberment and turnaround. It's worth the trouble to get both Black Fork and Sand Patch into one attic.

LOWER LEVEL

HAGERSTOWN HIDEAWAY

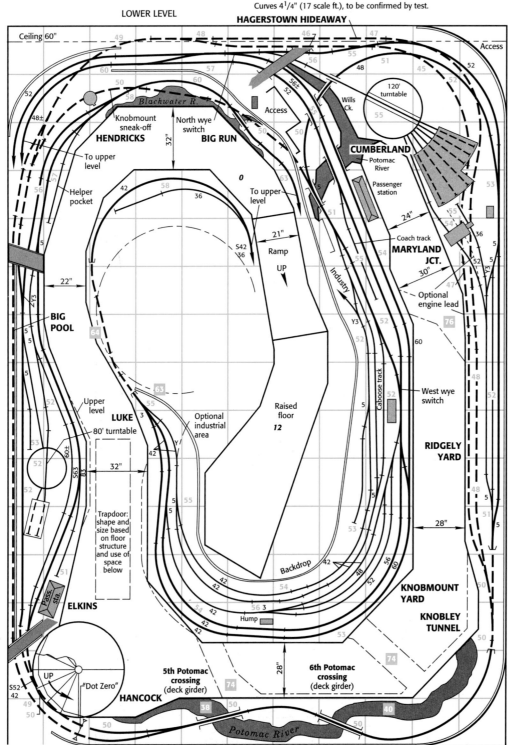

Ceiling 60"
Access
Knobmount sneak-off
HENDRICKS
North wye switch
BIG RUN
Blackwater R.
Access
Wills Ck.
120' turntable
CUMBERLAND
Potomac River
Passenger station
To upper level
Helper pocket
To upper level
Ramp
UP
MARYLAND JCT.
Coach track
Optional engine lead
BIG POOL
West wye switch
LUKE
80' turntable
Upper level
Optional industrial area
Raised floor 12
Caboose track
RIDGELY YARD
Trapdoor: shape and size based on floor structure and use of space below
ELKINS
Pass. sta.
"Dot Zero"
HANCOCK
UP
5th Potomac crossing (deck girder)
6th Potomac crossing (deck girder)
Backdrop
Hump
KNOBMOUNT YARD
KNOBLEY TUNNEL
Potomac River

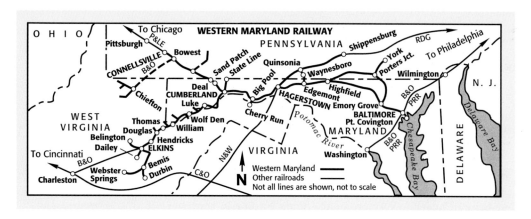

WESTERN MARYLAND RAILWAY

To Chicago · Pittsburgh · Bowest · CONNELLSVILLE · P&LE · B&O · OHIO · PENNSYLVANIA · Sand Patch · State Line · Quinsonia · Shippensburg · RDG · To Philadelphia · Waynesboro · York · Porters Jct. · Wilmington · Chiefton · Deal · CUMBERLAND · Luke · Big Pool · Big Pool · HAGERSTOWN · Edgemont · Highfield · Emory Grove · B&O PRR · N.J. · WEST VIRGINIA · Thomas · Douglas · William · Wolf Den · Cherry Run · Potomac River · BALTIMORE · Pt. Covington · Belington · Dailey · Hendricks · ELKINS · MARYLAND · B&O PRR · Delaware Bay · DELAWARE · To Cincinnati · B&O · Bemis · Durbin · Washington · Chesapeake Bay · Charleston · Webster Springs · C&O · N&W · VIRGINIA

Western Maryland ———
Other railroads ———
Not all lines are shown, not to scale

N

UPPER LEVEL

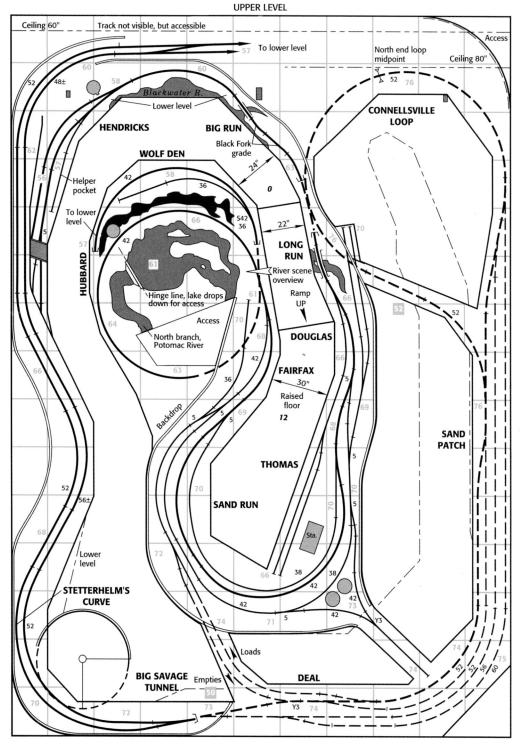

Ceiling 60" — Track not visible, but accessible — Access
North end loop midpoint — Ceiling 80"
To lower level — 57
CONNELLSVILLE LOOP
Blackwater R. — Lower level
HENDRICKS — BIG RUN
Black Fork grade
WOLF DEN
Helper pocket
To lower level
HUBBARD
Hinge line, lake drops down for access
Access
North branch, Potomac River
LONG RUN
River scene overview
Ramp UP
DOUGLAS
FAIRFAX
Raised floor
THOMAS
SAND RUN
SAND PATCH
Sta.
Backdrop
Lower level
STETTERHELM'S CURVE
Loads
BIG SAVAGE TUNNEL — Empties
DEAL

SANTA FE — ALTUS DISTRICT

Representing 70 miles of light-traffic railroad with a walk-in plan in less than 30 square squares

IN THE EARLY PART of this century entrepreneur Arthur Stilwell undertook the formidable task of building a new railroad from Kansas City to the Pacific Ocean port of Topolobampo, in the Mexican state of Sinaloa. The Kansas City, Mexico & Orient would be the shortest railroad from Kansas City to any harbor on the coast—1,659 miles. It was underfinanced and had little on-line traffic to nourish it as it pushed southwest from Wichita, Kansas, across Oklahoma into the desert country of the Texas panhandle. The Mexican revolution destroyed much of the two disconnected sections of the KCM&O in that country. The Orient scraped along from receivership to receivership until 1928, when the Santa Fe purchased it. The U. S. portion of the line extended from Wichita, Kansas, through San Angelo, Texas, to Alpine, Texas; the Mexican portion, which Santa Fe immediately sold, later became the nucleus of the Chihuahua-Pacific Railway.

This plan represents one of the more interesting sections of the old

Orient as it operated in the 1940s—a very secondary Santa Fe line in territory considerably pepped up by recent oil discoveries but still retaining a definite Wild West flavor. Walk-in access from the side leaves only 29 square squares available for the layout. The inclusion of several intermediate stations in the 67 miles between Clinton and Altus, Oklahoma, requires some doubling back to fit a fairly long main line into an E-shaped layout. The payoff is a walk-in, no-stoop railroad—at the cost of some initial confusion in following a train around the continuous-run main line.

Plenty of connections

Passenger service on the Orient line consists of a motor train (doodlebug) making a daily run over the 508 miles from Wichita to San Angelo at a respectable average of 31 mph, including a 25-minute lunch stop at Altus—"not Fred Harvey service," the Santa Fe warns. On the schematic, it comes out of a short "doodlebug haven" track in the staging and layover trackage

that must represent both ends of the main line. A reasonable simulation of the grain and stock rushes requires as much secluded staging capacity as is practical. Taking the right-hand route at semi-hidden Ewing, the gas-electric enters Clinton, taking the connection to the Panhandle & Santa Fe so that it can back down First Street to the station. (The Orient station was torn down shortly after the Santa Fe took over.) The gas-electric uncouples the trailing coach and leaves it in the middle of First Street while it sets out a baggage car of mail and express from Kansas City.

First Street station in Clinton is not exactly a hotbed of passenger traffic. The only trains are the doodlebug and a P&SF mixed train to Pampa, Texas. The mixed offers at best a leisurely 6-hour connection with the doodlebug schedule. The P&SF line was opened between 1910 and 1912 as far west as Cheyenne, Oklahoma, by the Clinton & Oklahoma Western; it was extended to Pampa in 1929 by the P&SF. It is provided for by a mostly

Santa Fe 2-8-0 No. 2509, photographed near Lugert, Oklahoma, was a former New York Central engine, purchased secondhand by the KCM&O and acquired along with the railroad in 1928. AT&SF photo by Preston George.

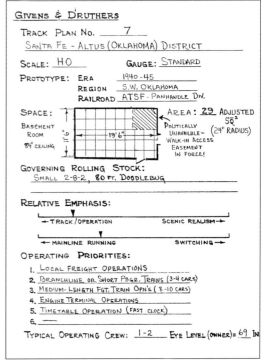

GIVENS & DRUTHERS

TRACK PLAN NO. ___7___

SANTA FE - ALTUS (OKLAHOMA) DISTRICT

SCALE: HO   GAUGE: STANDARD

PROTOTYPE: ERA   1940-45
             REGION   S.W. OKLAHOMA
             RAILROAD   ATSF-PANHANDLE DIV.

SPACE: AREA: 29 ADJUSTED SQ²
BASEMENT ROOM   POLITICALLY UNAVAILABLE - (24" RADIUS)
8'4" CEILING   19'6"   WALK-IN ACCESS EASEMENT IN FORCE!

GOVERNING ROLLING STOCK:
SMALL 2-8-2, 80 FT. DOODLEBUG

RELATIVE EMPHASIS:
← TRACK/OPERATION   SCENIC REALISM →
← MAINLINE RUNNING   SWITCHING →

OPERATING PRIORITIES:
1. LOCAL FREIGHT OPERATIONS
2. BRANCHLINE OR SHORT PSGR. TRAINS (3-4 CARS)
3. MEDIUM-LENGTH FGT. TRAIN OPN'S (8-10 CARS)
4. ENGINE TERMINAL OPERATIONS
5. TIMETABLE OPERATION (FAST CLOCK)
6.

TYPICAL OPERATING CREW: _1-2_   EYE LEVEL (OWNER) = 69 IN

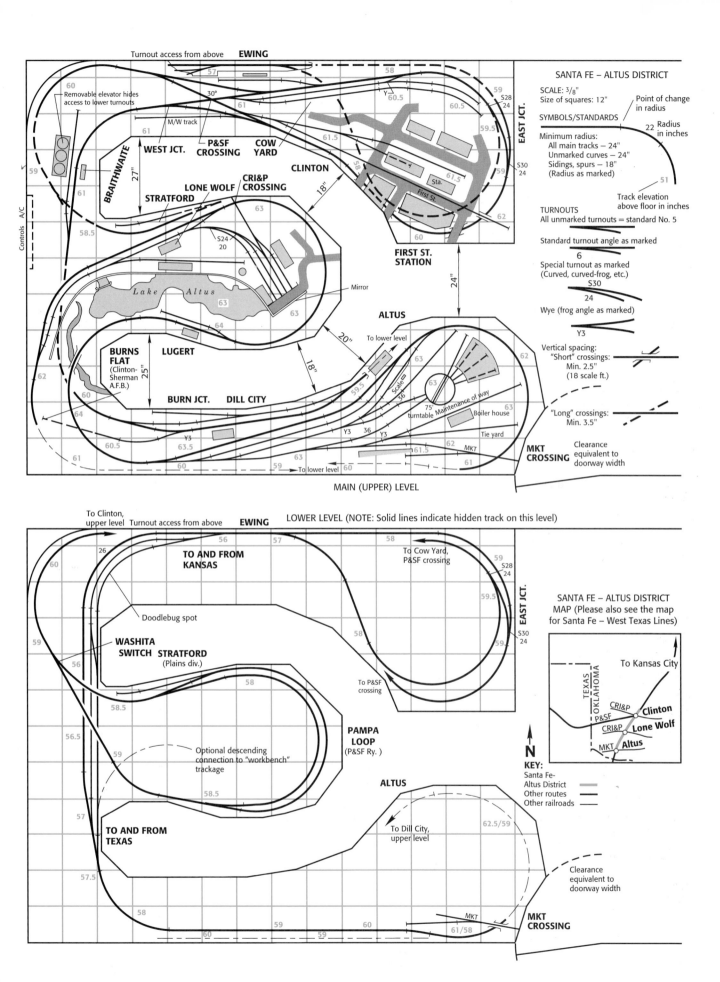

EWING

Turnout access from above

SANTA FE – ALTUS DISTRICT

SCALE: 3/8"
Size of squares: 12"

SYMBOLS/STANDARDS

Point of change in radius

22 Radius in inches

Minimum radius:
All main tracks — 24"
Unmarked curves — 24"
Sidings, spurs — 18"
(Radius as marked)

51 Track elevation above floor in inches

TURNOUTS
All unmarked turnouts = standard No. 5

Standard turnout angle as marked

6 Special turnout as marked (Curved, curved-frog, etc.)

S30 24 Wye (frog angle as marked)

Y3

Vertical spacing:
"Short" crossings:
Min. 2.5"
(18 scale ft.)

"Long" crossings:
Min. 3.5"

Clearance equivalent to doorway width

Removable elevator hides access to lower turnouts

60
60

M/W track
30°
57
61
58
60.5
59
60.5
59.5
S28 24

59
61

BRAITHWAITE 27"
WEST JCT.
P&SF CROSSING
COW YARD
CLINTON
61.5
58
61.5
Sta.
First St.
59
S30 24

58.5
STRATFORD
LONE WOLF
CRI&P CROSSING
18"
63
62

61

S24 20
63

Lake Altus
63
63
Mirror

64

62
BURNS FLAT
(Clinton-Sherman A.F.B.)
25"
LUGERT
18"
63

FIRST ST. STATION

ALTUS
To lower level
20"
63
62

60
54

BURN JCT. **DILL CITY**
Y3 63.5
60.5
24"
59.5
Scale 36
63
75' turntable Maintenance of way
63
Boiler house
63
Tie yard

61
360
59 → To lower level 60
Y3 36 Y3
61.5
62
MKT
61

MKT CROSSING

MAIN (UPPER) LEVEL

To Clinton, upper level   Turnout access from above   **EWING**

LOWER LEVEL (NOTE: Solid lines indicate hidden track on this level)

SANTA FE – ALTUS DISTRICT MAP (Please also see the map for Santa Fe – West Texas Lines)

60
26
56
57
58
59
S28 24

TO AND FROM KANSAS
To Cow Yard, P&SF crossing
59.5
S30 24

59
56

Doodlebug spot
58

WASHITA SWITCH STRATFORD
(Plains div.)

58
To P&SF crossing

58.5

PAMPA LOOP
(P&SF Ry.)

56.5
59

Optional descending connection to "workbench" trackage

58.5

ALTUS

57

TO AND FROM TEXAS
To Dill City, upper level
62.5/59

57.5

Clearance equivalent to doorway width

58
59 59 60 61/58 MKT

MKT CROSSING

EAST JCT.

To Kansas City
TEXAS OKLAHOMA
CRI&P **Clinton**
P&SF
CRI&P **Lone Wolf**
MKT **Altus**

N

KEY:
Santa Fe-Altus District
Other routes
Other railroads

Controls A/C

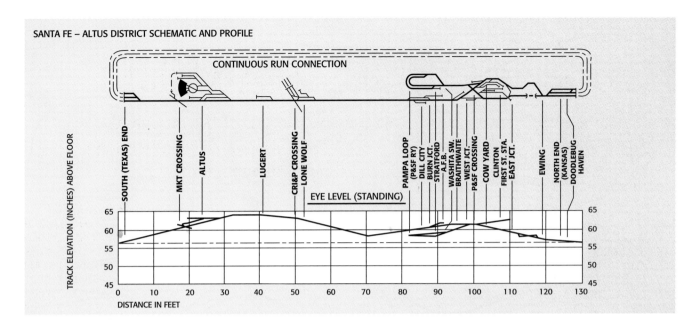

hidden loop that pops out to serve a grain elevator at Stratford. Cow Yard is, however, a scene of great activity during the rushes.

The trackage in Clinton is at least reminiscent of the prototype situation in the 1940s, but it doesn't give the doodlebug an easy way out of town in the direction of Braithwaite and its important track-hiding elevator. The line disappears briefly, then progresses past Burn Junction and Dill City. The vertical separation from the Altus trackage may disguise slightly that fact that the train is in the same area it will pass through again a scale mile later on. The route disappears again, and a short backward hike lets the viewer watch it swing into the most important intermediate station, Lone Wolf. Besides another passing track, there is interchange trackage with the Rock Island and a stockyard spur. A highway overpass provides an opportunity to use a well-framed mirror to make the interchange yard look twice as big and busy as it really is.

On the other side of the double-faced backdrop is the most scenic part of the Orient line, a lakeside stretch through Lugert and the bridge over the North Fork of the Red River of Texas. Altus is the largest town in southwest Oklahoma and home base for the locomotives (mostly those distinctive Santa Fe 2-6-2s) that power freights on both ends of the Orient.

To return to the secluded staging trackage (theoretically by way of Texas), the line leaves Altus on a 2.5 percent downward slant, ducking out of sight behind appropriate industrial buildings after crossing the Katy at grade. There is a steeply graded interchange connection between the two roads. If there were more room on the layout, there could be additional crossings and connections. The Frisco also crosses at Altus, and at Clinton are Rock Island's Memphis-Oklahoma City-Tucumcari main line and a Frisco branch served by a doodlebug.

Vertical considerations

Intertwining the routes with a comfortable vertical separation between tracks requires grades somewhat steeper than the prototype. In the compromise represented by the profile of the layout's Altus district there is at least 18 scale feet railhead to railhead where tracks cross briefly and minimum-thickness roadbed structure is practical. Flexible track alone is stiff enough to span a track or two (with a piece of cardboard or whatever to hide what's below) and leave clearance for rolling stock 16 feet high, plenty for railroading of this era. At other points, such as Braithwaite, where lower-level trackage is extensive and access is from the side, hand room is important and vertical separation is 4 inches (29 scale feet) or more.

Since train length is not going to strain even the modest-sized motive power assigned, grades on hidden track are in the 2.5 percent range. The Clinton-Altus segment of the old Orient is far from flat, with pitches up to 1 percent or so in crossing several shallow stream valleys in the foothills of the Wichita Mountains. To stay within reasonable bounds, grades on visible sections of the main line have been held to 2.0 percent or less. Within yard limits the slope has been held to 0.7 percent in the interest of realistic appearance and switching ease.

Built and checked out operationally from the bottom up, with terrain contours finalized on the spot and augmented with removable buildings, backdrops, and the like to keep separate scenes separate, the Altus District remains a single-decker—basically, the choice for convincing, comfortable model railroading when expansionist desires are held in check.

Isn't 63 inches awfully high for a principal yard and station area such as Altus? Not if you are 75 inches tall and own the railroad. As in all the other plans in this book, track elevations are planned to suit the eye level of the owner (height minus 6 inches, an approximation that holds for almost everyone). For those of other height, elevations can be adjusted by raising or lowering the entire railroad to suit.

SOUTHERN PACIFIC — SHASTA ROUTE

Intense mountain railroading in the shadow of Mount Shasta, with a logging branch and a busy division point complementing long-train, single-track mainline operations

WITH ITS DISTINCTIVE yet attractive steam locomotives succeeded by a variety of colorful first-generation diesels, the Southern Pacific has been a favorite of those who are collectors as well as model railroaders. When the time comes to provide a scenically characteristic right-of-way over which at least a major fraction of the accumulated late steam and early diesel roster can do its thing, SP's spectacular San Francisco-Portland "Shasta Route" in the vicinity of its division point at Dunsmuir, California, is a logical choice.

This HO scale representation is confined to an uncluttered enclosed-porch area about 11 × 19 feet in size but blessed with an 8-foot ceiling. It emphasizes staging-track capacity that provides a steady supply of impressive trains to weave in and out of a reasonable number of passing tracks along a convoluted main line of at least 30-inch radius. With the aid of overhead and lower-level turning and staging trackage—both out of view—and some

double-decking, it wraps a visible main line somewhat more than 2 scale miles long along a walk-around aisle. Furthermore, there is no need for backtracking in following a *Shasta Daylight* or Oregon lumber extra over its entire journey. The price includes multi-level construction, as well as the challenge of deciphering the relationship between a straightforward schematic and the four drawings needed to depict the various layers.

A first evaluation of the space comes out to only about 21 square squares. The layout must be approached from the side, and that calls for an 8 square squares deduction to allow for the desired walk-in entry. However, the summit of the line is certainly going to be up near eye level or perhaps above, and accepting a moderate duck-under (6 inches for the owner; taller operators still won't suffer much) will restore the space to a more comfortable 29 square squares, within which all of the desirable features above are possible.

When east is north
When you're trying to represent 70 miles of railroad in a moderate-size room, the compression ratio is something like 35 to 1. Most features and stations must be either condensed or omitted. Nevertheless, this layout can still be unmistakably the Shasta Route if the important characteristics are represented. For example, as far as the railroad is concerned, the end of the trail is San Francisco so all trains headed toward the City by the Bay are westbound. Therefore, Shasta Route trains headed north—and even west at points en route—are eastbound by timetable, and keeping in sync means that moving upward from the secluded turnaround loop representing the Oakland and Roseville end of the line is eastbound. Let's follow a cab-forward-powered freight out of Roseville, SP's huge yard east of Sacramento.

There's only a single 30-inch-radius track around the loop itself. Layover and staging capacity is provided by double-ended sidings approaching the

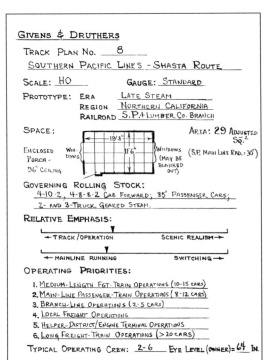

Two Decks (that's what Espee crews call their 2-10-2s) start an Oregon-bound freight out of Dunsmuir, while the 2-8-2 that works as a switcher heads down into the yard. Photo by Mac Lefebre.

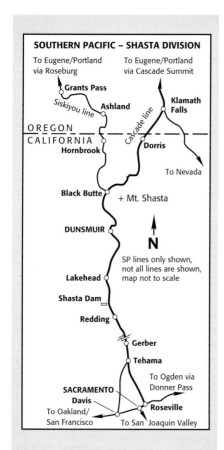

SOUTHERN PACIFIC – SHASTA DIVISION

(map showing SP lines only shown, not all lines are shown, map not to scale)

To Eugene/Portland via Roseburg
To Eugene/Portland via Cascade Summit
Grants Pass
Ashland
Siskiyou line
Cascade line
Klamath Falls
OREGON
CALIFORNIA
Hornbrook
Dorris
To Nevada
Black Butte
+ Mt. Shasta
DUNSMUIR
N
SP lines only shown, not all lines are shown, map not to scale
Lakehead
Shasta Dam
Redding
Gerber
Tehama
SACRAMENTO
Davis
To Ogden via Donner Pass
To Oakland/ San Francisco
Roseville
To San Joaquin Valley

The Portland-Oakland *Shasta Daylight* is more than halfway through its 715-mile journey as it rolls downgrade near Azalea, California, north of Dunsmuir, with namesake Mount Shasta in the background. SP photo.

loop plus three single-ended tracks (A, B, and C) into which trains must back if scheduled for layover. This is a downhill movement—no problem! In the rare event of some difficulty, all the key trackage (turnouts, particularly) is readily accessible from the side, with all lines on the next level above at least 6 inches higher, so that a hand can get in there.

From its emergence at Lakehead (the north end of the reservoir formed behind Shasta Dam in 1944) all the way uphill until it disappears beyond Black Butte at Dorris, the main line is viewed from the same side—the east, generally, so trains are in the sunlight during the forenoon. By timetable, west is to the left and east is to the right; this is desirable for continuity, but Mount Shasta itself is east of the track (as the sketch map shows) and therefore out of sight behind the viewer's back. Fortunately, the line doubles back at the Cantara Loop, so for a short distance the mighty mountain is visible behind an eastbound train. That's where you can legitimately locate the background "Shasta Vista."

The canyonized division point

Like most of the territory represented in the plan, Dunsmuir itself is squeezed into the Sacramento River

canyon—just as the trackage in any proper walk-around plan must fit between an aisle and a backdrop that are preferably no more than arm's length apart. This means that an HO-scale Dunsmuir yard can mimic its prototype fairly closely, except for being flipped east to west. The back wall of SP's Dunsmuir roundhouse is practically in the Sacramento River. On the layout that would be the aisle, and we would rather have the more interesting side of the roundhouse visible. Excellent plans for the original yard may be found in John R. Signor's *Rails in the Shadow of Mt. Shasta* (Howell-North Books, 1982).

Chopping off some of the rear of the roundhouse allows a not-too-condensed version to be confined within the depth limit; wedge plows, flangers, and single-unit diesels can be enlisted to conceal the shortness of those center stalls. When the long articulateds went into service, the SP lengthened the turntable but could provide the necessary stall length only in a separate "Mallet house," which can be duplicated to catch the flavor of this busy engine terminal.

West (compass south) of Dunsmuir the ruling grade is 1.8 percent, not too much of an exaggeration of the prototype's 1 percent, which continues

through the yard and requires the use of hand brakes on all cuts of cars left standing on any tracks. In the model the grade has been flattened to an average of 0.8 percent, but in the absence of working handbrakes you will probably have to resort to artificial means (a 'peg stuck in a hole between the rails?) to restrain any consists before their locomotives are attached.

Continuing east (compass north), the freight must overcome a stretch of 3.3 percent to climb out of the Sacramento River Canyon, so there's no doubt of the necessity for helper service: front, rear, or mid-train, steam or diesel, it's quite a show. At the top of the grade is a condensed version of Black Butte, where the horrendously graded Siskiyou line takes off toward Ashland and Grants Pass, Oregon. A wye lets the helpers return to Dunsmuir right-end-to. The Cascade line to Klamath Falls continues as double track on unprototypically separated grades; eastbound trains continue upgrade on the left-hand track into one of three tail tracks (now above head-height, so they can extend over the aisleway, effectively out of sight).

Turning these and the Siskiyou-bound trains (power for the latter is prototypically restricted to nothing larger than 2-10-2s) is accomplished

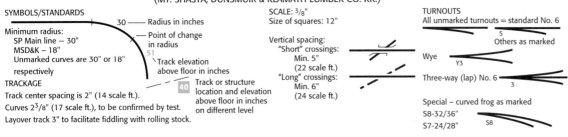

SYMBOLS/STANDARDS

Minimum radius:
SP Main line — 30"
MSD&K – 18"
Unmarked curves are 30" or 18"
respectively

TRACKAGE

Track center spacing is 2" (14 scale ft.).
Curves $2^3/8$" (17 scale ft.), to be confirmed by test.
Layover track 3" to facilitate fiddling with rolling stock.

30 — Radius in inches
Point of change
in radius
51 Track elevation
above floor in inches
40 Track or structure
location and elevation
above floor in inches
on different level

SCALE: $^3/8$"
Size of squares: 12"

Vertical spacing:
"Short" crossings:
Min. 5"
(22 scale ft.)
"Long" crossings:
Min. 6"
(24 scale ft.)

TURNOUTS

All unmarked turnouts = standard No. 6
Others as marked
Wye — Y3
Three-way (lap) No. 6 — 3

Special – curved frog as marked
S8-32/36"
S7-24/28" — S8

SOUTHERN PACIFIC LINES – SHASTA DIVISION
(MT. SHASTA, DUNSMUIR & KLAMATH LUMBER CO. RR.)

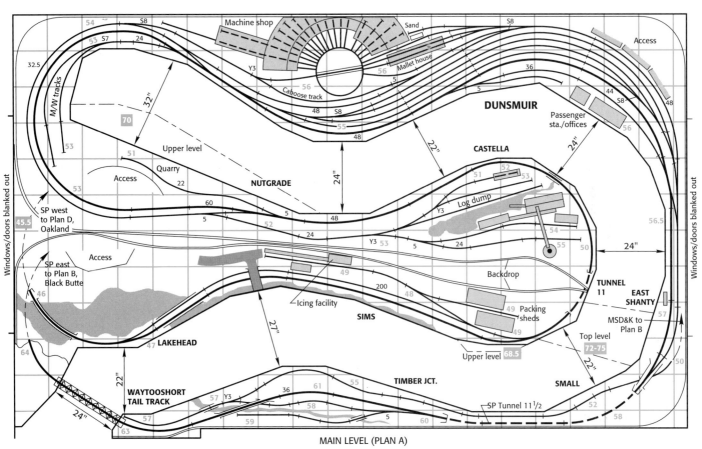

MAIN LEVEL (PLAN A)

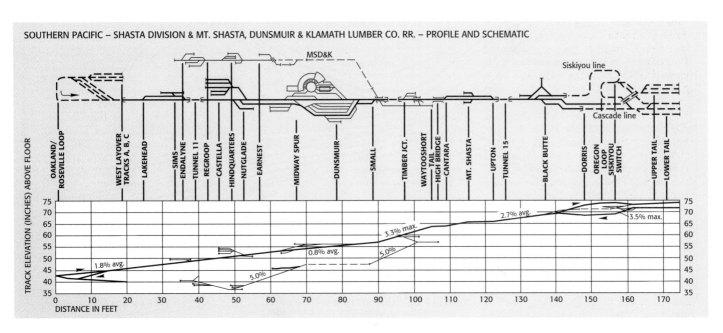

SOUTHERN PACIFIC – SHASTA DIVISION & MT. SHASTA, DUNSMUIR & KLAMATH LUMBER CO. RR. – PROFILE AND SCHEMATIC

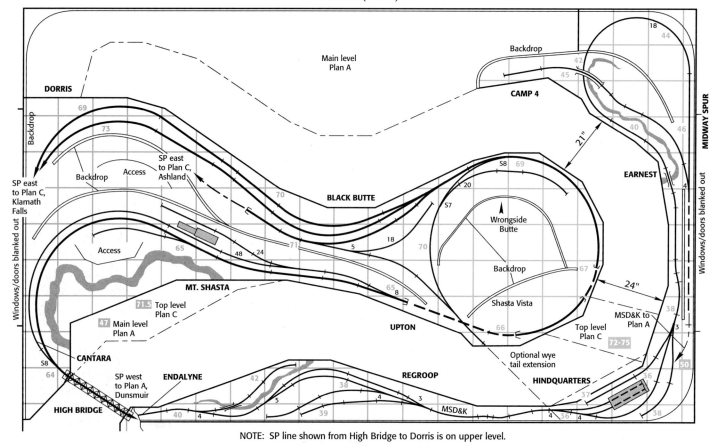

DORRIS

69

73

Backdrop

Access

SP east
to Plan C,
Ashland

SP east
to Plan C,
Klamath
Falls

Access

Backdrop

65

48   24

71

BLACK BUTTE

70

5

18

70

CAMP 4

Backdrop

42

45

18
44

40

46

MIDWAY SPUR

EARNEST

21"

S8   69

20

S7

Wrongside
Butte

Backdrop

Shasta Vista

67

24"

38

72-75

MSD&K to
Plan A

3

50

65
8

66

Top level
Plan C

Optional wye
tail extension

HINDQUARTERS

37

36

38

MT. SHASTA

71.5   Top level
Plan C

47   Main level
Plan A

CANTARA

S8

64

SP west
to Plan A,
Dunsmuir

ENDALYNE

42

5

38

4

REGROOP

4

3

39

MSD&K

4   36   4

40   4

HIGH BRIDGE

NOTE: SP line shown from High Bridge to Dorris is on upper level.
MSD&K line from Midway Spur to Endalyne is on a lower level, below main level (plan A).

Windows/doors blanked out

UPTON

Main level
Plan A

TOP LEVEL (PLAN C)

DORRIS

69

73

S8

Access

Oregon loop,
midpoint

SISKIYOU SWITCH

72

74

70

65

24

See Plan B

Access

73

71

71

LOWER THROAT

UPPER THROAT

72

70

5

18

Main level
Plan A

BLACK BUTTE

S8   69

20

S7

Upper level
Plan B

Backdrop

67

70

Upper tail:
optional space
for two tracks

72

68.5

Lower tail:
optional terracing for
better visibility,
track heights
71; 71.5; 72

CANTARA

S8

64

SP west
to Plan A,
Dunsmuir

HIGH BRIDGE

74

71

Main level
and lower level,
Plans A & B

NOTE: Top-level trackage is not scenicked,
tracks on top level are drawn with solid lines.

44

with a single reverted loop, around which all backing movements are comfortably downgrade. Overall staging and layover track capacity can be approximately as great as that at the Oakland and Roseville end of the line (100 40-foot cars); Dunsmuir yard has a similar capacity for absorbing the inevitable accretion of rolling stock.

Activities for the locals

Shasta Route territory is productive, if remote and sparsely populated. Within the confines of this layout you have considerable flexibility in selecting industries. The example emphasizes lumbering with the Mt. Shasta, Dunsmuir & Klamath Lumber Co. It exploits geared locomotives—and the 5 percent grades they make practical—to drop down sharply from Timber Junction to an extensive logging area 18 inches or so below the upper deck. Log loads from this branch are taken down to Dunsmuir by the East Local, to be forwarded in due course to the extensive Castella sawmill complex.

Agriculture is the thing in the Lakehead-Sims area, so a logical complex includes packing sheds for its produce and a small Pacific Fruit Express icing facility serving reefers loaded locally. With careful arrangement of the buildings and a switchback spur to annoy the local freight crew, there is still room for a sweeping cosmetic curve on the main line.

A cab-forward 4-8-8-2, practically a Southern Pacific trademark, leads a westbound freight through sparsely wooded lava-rock country a few miles east of Black Butte in 1949. SP photo.

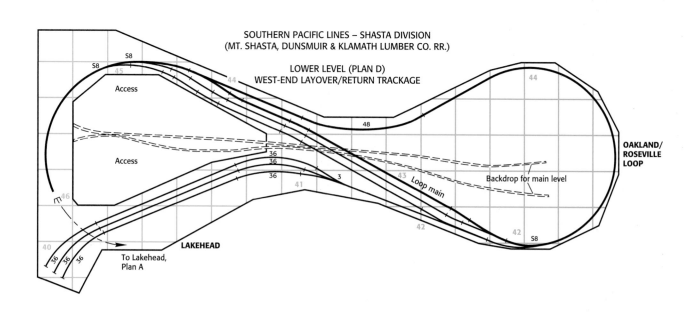

SOUTHERN PACIFIC LINES – SHASTA DIVISION
(MT. SHASTA, DUNSMUIR & KLAMATH LUMBER CO. RR.)

LOWER LEVEL (PLAN D)
WEST-END LAYOVER/RETURN TRACKAGE

S8
S8
45
44
44
48
Access
36
36
36
3
43
Loop main
Backdrop for main level
OAKLAND/ROSEVILLE LOOP
Access
41
42
42
42
S8
46
40
36 36 36
LAKEHEAD
To Lakehead, Plan A

ECLECTIC ELECTRIC LINES

A combination of East Coast urban-suburban and West Coast mountain railroading providing reasonably realistic settings for anything on rails that takes power from an overhead wire

IF WHAT ESPECIALLY turns you on about a train is not the railroad that owns it or where it's running but simply that it's electric, what do you ask for in a layout? No smoke, no cinder-filled stack talk, no scent of coal or diesel fuel, no Alco, EMD, or Baldwin rumble—just the whir of the blowers, a slight whiff of ozone, and perhaps the crunch of wheels on sanded rail as the electric puts its boundless horsepower to work. For pure realism in action no 12-volt K4 or PA can quite equal a GG1 of the same scale. Maybe the juice fans have something.

The Eclectic Electric plan does its best to rationalize squeezing two must-have electrified railroad operations—unfortunately separated by 2,000 miles in real life—into the confines of a single layout. The setup will also include assorted commuter, interurban, and streetcar lines.

The space is a T-shaped basement 34 × 41 feet overall and generally ideal, although the tracks must circumvent

or surmount such utilities as a furnace and a water softener. Access is by way of a central stairway far enough from the nearest wall to accommodate an aisle and two laps of trackage beneath it. No outside entrance spoils the perimeter of this layout. Any O-scale electric should be compatible with 54-inch radius curves, with some tinkering, perhaps, but no mutilation. On this basis the net area comes out to 41 square squares.

That is certainly enough for an ideal once-around, no backtracking, walk-in, single-deck plan—except that this pike is supposed to allow Eastern electrified railroading (Pennsy, of course, and perhaps some New Haven and even Lackawanna touches) to coexist with the Milwaukee Road in the Cascades. If that hodgepodge of prototypes is not to look like a hobby-shop display, there must be two mainline railroads, and they must be visually separate.

Whenever it doesn't show, they

must share space, particularly to provide staging and layover trackage accessible to both—but one road must run only through territory with the flavor of an East Coast metropolitan area, while the other must display at least a bit of Western spaciousness en route to a Pacific terminus. Overlapping is in order.

Generic communities

It would be preposterous to call the busy but modest-size eastern terminal New York, although no other East Coast city fits this situation, as far as electric traction is concerned. Wayside stations also probably shouldn't be tied down to specifics until the mix of railroads and rolling stock is better defined, so other points on this layout have been left unnamed. Junctions and other locations will have to be discussed in generic terms.

On the left as you come down the stairs is the single-platform stub passenger terminal of the Cascade divi-

Milwaukee Road bipolar E-2 arrives at Seattle's Union Station with the eastbound *Olympian* from Tacoma in August 1951. The train has run backward from Tacoma. The electric will run around the train here, then depart for Spokane, Butte, Minneapolis, and Chicago with the train properly pointed. Photo by Fred H. Matthews.

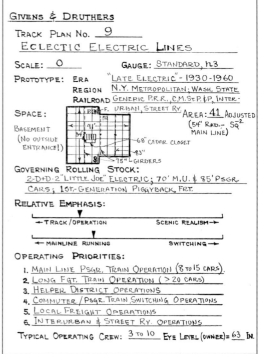

GIVENS & DRUTHERS

TRACK PLAN No. 9
ECLECTIC ELECTRIC LINES

SCALE: O   GAUGE: STANDARD, h3
PROTOTYPE: ERA "LATE ELECTRIC" - 1930-1960
           REGION N.Y. METROPOLITAN; WASH. STATE
           RAILROAD GENERIC P.R.R., C.M.ST.P.¿P., INTER-
                     -F. URBAN, STREET RY.
SPACE: AREA: 41 ADJUSTED
                                   (54" RAD.- SQ²
BASEMENT   MAIN LINE)
(NO OUTSIDE   -68" CEDAR CLOSET
ENTRANCE!)   -83"
           -75"L GIRDERS
GOVERNING ROLLING STOCK:
2-D+D-2 "LITTLE JOE" ELECTRIC; 70' M.U. & 85' PSGR.
CARS; 1ST-GENERATION PIGGYBACK FRT.

RELATIVE EMPHASIS:

    ◄─TRACK/OPERATION   SCENIC REALISM─►

    ◄─ MAINLINE RUNNING   SWITCHING ─►

OPERATING PRIORITIES:
1. MAIN LINE PSGR. TRAIN OPERATION (8 TO 15 CARS).
2. LONG FGT. TRAIN OPERATION (> 20 CARS)
3. HELPER DISTRICT OPERATIONS
4. COMMUTER / PSGR. TRAIN SWITCHING OPERATIONS
5. LOCAL FREIGHT OPERATIONS
6. INTERURBAN & STREET RY. OPERATIONS
TYPICAL OPERATING CREW: 3 TO 10 EYE LEVEL (OWNER)= 63 IN.

sion. Since there is only one electrified railroad in the West that reaches the coast, the station building itself can vaguely resemble a condensed version of Seattle's Union Station (which the Milwaukee Road used), though it must save space by being located above the tracks.

If the *Olympian* that the bipolar brings in every morning is so long that the switcher must cut off its rear cars and push them into the station on the adjacent track in a doubling maneuver, one of the tracks in the small freight yard must serve as an engine escape route so the locomotive can get to the motor barn. The consist itself will be turned on a wye that disappears behind buildings needed to hide some access openings in an otherwise hopelessly unreachable area. As the schematic shows ("west" is to the left), the wye tail extends into hidden layover trackage that is actually somewhere under New Jersey.

With similar tricks in these yards, where every track must serve more than one purpose, a heavy freight can be doubled together and dispatched up the 3 percent grade between a Little Joe and some boxcabs. The juice propelling it may come from a power plant down below. As seen from the schematic, the plant gets its coal from a mine that must be in Pennsylvania.

The stiff grade carries the line over a Milwaukee-style high, curved trestle to a comfortable walk-under elevation and past a transfer station for timber from a steam-powered narrow gauge line that pops up out of the woods. Apparently the exposed reciprocating action of the Shays on the 6 percent switchbacks is reminiscent enough of a siderod electric to make this interloper acceptable. At the end of a long passing track the single-track main disappears—for now.

Back east
Parallel with the west-end terminal but a continent away visually, thanks to urban building flats and contrasting backdrops, is the three-platform, stub passenger terminal of the Eastern Trunk. It features a station headhouse, also above the tracks, connecting with ferries to the big city. All five platform tracks funnel into a double-track main line carrying long-distance and commuter trains, the latter both locomotive-hauled and multiple-unit (MU) trains of various lengths. The electric locomotives don't have to be turned, but when time is short entire trains may be turned on the wye. Building flats hide the fact that the tail of the wye is located in Washington State.

Running on track equipped with both 11,000-volt catenary and 600-volt third rail, a Penn Central GG1 (still in Pennsylvania livery) heads toward the East River tunnels and Pennsylvania Station in Manhattan to pick up Florida-bound passengers in June 1970. Just beyond, a New York City Transit Authority train bound for Flushing climbs onto the elevated structure. In the distance the Empire State Building and the Chrysler Building punctuate the Manhattan skyline. Photo by Fred W. Schneider III.

Also entering the terminal on a steep (5 percent) single track connecting with the last three platforms are some of the MU trains of the Bi-State Commuter Railroad; many of its inbound runs turn back at an elevated-style station a few blocks away. Near the busy terminal throat is the joint locomotive and MU-car service yard and a shop for heavier repairs. The transfer table that furnishes access to the shop is a space-saver compared to a fan of tracks, and it provides a place to display locomotives.

Bi-State's trains, comfortable on 40-inch curves, first weave over four Eastern Trunk mains on one of those retaining-wall and tunnel bridges so characteristic of multiple-track territory. After dropping down alongside the Eastern Trunk to create the impression of another stretch of four-track main, the double tracks rise to soar over it again on another species of bridge and serve a high-platform station. Steep grades are nothing to MUs. Descending yet again, the commuters clatter across the Trunk at grade. Finally by themselves, the Bi-State tracks follow a scenic river on a bank so narrow that only an elevator can bring passengers down to the station from the town above. It's somewhat hokey, but it's Eastern electric railroading in a capsule.

The Eastern Trunk has also been doing its part to illustrate the complexities of interweaving lines. Three staging tracks, secluded beneath its double-track line, pop up between the two mains in an example of a flying junction. Finally approaching terrain conveniently moved east from the Delaware Water Gap and the Poconos, the line ascends a 3 percent grade until it, too, is at walk-under elevation.

Out and back—or coast to coast
The Cascade Division and Eastern Trunk have both ascended from tidewater terminals to summits high enough to present no impediment to aisleway traffic. When operating in "pure" mode—no trains allowed out in the open on the wrong side of the continent—each must be provided with its own private way to turn around. As the upper-level diagram shows, this means two loops, but they can share common trackage. Since there is room up there, a double-tracked arrangement provides some much-needed layover trackage.

Now we can operate in impure fashion! Is it depraved to have a New Haven EP-5 show up in the Northwest? The two areas have probably already been contaminated with inappropriate power (Great Northern and Virginian have interestingly different

Text continued on page 50.

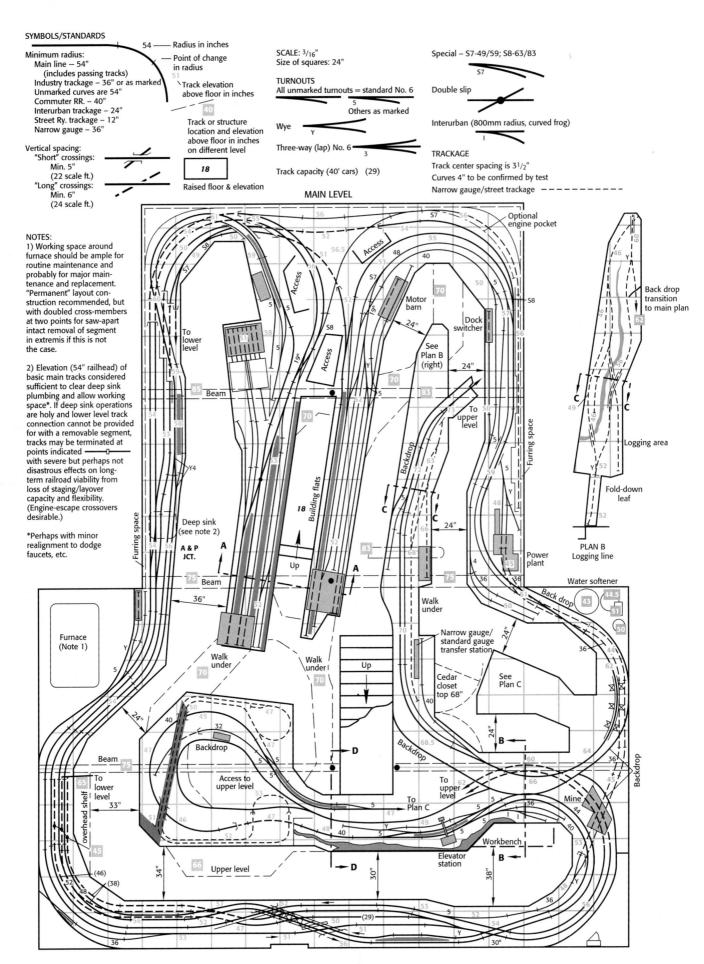

SYMBOLS/STANDARDS

Minimum radius:
Main line — 54"
(includes passing tracks)
Industry trackage — 36" or as marked
Unmarked curves are 54"
Commuter RR. – 40"
Interurban trackage – 24"
Street Ry. trackage – 12"
Narrow gauge – 36"

54 — Radius in inches
— Point of change in radius
Track elevation above floor in inches
40 — Track or structure location and elevation above floor in inches on different level
18 — Raised floor & elevation

Vertical spacing:
"Short" crossings:
Min. 5"
(22 scale ft.)
"Long" crossings:
Min. 6"
(24 scale ft.)

SCALE: 3/16"
Size of squares: 24"

TURNOUTS
All unmarked turnouts = standard No. 6
Others as marked
Wye
Three-way (lap) No. 6
Track capacity (40' cars) (29)

Special – S7-49/59; S8-63/83
Double slip
Interurban (800mm radius, curved frog)

TRACKAGE
Track center spacing is 3 1/2"
Curves 4" to be confirmed by test
Narrow gauge/street trackage – – – – –

MAIN LEVEL

NOTES:
1) Working space around furnace should be ample for routine maintenance and probably for major maintenance and replacement. "Permanent" layout construction recommended, but with doubled cross-members at two points for saw-apart intact removal of segment in extremis if this is not the case.

2) Elevation (54" railhead) of basic main tracks considered sufficient to clear deep sink plumbing and allow working space*. If deep sink operations are holy and lower level track connection cannot be provided for with a removable segment, tracks may be terminated at points indicated with severe but perhaps not disastrous effects on long-term railroad viability from loss of staging/layover capacity and flexibility. (Engine-escape crossovers desirable.)

*Perhaps with minor realignment to dodge faucets, etc.

Optional engine pocket
Access
Motor barn
Dock switcher
See Plan B (right)
To upper level
Backdrop
Building flats
Power plant
To lower level
Beam
Deep sink (see note 2)
A & P JCT.
Up
Walk under
Walk under
Up
Narrow gauge/ standard gauge transfer station
Cedar closet top 68"
See Plan C
Walk under
Furnace (Note 1)
Beam
To lower level
overhead shelf
Access to upper level
To Plan C
Backdrop
Upper level
Elevator station
Workbench
Mine
Water softener
Back drop

PLAN B
Logging line
Back drop transition to main plan
Logging area
Fold-down leaf

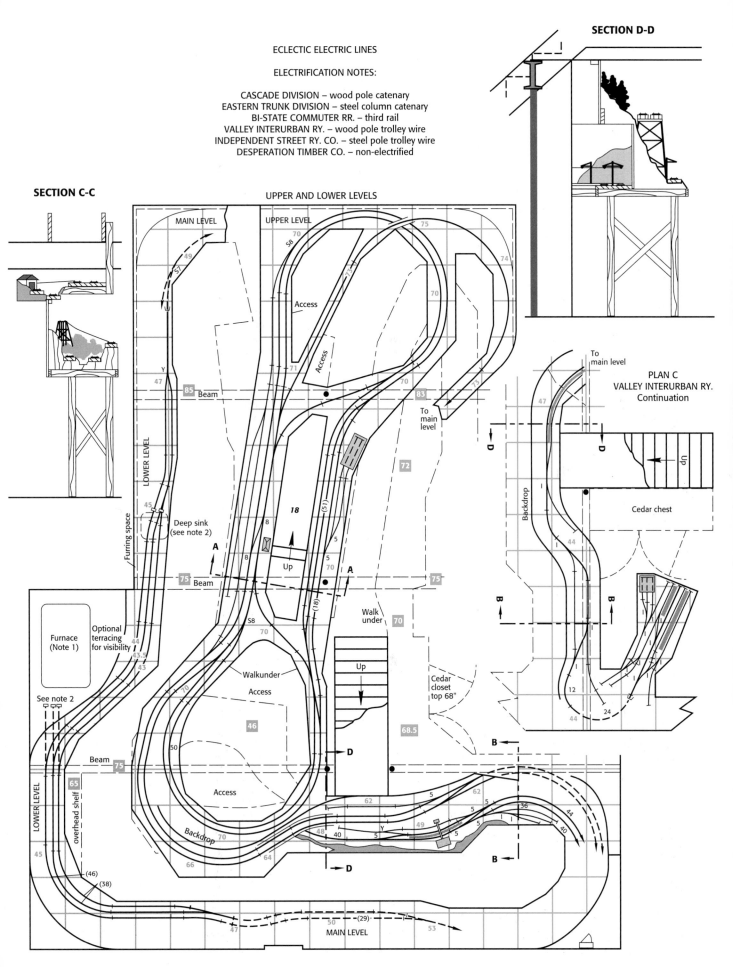

SECTION D-D

ECLECTIC ELECTRIC LINES

ELECTRIFICATION NOTES:

CASCADE DIVISION – wood pole catenary
EASTERN TRUNK DIVISION – steel column catenary
BI-STATE COMMUTER RR. – third rail
VALLEY INTERURBAN RY. – wood pole trolley wire
INDEPENDENT STREET RY. CO. – steel pole trolley wire
DESPERATION TIMBER CO. – non-electrified

SECTION C-C

UPPER AND LOWER LEVELS

MAIN LEVEL

UPPER LEVEL

70

75

S8

74

70

Access

Access

49

57

Y

47

85 Beam

71

70

73

83

To main level

72

LOWER LEVEL

PLAN C
VALLEY INTERURBAN RY.
Continuation

To main level

47

Backdrop

Cedar chest

45

Deep sink
(see note 2)

Furring space

18

(51)

8

5

5

A

8

5

70

A

44

12

24

44

Up

(18)

Walk under

70

Furnace
(Note 1)

Optional
terracing
for visibility

44

43.5

43

S8

70

Up

Cedar
closet
top 68"

68.5

See note 2

Walkunder

Access

46

Beam 75

50

D

Beam 75

LOWER LEVEL

65

overhead shelf

Access

Backdrop

70

62

5

62

5

36

44

45

64

48

40

Y

49

5

40

66

(46)

(38)

D

5

5

B

47

50

(29)

53

MAIN LEVEL

49

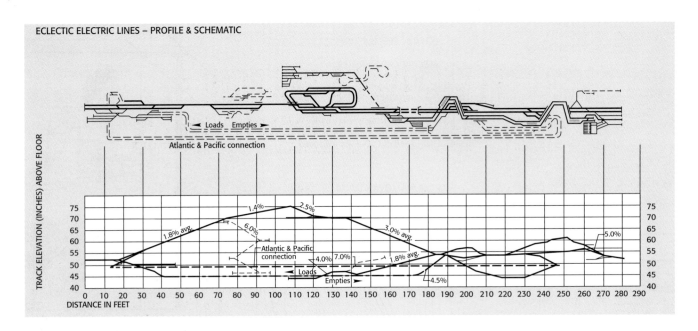

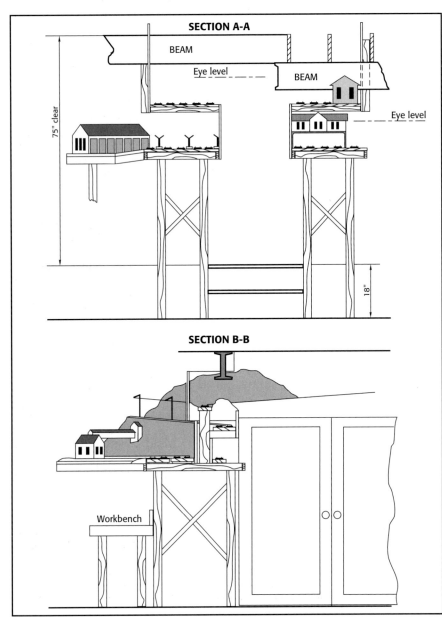

locomotives, too), so the ability to run trains round and round at times may not represent much further moral deterioration. A&P Junction down below completes the loop.

As Section A-A shows, separating the two passenger terminals with a raised aisle makes a "mushroom" configuration possible. Now that it's so reachable and viewable, some of the upper level may well be promoted to scenicked status, with some railroad structures, spurs, and industries.

Interurbans and streetcars

Down below, the Bi-State Commuter Railroad—which could well resemble the Long Island by using third-rail rather than catenary—comes down to single track as it passes under the high trestle and continues to its far terminal on track shared with the Valley Interurban. Perhaps more reminiscent of the Midwest, the Valley is the real thing, with wood poles supporting the trolley wire, box-motor package-freight service, and some interchange of steam-road freight cars. It ends up in a very cramped industrial area switched by its steeple-cab loco. Why such a complex of switchback spurs? A dozen 24-inch radius turnouts are already at hand. Nothing could be better for making good use of that awkward space without blocking access to an immovable cedar closet.

Passing beneath the small city's streets, the Valley Interurban also connects with the Independent Street Railway's Birney cars. Taking advantage of their grade-climbing propensities, its loop crosses back over the Valley on Industrial Avenue before squealing around some 12-inch curves into Main Street.

PENNSYLVANIA RAILROAD MIDDLE AND PITTSBURGH DIVISIONS

Jack's Narrows, Altoona, and the Horse Shoe Curve in S scale

A WELL-BUILT, fully scenicked, one-person layout that avoids the "bowl of spaghetti" approach of yesteryear typically has a "sincere" main line (it goes past any point only once) no more than 2 to 4 scale miles long. That's short, even in comparison with the typical distance between adjacent small-town stations. Nevertheless, it is possible to create a recognizable representation of even the mightiest railroad so that trains can duplicate the maneuvers of their prototypes. This is done by modeling only the most interesting and characteristic segments of a far-flung main line, shrinking them in proportion to the length of the trains, selectively compressing structures, and rigorously leaving out everything in between. To make up for those omitted miles of dullness that separate the interesting parts, it is necessary to group the surviving elements into concentrated but believable scenes.

What if those best parts are spread out along two divisions? That's actually beneficial. Only the single division point between them needs to be represented, with those mega-distances toward both ends of the railroad represented by return loops and staging trackage. This version of the Pennsy's busiest divisions doesn't skimp on highly recognizable scenes based on such features as the Susquehanna crossing and the summit of the Alleghenies—in reality, 185 miles apart. It omits everything from the west end of a shortened Rockville bridge to East Altoona except the photogenic trackage through Jack's Narrows and Spruce. Altoona itself takes full advantage of the length of the building (43 boxcar lengths) and exploits the space economy of overlapping freight yard and passenger station trackage. More than half the length of the main line is devoted to the central theme—the climb to and around Horse Shoe to Gallitzin and Cresson.

Hopper cars by the score

Eastbound coal is a major part of the Curve's traffic, so a loop-to-loop schematic must be supplemented with a continuous operating pattern to maintain the steady flow of empties and loads. In the preliminary sketch this was accomplished by connecting the two ends of the line with a three-turn helix. Sandwiched between the two end loops, the helix took no extra space.

Since the scheme represents a mountain crossing, there was no problem in lifting the main high enough for full walk-in entrance to the railroad. Getting the route in position to traverse the essential four-track version of the Curve, however, entailed adding a second blob near the center of the area. This was too much wasted space, especially since a multiple-track mainline this long absorbs a lot of square feet all by itself.

The adopted plan is a one-blob rearrangement in which moving the Curve to a corner allows the helix blob to double as the turnback at the end of the spiral peninsula. The 60 square feet or so saved can then be used for an expansive representation of the scenic Rockville bridge near Harrisburg.

The trade-off is a 43-inch duck-under entry to the walk-around aisle or the annoyance of a multi-track drawbridge or removable section. But wait! If the whole plan were flipped right to left (but not top to bottom) and grades throughout were revised (but not increased), track at the doorway could be a foot or more higher, promoting it to stoop-under rather than duck-under status. The catch? Horse Shoe Curve would then go around the wrong way, and much of the impact of its

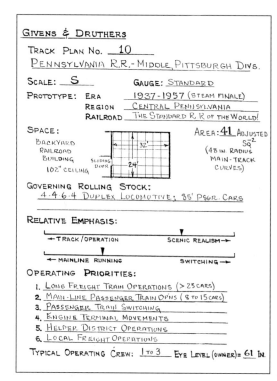

GIVENS & DRUTHERS

TRACK PLAN No. __10__
PENNSYLVANIA R.R.- MIDDLE, PITTSBURGH DIVS.

SCALE: __S__   GAUGE: STANDARD

PROTOTYPE: ERA   1937-1957 (STEAM FINALE)
           REGION   CENTRAL PENNSYLVANIA
           RAILROAD   THE STANDARD R.R. OF THE WORLD!

SPACE:
   BACKYARD   AREA: __41__ ADJUSTED
   RAILROAD   SQ²
   BUILDING   (48 IN. RADIUS
   102" CEILING   SLIDING DOOR   MAIN-TRACK
                   32'   24'   CURVES)

GOVERNING ROLLING STOCK:
   4-4-6-4 DUPLEX LOCOMOTIVE; 85' PSGR. CARS

RELATIVE EMPHASIS:
   ←TRACK/OPERATION   SCENIC REALISM→
   ←MAINLINE RUNNING   SWITCHING→

OPERATING PRIORITIES:
   1. LONG FREIGHT TRAIN OPERATIONS (>25 CARS)
   2. MAIN-LINE PASSENGER TRAIN OPNS (8 TO 15 CARS)
   3. PASSENGER TRAIN SWITCHING
   4. ENGINE TERMINAL MOVEMENTS
   5. HELPER DISTRICT OPERATIONS
   6. LOCAL FREIGHT OPERATIONS

TYPICAL OPERATING CREW: __1 TO 3__   EYE LEVEL (OWNER)= __61__ IN.

An M1 4-8-2 brings a freight across the Susquehanna River between Rockville and Marysville, Pennsylvania, on the world's longest stone arch bridge spanning a river—3,680 feet long. It was built in 1902 to replace an iron truss bridge. Photo by Philip R. Hastings.

SYMBOLS/STANDARDS

48 — Radius in inches

— Point of change in radius

51 — Track elevation above floor in inches

Minimum radius:
Main line East-West
No. 1 & 2 tracks – 48"
Reversing loops, No. 1 track – 45"
Layover tracks, wye
No. 3 & 4 main tracks – 42"
Industry trackage – 27"
Unmarked mainline curves – 48" or to match marked parallel curves

40 — Track or structure location and elevation above floor in inches on different level

SCALE: ¼"
Size of squares: 24"

TRACKAGE
Track center spacing is 2⁵⁄₈" (14 scale ft.).
Curves 3¹⁄₈", to be confirmed by test.

TURNOUTS
All unmarked turnouts = standard No. 6

5 — Others as marked

TURNOUTS, continued

Wye — Y

No. 3 frog, radius approx. = No. 6
Special – curved frog, radii as marked

63
50

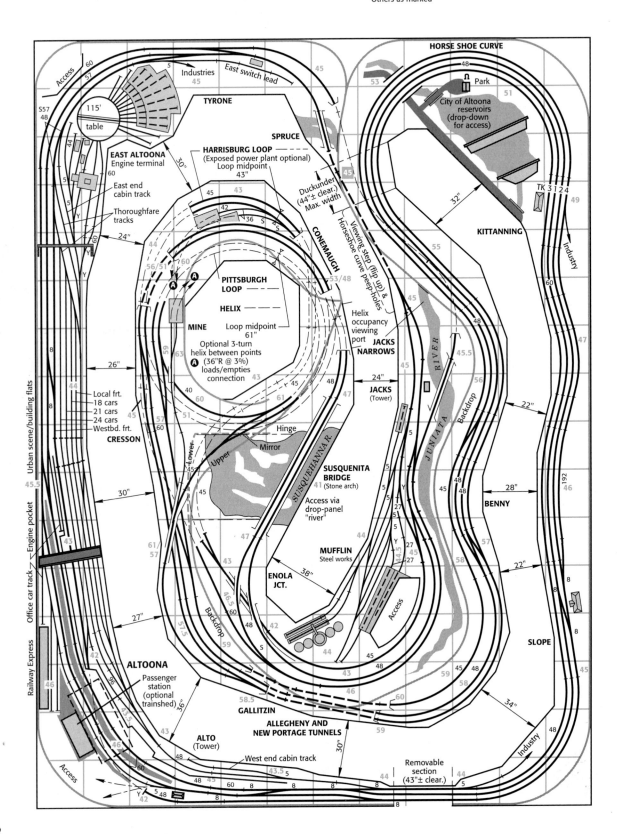

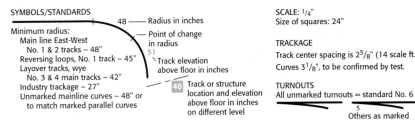

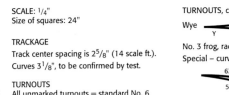

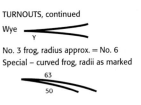

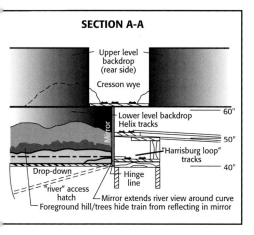

remarkably close agreement with the details of the real area would be lost. So realism prevails over comfort or convenience. For any less famous piece of roadway that probably wouldn't be the case.

Improving on the prototype

This part of the Pennsy line is so studded with features to model that the plan calls for little rearrangement. At 2.5 percent, the westbound grade is only 0.7 percent greater than the prototype—just enough to differentiate it from the 1.6 percent eastbound grade. In general, you want to avoid helpers in that direction, and that's about the minimum grade that will provide for a comfortable 6 inches between helix turns.

The twin tunnels at the summit are short, of course, but at those well-known different elevations suggestive of the real scene; a typical Pennsy "jumpover" track lets you work in a wye at Cresson so I1 2-10-0 helpers can come back down right-end-to. Its 40-inch radius won't necessarily accommodate longer engines, but there is at least one track over the entire main line with 48-inch curvature that should allow operation of a rigid-frame Q2 4-4-6-4 in this territory—something the Pennsy never did, at least regularly. Only the innermost track of the horseshoe is sharper than 48 inches and the outer tracks of the reversing loops are 45-inch radius.

Not shown on the track plan is a second double-track, 36-inch-radius helix. Located inside the mainline twister, it provides empties/loads exchange between a topside mine and a power plant served by a short exposed section of the Harrisburg loop down below.

Aside from the sidings on the reverse loops, there is little staging trackage on this railroad. Crossovers are such that trains can be parked on the inner track of the helix without blocking traffic when the outer track is operated as a single track. The main justification for this paucity of layover trackage is the large capacity of the Altoona yard, engine terminal, and caboose (oops, cabin—this is the Pennsy) sidings. Although not a major classification point, Altoona's trackage can absorb a fair share of the layout's roster of rolling stock. Several trains at a time can logically be awaiting helpers and exchanging engines and cabins at this choke point, where the easy water-level grade ends and the mountain climb demands more and heavier power. Eastbound trains must spend some time cooling their wheels after the descent.

Since passenger switching is another priority, some enhancement of the prototype is in order. Like other railroad towns where most of the passengers were traveling on passes, it made do with modest station facilities, although in the 1930s there was a short train shed over the tracks. Only a handful of mainline local trains origi-

nated or terminated at Altoona, and express and mail loadings were light. In this design, routing the westbound freight main through a tunnel beneath the platform enhances the prominence of the passenger area. The layout also contains spurs for the division superintendent's office car, headend loading, and the restocking of dining cars cut out of the fleet of westbound limiteds after dinner, pending their eastbound pickup for breakfast—a fairly common pre-World War II practice you can well extend into this era to keep the switch crews busy.

This is basically a single-level layout, but by extending the lower scene beneath Cresson for a few feet, you can jazz up the junction to the Harrisburg turning loop to look something like the flyover junction that separates traffic to Enola from that headed across the Susquehanna to Harrisburg. A mirror can visually extend the broad, rocky river around a bend into space actually full of helixes. (Be careful to hide trains at points where their motion would give away the illusion.) The Rockville stone arch bridge is half as wide and a fifth as long as its prototype but it is still impressive by model standards.

With a radius this large, there is always room inside an ox-bow of main line for more than just an aisle. Reaching a few miles east of Harrisburg, we can grab a Bethlehem Steel mill of respectable proportions and transplant it to Mifflin Haven. (Governor Mifflin's name is memorialized in towns all over central Pennsylvania.) It will give a plant switcher and the Pennsy local freight plenty of work. Access problems in a scene this deep are eased by the presence of an open-hearth or rolling-mill structure big enough to hide a generous hatch.

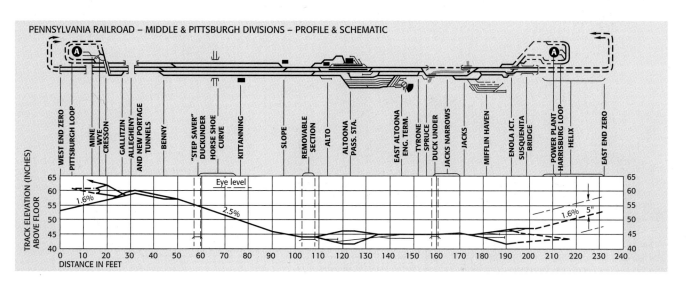

PENNSYLVANIA RAILROAD – MIDDLE & PITTSBURGH DIVISIONS – PROFILE & SCHEMATIC

SAN JOAQUIN SOUTHWESTERN

A plausible (if unlikely) line through new territory

LOOK AT ANY railroad map of California, and you'll find no line crossing the Coast Range between the Western Pacific (now Union Pacific) route over Livermore Pass southeast of San Francisco and the Southern Pacific track through Saugus Canyon some 325 miles to the southeast. The SP line still requires a struggle over Tehachapi Pass to connect the coast with the south end of the San Joaquin valley. For years the Santa Fe considered building a line over Tejon Pass that would bring Bakersfield and Los Angeles almost 150 miles closer together than by its long-way-around route through Barstow; but the company never took the plunge—thus leaving an opening for the S-scale San Joaquin Southwestern to fill.

Jointly backed by the SP and Santa Fe, the San J took off like a shot across the level country southwest of Bakersfield and then fought its way up and over Pine Mountain summit and down a precipitous canyon to Wheeler Springs, a wide spot in the road that immediately blossomed into the line's well-populated operating hub. (You'll find the San J's line on the map as

state highway 33.) During the 1920s the San J's tentacles made connections with its parent railroads at several points and even established a Pacific port at Point Dume.

In the era depicted the San J has settled down to a prosperous middle age as a bridge route for Valley-to-Coast freight. The Santa Fe operates through passenger service to Los Angeles instead of busing its Valley patrons from Bakersfield. Business isn't what it would have been over the shorter Tejon route but rates respectable Pullman-equipped consists. As a terminus for branch-line doodlebug or mixed-train connections, Wheeler Springs has more metropolitan-looking platforms than you might expect.

One side of the mountain

Now, how does the San J fit into its space, a separate building about 17 × 27? The railroad has dipped its toe into the Superpower era with a 2-8-4 to supplement its Pacifics and Mikados, so for S scale a 36-inch minimum radius—between conventional and broad standards—is appropriate. On this basis the area amounts to 41

square squares. Ordinarily you would subtract 8 square squares to reflect the unfortunate fact that entrance is via side doors, precluding full use of the walls in a walk-in plan. However, it should be possible to come up with a walk-under plan that makes efficient use of the whole area. It probably isn't possible to model both sides of the divide without doubling back unrealistically, so one terminal of the main line will be just past the summit, in the form of an overhead loop.

How does the line get back down? Well, it doesn't. If the San J carried a lot of mineral traffic in open-top cars displaying their empty or loaded state for all to see, you would probably want to provide for continuous operation (round-and-round, to put it bluntly); it could be done with a multi-turn helix. With practically all its freight carried in reefers, boxcars, and tankers, however, the San J gets along just fine with loop-to-loop and loop-to-wye operation between Bakersfield (miraculously raised about 3,500 feet above its actual elevation) and the principal SP and Santa Fe connections down near sea level.

A Santa Fe 4-6-2 built in 1905 leads a short train of refrigerator cars through the yard at Bakersfield, California, in 1940. It might well be a transfer run heading for the San Joaquin Southwestern interchange. Photo by R. H. Kindig.

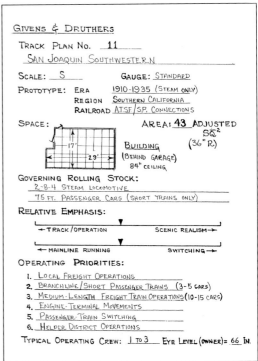

GIVENS & DRUTHERS

TRACK PLAN No. __11__

SAN JOAQUIN SOUTHWESTERN

SCALE: S   GAUGE: STANDARD

PROTOTYPE: ERA 1910-1935 (STEAM ONLY)
REGION SOUTHERN CALIFORNIA
RAILROAD ATSF/S.P. CONNECTIONS

SPACE: AREA: 43 ADJUSTED SQ²
                                        (36" R.)
                          BUILDING
                          (BEHIND GARAGE)
                          84" CEILING

GOVERNING ROLLING STOCK:
2-8-4 STEAM LOCOMOTIVE
75 FT. PASSENGER CARS (SHORT TRAINS ONLY)

RELATIVE EMPHASIS:

←TRACK/OPERATION   SCENIC REALISM→

←MAINLINE RUNNING   SWITCHING→

OPERATING PRIORITIES:
1. LOCAL FREIGHT OPERATIONS
2. BRANCHLINE/SHORT PASSENGER TRAINS (3-5 CARS)
3. MEDIUM-LENGTH FREIGHT TRAIN OPERATIONS (10-15 CARS)
4. ENGINE-TERMINAL MOVEMENTS
5. PASSENGER-TRAIN SWITCHING
6. HELPER DISTRICT OPERATIONS

TYPICAL OPERATING CREW: 1 TO 3   EYE LEVEL (OWNER) = 66 IN.

An appropriate loop

With the aid of a Tehachapi-style loop—jazzed up a bit with two impressive trestles, which also span a short branch headed for a timbering area upstream—a grade of just over 3 percent suffices to get the main line above head-height elevation at both entrance doors. Thus you have comfortable access to a serpentine aisleway, from which you can follow trains for a bit over 2 scale miles without backtracking. Orientation of the line corresponds to viewing it from the west side.

Aisle width varies from 24 to 36 inches. The optimum length, location, and capacity of yard, passing siding, and industry trackage is greatly facilitated by nine curved turnouts—included because the experienced modeler building this railroad is not only unfazed by the prospect of hand-laying them but likes their authentic, somewhat slinky appearance. The standard No. 5 turnout is compatible with the 36-inch minimum radius and greatly increases yard capacity as compared to that which would result with No. 6 turnouts, but the latter are used in crossovers and at any other points where reverse curves might pose a operational problem.

With the aid of a couple of open-top mountains extending above eye level to hide access openings without the need for hatch covers, the plan observes the 27-inch rule. All trackage and scenery that might require attention is within arm's reach of an aisleway or other reasonably comfortable access. It should be noted that the staging trackage at Maricopa, suspended from the overhead and unscenicked, has been located away from the wall to be accessible from the aisle.

The arrival of a San J passenger train at one of the small stations could resemble this scene on the Southern Pacific at Felton, California, back in the late 1920s. SP photo.

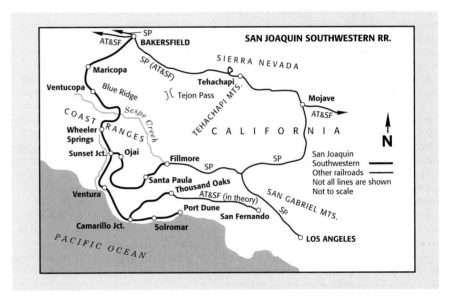

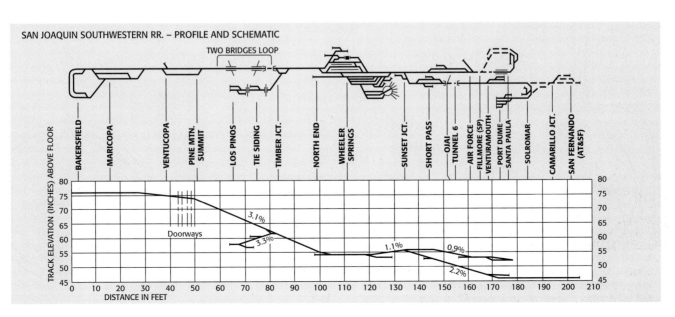

SAN JOAQUIN SOUTHWESTERN RR.

SCALE: ¼"
Size of squares: 24"

SYMBOLS/STANDARDS

Minimum radius:
Main line — 36"
Passing tracks — 33"
Industry trackage — as marked
Unmarked mainline curves — 36"

36 —— Radius in inches
Point of change in radius
Track elevation above floor in inches

40 — Track or structure location and elevation above floor in inches on different level

TURNOUTS
All unmarked turnouts = standard No.5

Others as marked

Wye

Three-way (lap) No. 6

Special – curved frog, radii as marked

TRACKAGE

Track center spacing is 2¾" (14 scale ft.).
Curves 3", to be confirmed by test.
Staging trackage is 4" (21 scale ft.) for "finger room" and rear-track consist visibility

MAIN LEVEL

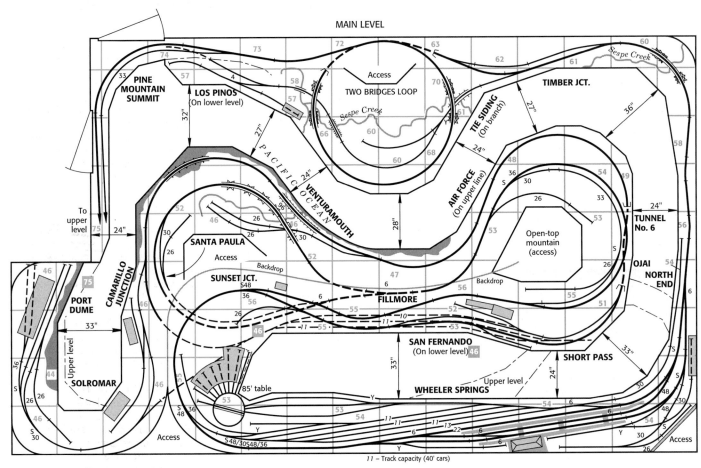

11 – Track capacity (40' cars)

UPPER LEVEL

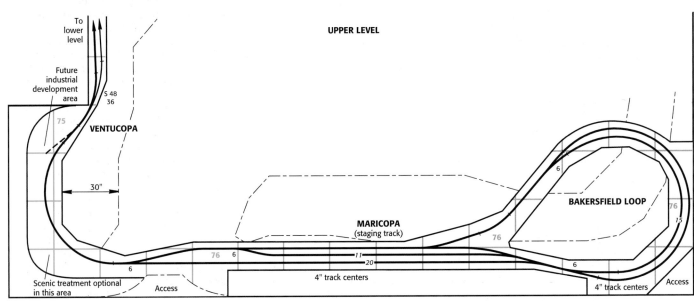

ERIE-LACKAWANNA RAILROAD

Parallel routes from Hoboken and Jersey City through the suburbs and over the mountains to upstate New York carry dense commuter, passenger, and freight traffic over two long viaducts in an N-scale version of the merged lines.

An Erie Lackawanna freight rolls east over Starrucca Viaduct. The track beneath belongs to Delaware & Hudson. Photo by Jim Shaughnessy.

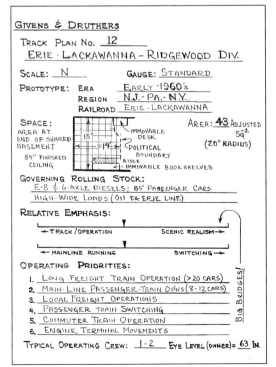

plan with no backtracking, even though it should be possible for both main lines to reach walk-under elevations with the aid of helixes.

The result is a partially double-deck plan with railhead-to-railhead separation between the layers in the range of 11 to 14 inches, not lavish but okay in N scale. Two helixes—one of them on the Erie and the other on the Lackawanna (the latter also provides a continuous route for the Erie in conjunction with the loop under the Hoboken terminal)—ease the problem of making unobtrusive transitions between single- and double-deck areas. Equipped with alternating facing-point and trailing-point crossovers, each helix can stage a pair of 30-car trains while leaving a clear route for through traffic. As noted on the schematic, these crossovers have been named for some important points on the two routes that had to be eliminated in bringing the main line down to size.

For once, *high* bridges

Interrupting the usual visual separation between decks are two famous bridges that reach almost scale height, Lackawanna's concrete-arch Tunkhannock Viaduct and Erie's stone-arch Starrucca Viaduct. They tower above notches in the lower-level terrain to carry upper-level trains at dizzying altitudes. Located near the end of the cul-de-sac by the bookcase, Tunkhannock can be lengthened optically from 30 percent to a respectable 60 percent of the protoypical span count with a carefully aligned mirror. The mirror must be precisely at 90 degrees to the bridge to avoid bending the structure, and its top must not extend above track level; if it did, the resulting "continuous collision" effect on a passing train could be hilarious.

As the schematic shows, two protoypically double-track routes start at a ferry-served stub passenger terminal at Hoboken. They extend north and west separately and reconnect near Binghamton. On the Erie the busy commuter run to Suffern is compressed but visible, with a stretch of triple

THE 1960 MERGER creating the Erie-Lackawanna slowed but did not ultimately solve the financial deterioration of the "Weary Erie" and the "Road of Anthracite." It did, however, result in new and interesting traffic patterns over some of the more scenic routes in the East. This "Ridgewood Division" plan (named for the suburban New Jersey city in which it is being built) represents in condensed form the widely separated routes by which the two railroads reached Binghamton, New York, from the west bank of the Hudson River opposite New York City.

The area available is amply large for an N-scale railroad with such ambitions, but entry from the side means that a walk-in design will require at least two blobs. The mandatory aisleway to allow access to that fixed bookcase must come to a dead end, precluding a fully walk-around

Text continued on page 60.

SYMBOLS/STANDARDS

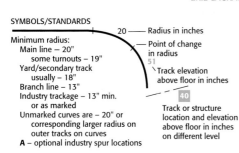

20 —— Radius in inches

—— Point of change
in radius

Minimum radius:
Main line – 20"
some turnouts – 19"
Yard/secondary track
usually – 18"
Branch line – 13"
Industry trackage – 13" min.
or as marked
Unmarked curves are – 20" or
corresponding larger radius on
outer tracks on curves
A – optional industry spur locations

Track elevation
above floor in inches

Track or structure
location and elevation
above floor in inches
on different level

SCALE: 3/8"
Size of squares: 12"

TURNOUTS
Unmarked turnouts are Peco "medium"
curved frog 19" rad. ±, equivalent to
straight frog no. 5

L – indicates location where Peco "long"
turnout is preferred (36" rad. ±)

Area available for upper deck support,
typically disguised as buildings

TRACKAGE
Track center spacing is 1 1/4" (16 2/3 scale ft.).
Curves 1 3/8" min., to be confirmed by test.
Helix or other layover/staging trackage – 2"

Vertical spacing:
"Short" crossings:
min. 1.5"
(20 scale ft.)
"Long" crossings:
min. 3.25"
standard 4"

LOWER LEVEL

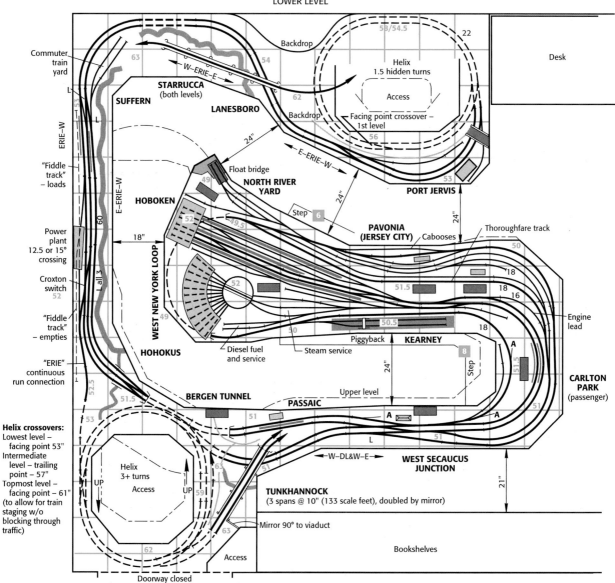

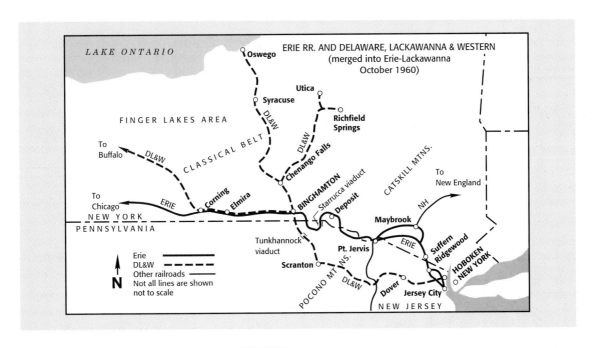

ERIE RR. AND DELAWARE, LACKAWANNA & WESTERN
(merged into Erie-Lackawanna
October 1960)

LAKE ONTARIO

Oswego

Utica

Syracuse

Richfield Springs

FINGER LAKES AREA

CLASSICAL BELT

DL&W

DL&W

Chenango Falls

To Buffalo

DL&W

BINGHAMTON

Starrucca viaduct

CATSKILL MTNS.

To New England

NH

To Chicago

ERIE

Corning   Elmira

Deposit

NEW YORK

Maybrook

PENNSYLVANIA

Tunkhannock viaduct

Pt. Jervis

ERIE

Suffern Ridgewood

HOBOKEN

NEW YORK

Scranton

POCONO MTNS.

DL&W

Dover

Jersey City

NEW JERSEY

Erie ——————
DL&W ‑ ‑ ‑ ‑ ‑
Other railroads ———
Not all lines are shown
not to scale

N

UPPER LEVEL

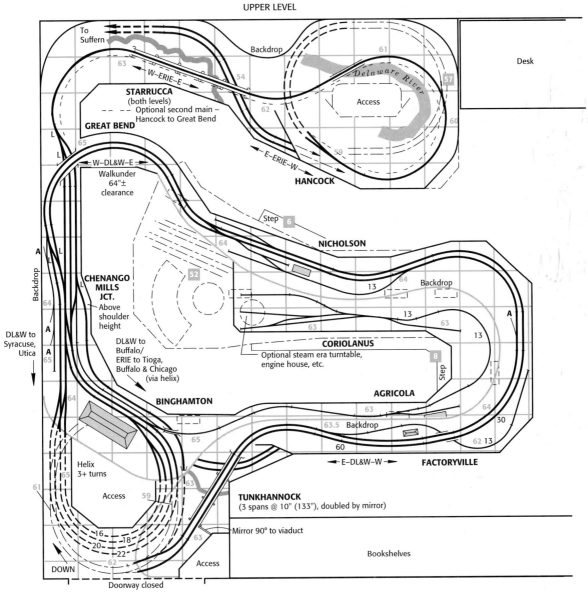

To Suffern

Backdrop

Desk

63

W–ERIE–E

54

Delaware River

57

61

STARRUCCA
(both levels)
– – – Optional second main –
Hancock to Great Bend

Access

62

60

59

GREAT BEND

L

65

L

W–DL&W–E

E–ERIE–W

Walkunder
64"± clearance

HANCOCK

Step   6

NICHOLSON

A

64

52

CHENANGO MILLS JCT.
Above shoulder height

13

64   Backdrop

DL&W to Syracuse, Utica

A

DL&W to Buffalo/
ERIE to Tioga,
Buffalo & Chicago
(via helix)

13

63

63

13

A

65

A

CORIOLANUS

Optional steam era turntable,
engine house, etc.

8

Step

BINGHAMTON

AGRICOLA

64

64

63

30

65

63.5   Backdrop

62 13

61

65

Helix
3+ turns

60

E–DL&W–W

FACTORYVILLE

Access

59

63

TUNKHANNOCK
(3 spans @ 10" (133"), doubled by mirror)

16
18
20
22

63

Mirror 90° to viaduct

Bookshelves

DOWN

62

Access

Doorway closed

track west of the Bergen tunnel and three intermediate suburban stations that have been chosen on the basis of their modest size. Ridgewood itself rates a station far too impressive to be compressed to fit.

Lanesboro is unprotoypically east of Port Jervis (the terminus of a few long-run commuter trains) but left visible because the scene of tracks curving under Starrucca is familiar and irresistibly attractive. Scores of miles have been shrunk into the helix trackage; visibility resumes atop the viaduct.

On the Lackawanna route, which peels off in the correct direction at West Secaucus Junction, it's the commuter territory that's omitted. The line, which carries mostly passenger traffic, is out in the open as it passes under Tunkhannock Viaduct—another irresistible scene—then disappears to start its 2.8 percent climb. This is correctly steeper than the Erie's 2 percent and comfortably adds ¾ inch to the finger room between levels. The Lackawanna line emerges, still westbound but now traveling in an opposite (right-to-left) direction—one of the side-effects of a helix cure—and crosses the span into a rural area. It serves Factoryville and Nicholson industries before crossing the walk-under aisle to rejoin the Erie at Chenango Mills Junction via a rather contrived overhead approach to Binghamton.

A bonus branch

Since an important Lackawanna secondary main line to Syracuse and Lake Ontario branches north at Binghamton, it's no great strain on

reality to leave exposed the approaches to the turning loop and its concentric staging tracks that represent the lines west through the Southern Tier counties of New York. One direction looks like the line to Buffalo, the other the Syracuse main. Trains coming in from the east on the ex-Erie have the choice of turning via the same loop or sneaking down the Lackawanna helix to retain their westbound status—handy for trains of empty hoppers.

Behind the backdrop along the Factoryville-Nicholson section of the main line is some real estate that is practically free for the taking but difficult to utilize. There's no way out for a track entering from Binghamton, so it can't be used to extend a main line, but it is ideal for a branch. The Lackawanna had branches serving central New York's "Classical Belt," so known because of the dozens of localities named for ancient Greek and Roman places and notables. Since Coriolanus wasn't among those honored, using his name for the destination of the milk-train branch will suggest its locale, while keeping it thoroughly fictitious. Coriolanus is above eye level, and the floor level in this area can't be raised because New Jersey is down below, but there is room for a permanent 8-inch step to bring the scene into focus.

Back by the Hudson River are the parallel passenger and freight terminals serving both routes. Several years before the merger all Erie passenger trains, including commuter runs, moved into the Lackawanna's Hoboken station, and Erie abandoned its Jersey City terminal. Pavonia-area freight

facilities remained and are represented in this condensation by a skinny yard leading to a mostly hidden return loop. Maintaining a sufficient flow of mainline freight traffic with the number of trains that can be turned in a purely stub yard could be wearying. Commuter trains are easily "turned" (we are not yet in the push-pull era) by putting the motive power on the other end, but readying the *Phoebe Snow* and other limiteds featuring sleepers and observation-lounge cars will also be expedited by a trip around the loop.

In prime viewing territory on the opposite side of the Hoboken terminal are the engine service facilities and one of the early piggyback-era intermodal terminals. While both roads were dieselized by the time of the merger, some steam-era structures have remained in use as fuel facilities for the newcomers. N scale comes to the rescue, since these sub-terminals can be placed side by side and yet remain within arm's reach.

Connecting all these elements is a sprawling throat, extending out as far as West Secaucus, allowing all the necessary movements to be made, though in some cases in ways more interesting than convenient. Departing from normal practice, it is recommended that there be only a partial view block (mostly to help support the upper deck) between the two sides of the peninsula. The ability to see and control a departing Lackawanna or Erie train from the opposite side of the terminal makes the subsequent mainline trip possible without backtracking. Try it!

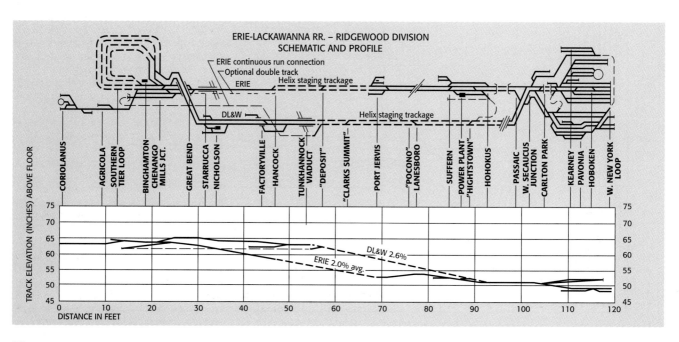

THE UPPER MISSISSIPPI RAILROAD

A composite of the Burlington, Milwaukee, and North Western lines
along the scenic Mississippi in Wisconsin and Minnesota,
with abundant, accessible staging and layover trackage

WHEN THE AREA must be approached from the side rather than from above or below, coming up with a walk-in plan is a challenge. If the area is fairly large—30 square squares or more—it may be practical to have the main line rise to a summit near or above head height, alleviating the entry problem and giving the layout no-stoop or at least slight-stoop status. If the layout is to represent a midwestern granger railroad, however, mountain-scaling grades are out of place and we are faced with accepting a "two-blob" space penalty in providing an entryway between two lobes of main line. That's the reasoning behind that eight-square-square subtraction in coming up with the adjusted rating for space usability.

Such is the situation with the Upper Mississippi Railroad, an HO plan designed to exploit the calm beauty of the river south of the Twin Cities toward the Iowa and Illinois borders—as the Burlington used to say in ads for its *Zephyrs*, "Where Nature smiles 300 miles." While the area is generally flat to gently rolling in character, along many miles of the river are imposing bluffs which should provide a similarly imposing backdrop for the .

The classic approach for such a side-entry plan is a folded shank connecting the two end loops of a dogbone. Aside from the space taken up by those two ends, what do you do with the back track of that shank? It can be presented as the second track of a two-track main line, but that's an awfully short run. The end loops, which usually have to be hidden to avoid the appearance of a toy-train oval, could be augmented with at best two or three parallel staging and layover sidings. Maintaining the minimum radius on the inner tracks means that the knobs of track grow too big for the space— and this pike needs a great deal more such trackage. Rolling stock already at hand has passed the 250-car mark, and population control is no more likely to work in the future than it has in the past. As the model manufacturers know, all three prototype railroads have some irresistible items.

The compromise is to put one side of the dogbone shank "downstairs" as a secluded but accessible return route paralleled by extensive staging trackage (Yards A and B). The ladders are arranged so that traffic can still get by on the main line with all yard tracks occupied and yet trains laying over can leave in any order in either direction. The two yards can thus absorb about 160 freight-car lengths worth of trains.

Where did that train go?

These tracks are on wider centers (3 inches) to provide finger room, should fiddling or re-railing be needed. It's also recommended that the yards be "terraced" as indicated; even a slight elevation of the rear tracks makes it a lot easier to identify a particular consist when you're looking for it.

As the plan develops, it turns out there is room (some of it required for access to the workbench area) to provide aisles alongside much of the end-loop trackage, so most of the overall dogbone route can be left visible without having a train go through the same scene more than once. When a southbound train goes past Quarryville and quietly disappears, how does the engineer who has been following it get it safely parked without having to backtrack around the peninsula for a peek? With today's readily available technology, it's not too hard. One thing that will do the trick is to provide stopping sections at the ends of the staging tracks; when turned off, they will bring any train approaching the clearance point to a halt. The sections will, however, require a fair amount of wiring to provide status information at the disappearance points.

Making those end loops
earn their keep

Mainline traffic will undoubtedly move predominantly in round-and-round fashion. In the era being modeled there wasn't much coal traffic in open-top cars that would have to be so routed to make it appear that loads and empties were moving in logical directions. Nevertheless, reversing connections are desirable, and those end loops provide both north-to-south and south-to-north connections. There is even room on the north-to-south loop for another staging track to stash away another 22 cars' worth of trains. Topside on one loop a reduced-radius branch can curve its way up to Chatsworth and a switchback to a lead mine, an appropriate industry for this territory.

The other return bend gets a less traditional treatment. Rather than leave a doughnut hole unoccupied behind a tear-drop backdrop, you can have a wide Mississippi oxbow within an aisle-side backdrop, notched at some points to provide broad views of

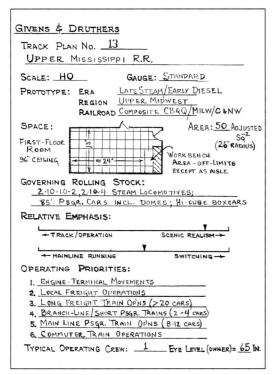

GIVENS & DRUTHERS

TRACK PLAN No. __13__

UPPER MISSISSIPPI R.R.

SCALE: __HO__   GAUGE: STANDARD

PROTOTYPE: ERA   LATE STEAM/EARLY DIESEL
                REGION   UPPER MIDWEST
                RAILROAD Composite CB&Q/MILW/C&NW

SPACE: AREA: 50 ADJUSTED
FIRST-FLOOR   SQ²
ROOM   (26" RADIUS)
96" CEILING
                                  WORK BENCH
              ≈ 24'   AREA - OFF-LIMITS
                                EXCEPT AS AISLE

GOVERNING ROLLING STOCK:
   2-10-10-2, 2-10-4 STEAM LOCOMOTIVES;
   85' PSGR. CARS INCL. DOMES; HI-CUBE BOXCARS

RELATIVE EMPHASIS:
   ◄─ TRACK/OPERATION   SCENIC REALISM ─►

   ◄─ MAINLINE RUNNING   SWITCHING ─►

OPERATING PRIORITIES:
   1. ENGINE-TERMINAL MOVEMENTS
   2. LOCAL FREIGHT OPERATIONS
   3. LONG FREIGHT TRAIN OP'NS (>20 CARS)
   4. BRANCH-LINE/SHORT PSGR. TRAINS (2-4 CARS)
   5. MAIN LINE PSGR. TRAIN OP'NS (8-12 CARS)
   6. COMMUTER TRAIN OPERATIONS

TYPICAL OPERATING CREW: __1__   EYE LEVEL (OWNER) = 65 IN.

UPPER MISSISSIPPI RAILROAD

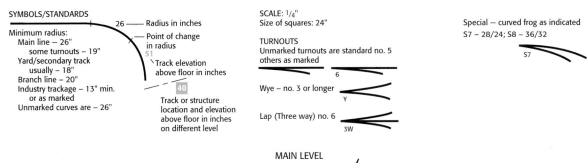

SYMBOLS/STANDARDS

Minimum radius:
 Main line — 26"
  some turnouts – 19"
 Yard/secondary track
  usually – 18"
 Branch line – 20"
 Industry trackage – 13" min.
  or as marked
 Unmarked curves are – 26"

26 — Radius in inches

Point of change in radius

51 — Track elevation above floor in inches

40 — Track or structure location and elevation above floor in inches on different level

SCALE: ¼"
Size of squares: 24"

TURNOUTS
Unmarked turnouts are standard no. 5
others as marked

Wye – no. 3 or longer

Lap (Three way) no. 6

Special — curved frog as indicated
S7 – 28/24; S8 – 36/32

MAIN LEVEL

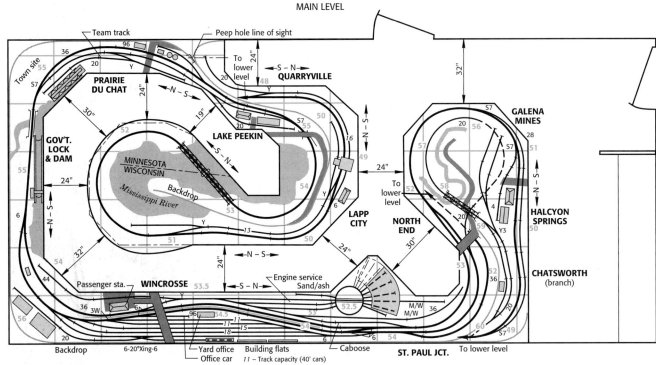

Team track
Peep hole line of sight
To lower level
QUARRYVILLE
PRAIRIE DU CHAT
LAKE PEEKIN
GOV'T. LOCK & DAM
MINNESOTA
WISCONSIN
Mississippi River
Backdrop
GALENA MINES
LAPP CITY
NORTH END
HALCYON SPRINGS
CHATSWORTH (branch)
WINCROSSE
Passenger sta.
Engine service Sand/ash
M/W
M/W
ST. PAUL JCT.
To lower level
Backdrop
6-20°Xing-6
Yard office
Office car
Building flats
11 – Track capacity (40' cars)
Caboose

LOWER LEVEL
STAGING AND REVERSING
TRACKAGE ONLY

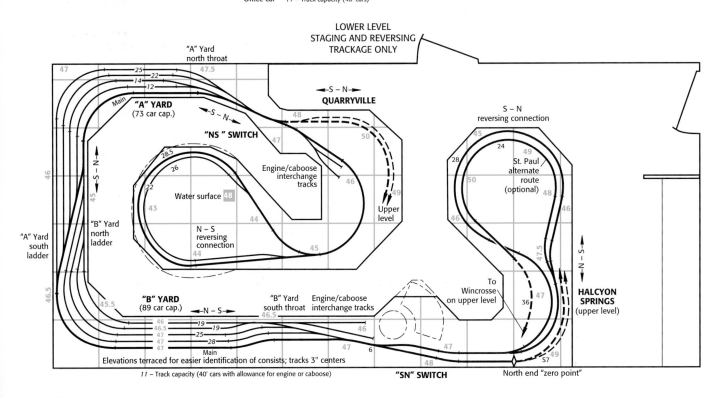

"A" Yard north throat
Main
"A" YARD (73 car cap.)
"NS " SWITCH
Engine/caboose interchange tracks
QUARRYVILLE
S – N reversing connection
St. Paul alternate route (optional)
Upper level
"B" Yard north ladder
Water surface 48
N – S reversing connection
"A" Yard south ladder
"B" YARD (89 car cap.)
"B" Yard south throat
Engine/caboose interchange tracks
To Wincrosse on upper level
HALCYON SPRINGS (upper level)
Main
Elevations terraced for easier identification of consists; tracks 3" centers
11 – Track capacity (40' cars with allowance for engine or caboose)
"SN" SWITCH
North end "zero point"

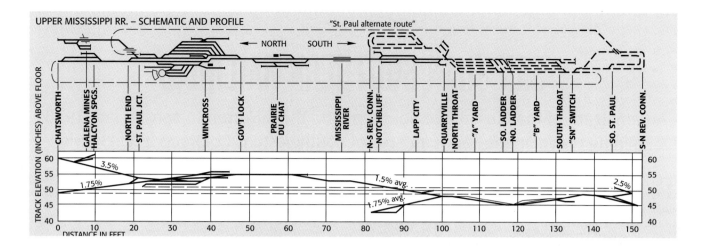

Old Man River while hiding the fact that the majestic stream must shortly expire against a backdrop. The oxbow itself represents a modeler's license import from farther south; the Father of Waters actually follows a generally straight course through this broad section, properly known as Lake Pepin.

Featured up front are the through truss spans taking the main line from Minnesota to Wisconsin. Much of the river and the terrain on the far bank is well beyond arm's reach, but if solidly executed, this scenicking job should be well worth the strain.

A matter of balance: grades vs. access

Is all that secluded trackage practical? It can be, but only if carefully located horizontally and vertically. The turnouts are kept as close to the aisle as possible, and all tracks are within about 15 inches of the layout edge on straightaways and ladders. There is a vertical separation of 7 to 10 inches (railhead to railhead) between the visible and secluded layers—room for those minor emergency trackwork adjustments that really shouldn't be necessary because of the thorough operational checkout given the lower-level trackage before the top-level structure is put in place.

The Upper Mississippi should be close to level. As the profile shows, grades in the range of 1.5 to 1.75 percent are needed to maintain those ample lower-level clearances. Our relatively powerful locomotives should be able to handle typical model-length consists with little difficulty, but will the grade look too steep? Probably not, if care is taken to tailor scenic details—water surface elevations and the pitch of rock strata, for example—to create a deceptive impression of levelness. In any case, balancing the opposing considerations of gradient

Milwaukee Road train 100, the *Afternoon Hiawatha*, rolls south along the west bank of the Mississippi a few miles north of Winona, Minnesota, on June 10, 1950. Photo by James G. La Vake.

and access is the crux of effective layout planning in a midwestern context.

The classic division point

Wincrosse—an obvious amalgam of La Crosse, Wisconsin, and Winona, Minnesota—is arranged as a classic steam-era division point where changing engines, originating local freights, and servicing through passenger trains kept an army of employees and an ocean of yard trackage busy. Accommodating all this activity within the length and width available is a matter of arranging the trackage so that it can serve multiple purposes.

The second main track serves as the switching lead for both ends of the freight yard, as well as the bypass (via the thoroughfare track at the rear of the classification tracks) for through traffic when a passenger train is occu-

pying the station track. The busy lead to the three engine-terminal tracks also leads to the passenger station siding and doubles as the south lead to the caboose and maintenance equipment tracks. The latter are more than usually important on this railroad because super-detailed cranes, plows, ditchers, and such are a particular liking of the management.

By wrapping the south ladder around a curve in pinwheel fashion and using the No. 5 turnouts appropriate for a layout with 26-inch main line curves throughout (except in crossover alignments, where No. 6 turnouts eliminate any S-curve problems), yard tracks are long enough to justify the use of heavy switchers, while keeping most of the north ladder clear of the marginally accessible area behind the engine terminal.

SAN JUAN SOUTHERN RAILROAD

An amalgam of the Rio Grande Southern and the Silverton to serve a late-1930s mining revival in the San Juan area of southwestern Colorado in On3 style

THE SILVERTON and the Rio Grande Southern were the two most uniformly spectacular narrow gauge railroads in Colorado. Otto Mears intended the Silverton Railroad to connect Silverton and Ouray, which are 15 miles apart, straight-line distance, but the last few miles of terrain between Ironton and Ouray ultimately proved impassable for a railroad. (Mears's wagon road was already in place there, anyway.) Mears then built the Rio Grande Southern between Ridgway, 10 miles north of Ouray, and Durango, 45 miles south of Silverton, primarily to serve the mining area west of Silverton and Ouray. The long life of the Rio Grande Southern was surprising, considering the boom-and-bust character of the San Juan area mining industry supporting it.

Taking full advantage of modeler's license, the San Juan Southern melds these lines into a composite route hauling ore and concentrates from the mines and mill in the Corkscrew area up and over Red Mountain pass, down past a Denver & Rio Grande Western connection at Ridgway, then over a Rio Grande Southern-like summit at Serpent Head to a smelter just beyond another connection with the D&RGW at Durangisson.

The 270 feet of On3 main line is wrapped into an area evaluated at about 60 square squares in a newly-built "basement with a house over it." The main line has a liberal 42-inch radius, and it can certainly rise high enough to provide walk-in access to the relatively uncluttered railroad room. The Red Mountain Extension can be more sharply curved. There is room for track to pass behind the furnace and water heater, and a window, intended to admit G-gauge trains from the garden rather than light or air, can be permanently blanked out otherwise.

An existing 4 × 16-foot module with a laboriously hand-laid yard and an engine terminal complete with structures is to be incorporated in the new railroad; two tracks are to be dedicated to the storage—display, rather—of the rotary, wrecker, and other pieces of superdetailed maintenance-of-way equipment that are already on hand.

Staged construction

Completion of a railroad of this scope is a matter of years. The lowest-level trackage, including two end loops, a staging yard, and the Durangisson yard, constitute a logical first stage. Fortunately most of that will go down quickly, since no scenic treatment is involved. As the schematic shows, a variety of continuous and out-and-back routes will then serve to provide early-on operating interest and thoroughly test the quality of the trackwork that will later be hidden away. This "Hernando" trackage will become a staging hideaway when the track above is put in place. It is designed for continuing maintainability—all the turnouts are located close to the aisle.

The next stage of construction takes the line on a climbing path across a roaring stream from the previously laid track. It goes up and over Serpent Head Pass toward Welcome Arch, a bridge high and long enough for full walk-in entry to the railroad.

Rio Grande Southern 461 and Denver & Rio Grande Western 451 lift a 13-car freight up Lizard Head Pass on September 4, 1951. Photo by R. H. Kindig.

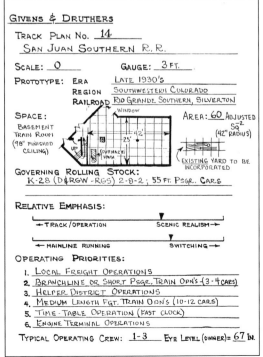

GIVENS & DRUTHERS

TRACK PLAN No. 14
SAN JUAN SOUTHERN R. R.

SCALE: O   GAUGE: 3 FT.

PROTOTYPE: ERA   LATE 1930's
           REGION SOUTHWESTERN COLORADO
           RAILROAD RIO GRANDE SOUTHERN, SILVERTON

SPACE: AREA: 60 ADJUSTED SQ²
BASEMENT   (42" RADIUS)
TRAIN ROOM
(98" FINISHED
CEILING)   EXISTING YARD TO BE INCORPORATED

GOVERNING ROLLING STOCK:
K-28 (D&RGW -RGS) 2-8-2 ; 55 FT. PSGR. CARS

RELATIVE EMPHASIS:

← TRACK/OPERATION   SCENIC REALISM →

← MAINLINE RUNNING   SWITCHING →

OPERATING PRIORITIES:
1. LOCAL FREIGHT OPERATIONS
2. BRANCHLINE OR SHORT PSGR. TRAIN OPN'S -(3-4 CARS)
3. HELPER DISTRICT OPERATIONS
4. MEDIUM LENGTH FGT. TRAIN OPN'S (10-12 CARS)
5. TIME-TABLE OPERATION (FAST CLOCK)
6. ENGINE TERMINAL OPERATIONS

TYPICAL OPERATING CREW: 1-3   EYE LEVEL (OWNER)= 67 IN.

At the summit of this 4 percent helper grade there is a wye. Its tail over toward the furnace is above head height and high enough that it will not be part of the scenery of San Juan Junction far below. The fact that two legs of the wye must poke through the backdrop is well hidden by rickety snow sheds like those on the RGS at Lizard Head. The combination of the wye and the passing track at Serpent Head will permit out-and-back operations from Durangisson with all the locomotives pointed correctly—an immediate payoff in enjoyment.

Next it's down toward the already-built Ridgway terminal module, via scenic features swiped from Colorado Central's Georgetown loop and Rio Grande's line through the Black Canyon of the Gunnison. Both loop and canyon involve watercourses; to get the most scene for the square foot, the two have been combined into a single convoluted stream. To conceal this fact, the walls of Opaque Canon are configured so viewers peering into the gorge from opposite ends won't see each other or otherwise suspect deception.

On to Corkscrew

The Silverton Railroad surmounted Red Mountain Pass and got as far down toward Ouray as Corkscrew in the fabulously wealthy Mineral Creek area. Switchback tracks serving the numerous mines and mills in this cramped gorge were so steep and crooked that nothing we can do in On3 can be an exaggeration. Dropping down to a 36-inch radius, the SJS Red Mountain Extension climbing back from Ridgway uses nothing larger than

Rio Grande Southern Galloping Goose No. 5 pauses in front of the heavy timber station at Lizard Head on August 14, 1942. Snowsheds protect not only the main track but the turning wye. Photo by R. H. Kindig.

2-8-0s on its 5 percent slopes, with Galloping Geese to handle the mail, express, and passengers. The last mines on the Silverton actually played out in 1931, but this version of the area experienced enough of a revival later in the decade to match RGS's uranium rush and survive (with the aid of the Geese) through the 1940s.

The Extension enhances the canyon scene with another pair of bridges in the process of horseshoeing and switchbacking its way up and down to the Big Juan concentrator—which just happens to be at the right elevation for a comfortable empties-in–loads-out exchange connection with the smelter back near Durangisson.

Corkscrew itself turned its tiny trains with the aid of a covered turntable completing the run-around track. Compounding the joys of running the precipitous railroad was its location in a snowbelt area. Down below timberline at Woodzee the SJS might as well

gather itself some lumbering traffic.

The Georgetown-style loop and the first horseshoe on the Extension can be fitted into the same blob, but keeping them scenically separate widens this section of benchwork to about 11 feet, so access requires attention. Fortunately, the central mountain core is well above eye-level, even from the raised aisleway needed to make the Serpent Head scene attractive. So a large but out-of-sight opening within the fabled Peaks of San Juan can not only ease the reach all around but provide a glorious panorama of the little trains struggling up, down, and around the topography.

Ridgway yard is also too wide for one-side access. Adding a one-person raised aisleway (18 inches) concealed by a low backdrop that also enhances the yard scene corrects this and offers a better view of the lofty Red Mountain Pass area.

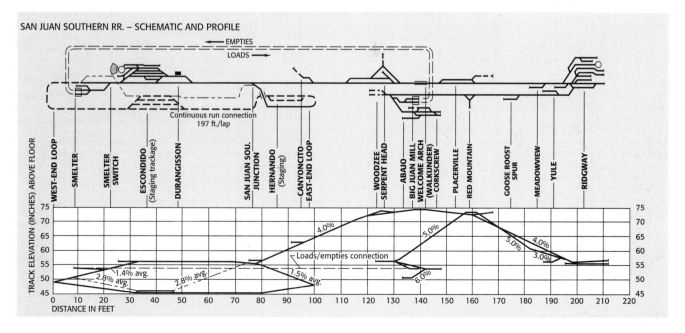

SAN JUAN SOUTHERN RR. – SCHEMATIC AND PROFILE

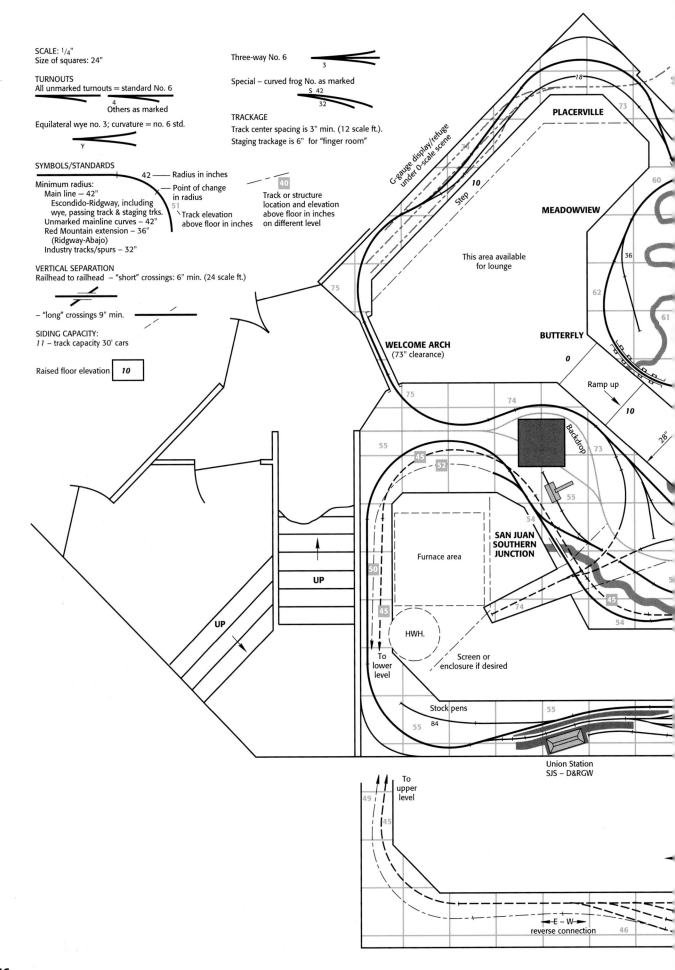

SCALE: ¹/₄"
Size of squares: 24"

TURNOUTS
All unmarked turnouts = standard No. 6
                    4
          Others as marked

Equilateral wye no. 3; curvature = no. 6 std.

          Y

SYMBOLS/STANDARDS
          42 ——— Radius in inches
          —— Point of change
             in radius
   51   Track elevation
           above floor in inches

Minimum radius:
   Main line – 42"
      Escondido-Ridgway, including
      wye, passing track & staging trks.
   Unmarked mainline curves – 42"
   Red Mountain extension – 36"
      (Ridgway-Abajo)
   Industry tracks/spurs – 32"

VERTICAL SEPARATION
Railhead to railhead – "short" crossings: 6" min. (24 scale ft.)

– "long" crossings 9" min.

SIDING CAPACITY:
11 – track capacity 30' cars

Raised floor elevation   10

Three-way No. 6
                    3

Special – curved frog No. as marked
          S 42
          32

TRACKAGE
Track center spacing is 3" min. (12 scale ft.).
Staging trackage is 6" for "finger room"

   40   Track or structure
        location and elevation
        above floor in inches
        on different level

G-gauge display/refuge
under O-scale scene

Step   10

PLACERVILLE   73

MEADOWVIEW

18

60

36

62

61

This area available
for lounge

75

BUTTERFLY

0

Ramp up

10

WELCOME ARCH
(73" clearance)

75   74   73   28"

55

45

52   Backdrop

55

54

SAN JUAN
SOUTHERN
JUNCTION

45

UP

50

45

74

54

UP

HWH.

To
lower
level

Screen or
enclosure if desired

Stock pens   55
              84

55

Union Station
SJS – D&RGW

To
upper
level

49

45

←E – W→
reverse connection

46

66

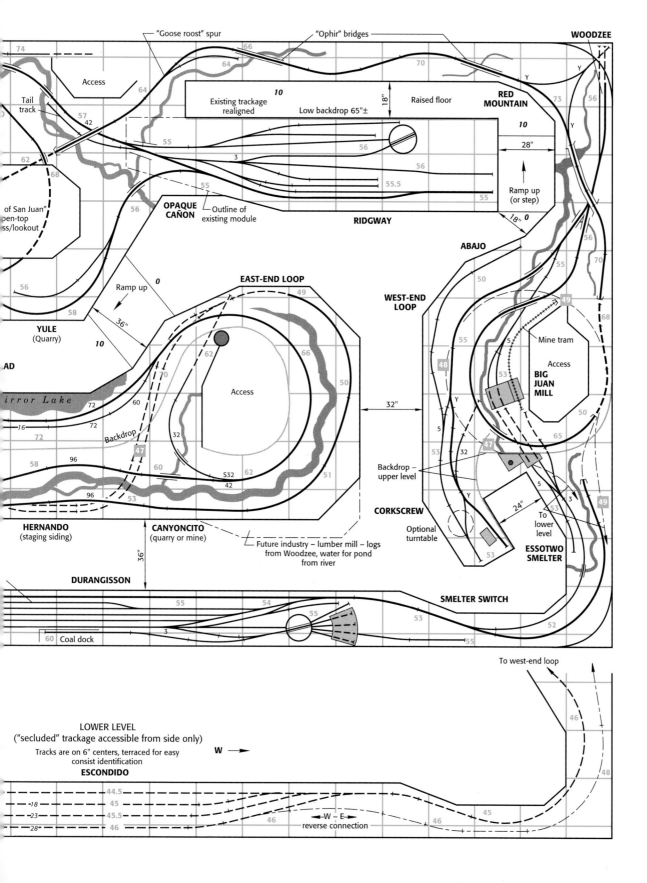

"Goose roost" spur   "Ophir" bridges

WOODZEE

74

Access

Tail track

Existing trackage realigned

18"

Low backdrop 65"±

Raised floor

RED MOUNTAIN

10

28"

Ramp up (or step)

OPAQUE CAÑON

Outline of existing module

RIDGWAY

18" 0

of San Juan" pen-top ss/lookout

ABAJO

EAST-END LOOP

WEST-END LOOP

Ramp up

36"

YULE (Quarry)

10

Mine tram

Access

BIG JUAN MILL

AD

irror Lake

Access

32"

Backdrop

Backdrop – upper level

CORKSCREW

Optional turntable

HERNANDO (staging siding)

CANYONCITO (quarry or mine)

Future industry – lumber mill – logs from Woodzee, water for pond from river

24"

To lower level

ESSOTWO SMELTER

36"

DURANGISSON

SMELTER SWITCH

Coal dock

To west-end loop

LOWER LEVEL
("secluded" trackage accessible from side only)

Tracks are on 6" centers, terraced for easy consist identification

ESCONDIDO

W →

←W – E→
reverse connection

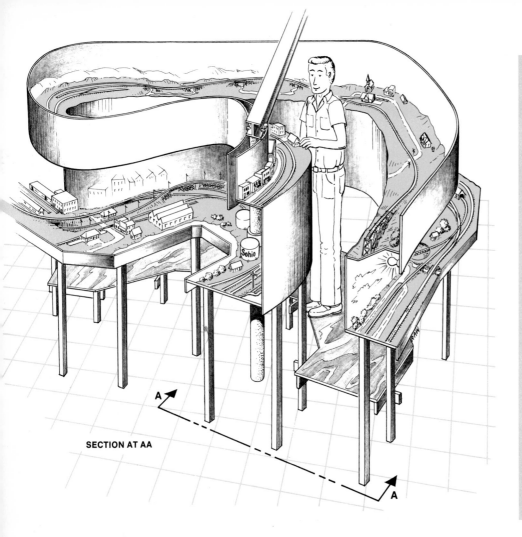

SECTION AT AA

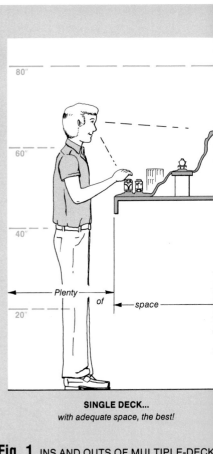

SINGLE DECK...
with adequate space, the best!

Fig. 1 INS AND OUTS OF MULTIPLE-DECK

MEET THE MUSHROOM

A double deck layout with both decks at the perfect height

IS THERE a single best height for a model railroad? Sure, but it varies with the tastes and statures of the individuals arguing the point. Among 6-footers, the optimum rail height might range from as low as 42 inches to near eye-level—60 inches or so.

Why so much difference of opinion? Perhaps as much as anything it comes from train-watching preferences. Those who get their biggest thrills from up-close views of passing trains will tend to like the trackside realism of eye level; those who prefer a broader view, say, from a hill or an overpass, are more likely to accept a lower layout (along with its crawl-under construction and maintenance discomforts). In any case, in recent times most single-deck pikes have been planned for base elevations of 48 inches, give or take, as shown in Figure 1. It follows, then, that a multideck pike can't have 'em all at that optimum elevation. If a dou-

ble-deck layout is to be reasonably practical, comfortable, and scenically convincing, the decks should be 14 to 20 inches apart (at least in HO and larger scales). This means that either the lower one must be too low or the upper one too high; the most likely compromise has neither at a really ideal elevation.

Fiddling with "sea level"

In a more logical compromise, the lower deck is set at a normal elevation, as if for a single-deck railroad. The upper deck is then viewed and operated from elevated step-up areas—permanent, movable, or fold-up. Another approach, particularly appropriate for walkaround pikes in sloping-ceiling locations (usually attics), is to operate and view the lower level from a roll-around chair.

With this approach aisleways should be widened, either to accommo-

date step-up areas or to make way for chairs and their occupants' horizontal thighs. This widening in turn dilutes the increase in space efficiency that prompted the bilevel approach in the first place.

Conceptually, there is an approach to multilevel model railroading free from these negative aspects—build the layout so you look at the two layers from opposite directions! The floor levels for each layer are then independent, and both can be ideal. The arrangement also eliminates the possibility of visual distraction from tracks and trains on another level.

Enter the Mushroom

Such a back-to-back configuration—hereafter called the Mushroom—is the centerpiece of the layout presented here. Its large hollow stem supports a wide cap that encloses the upper level of the layout.

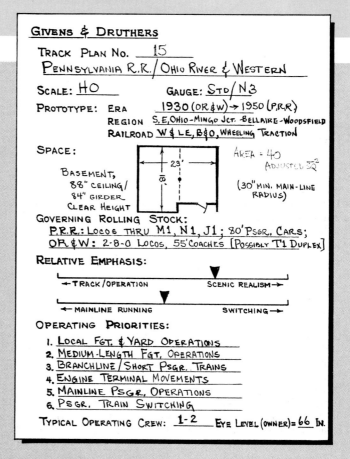

MULTIPLE DECKS...
*bottom too low or top too high...
take your pick!*

A STEP UP HELPS A BIT...
*but watch out
when you back up!*

ROLL AROUND *and* STAND UP...
*nice, if you have
plenty of space.*

DOUBLE DECKS, BACK-TO-BACK...
*ideal...we'll call it
"the Mushroom"!*

The resulting layout combines HO and HOn3 based on—unlikely as it might seem—late-steam Pennsylvania Railroad operations in southeastern Ohio. The layout space is nearly ideal in shape and size. The challenge lies in wanting to represent realistically the whole spectrum of railroading in the Ohio River valley south and west of Steubenville, Ohio: Pennsy's Pittsburgh-St. Louis main line through Steubenville; heavy-duty Pennsy branches along each side of the densely industrialized river valley, interlaced with tracks of the Baltimore & Ohio, Pittsburgh & West Virginia, Wheeling & Lake Erie, and local streetcar and interurban lines; and (as late as 1931) a 42-mile remnant of the rural Ohio River & Western, a 3-foot-gauge Pennsylvania Railroad affiliate that once reached 112 miles from Bellaire to Zanesville.

Three "railroads" in one space

To represent all this prototype activity, the plan features what amounts to three separate railroads. The first is the big-time mainline Pennsy. As indicated on the schematic, it's a double-track dogbone over which trains can shuttle to represent

Text continued on page 72.

GIVENS & DRUTHERS

TRACK PLAN NO. ___15___
PENNSYLVANIA R.R./OHIO RIVER & WESTERN

SCALE: HO   GAUGE: STD/N3

PROTOTYPE: ERA   1930 (OR&W) → 1950 (P.R.R.)
REGION   S.E.OHIO-MINGO JCT.-BELLAIRE-WOODSFIELD
RAILROAD   W&LE, B&O, WHEELING TRACTION

SPACE:

BASEMENT,
88" CEILING/
84" GIRDER
CLEAR HEIGHT

AREA = 40
ADJUSTED 38?

(30" MIN. MAIN-LINE
RADIUS)

GOVERNING ROLLING STOCK:
P.R.R.: LOCOS THRU M1, N1, J1; 80' PSGR. CARS;
OR&W: 2-8-0 LOCOS, 55' COACHES [POSSIBLY T1 DUPLEX]

RELATIVE EMPHASIS:

←TRACK/OPERATION   SCENIC REALISM→

←MAINLINE RUNNING   SWITCHING→

OPERATING PRIORITIES:

1. LOCAL FGT. & YARD OPERATIONS
2. MEDIUM-LENGTH FGT. OPERATIONS
3. BRANCHLINE/SHORT PSGR. TRAINS
4. ENGINE TERMINAL MOVEMENTS
5. MAINLINE PSGR. OPERATIONS
6. PSGR. TRAIN SWITCHING

TYPICAL OPERATING CREW: ___1-2___   EYE LEVEL (OWNER) = 66 IN.

Fig. 2 TRACK PLANNING CRITERIA

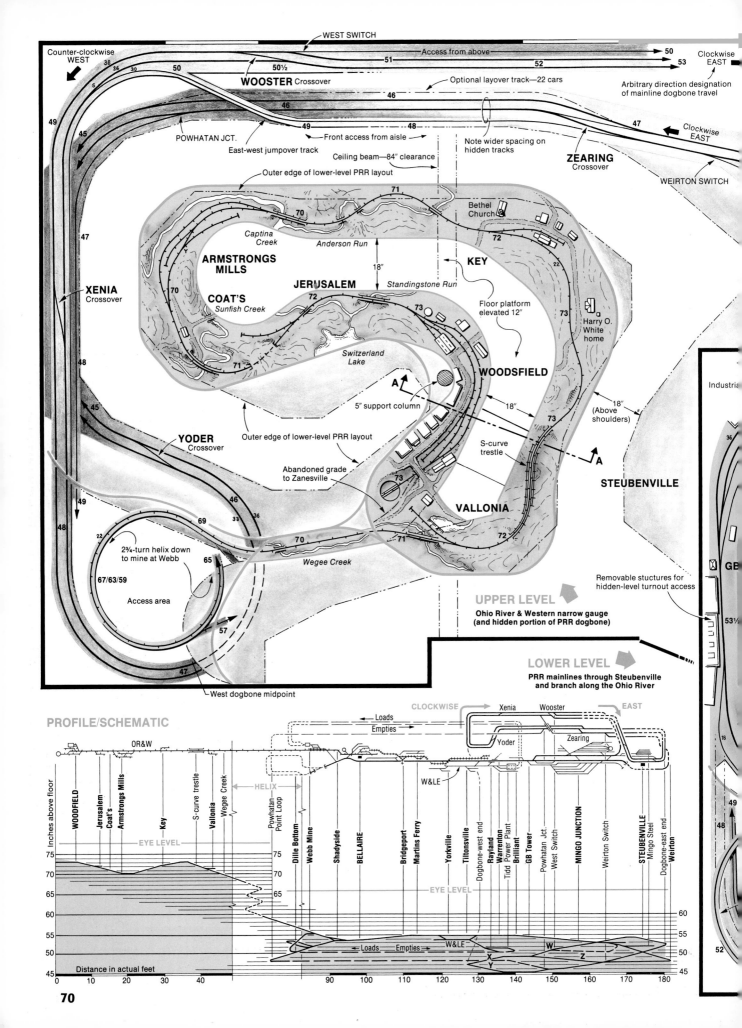

WEST SWITCH

Counter-clockwise WEST

Access from above → 50

Clockwise EAST

38
36
30
S
50
51
52
53

Arbitrary direction designation of mainline dogbone travel

50½

WOOSTER Crossover

Optional layover track—22 cars

46

49

POWHATAN JCT.

46

45

East-west jumpover track

49

48

Front access from aisle

Note wider spacing on hidden tracks

47

Clockwise EAST

Ceiling beam—84" clearance

ZEARING Crossover

WEIRTON SWITCH

Outer edge of lower-level PRR layout

71

47

70

Bethel Church

72

Captina Creek

Anderson Run

KEY

ARMSTRONGS MILLS

18"

22

XENIA Crossover

70

COAT'S Sunfish Creek

JERUSALEM

72

Standingstone Run

73

Floor platform elevated 12"

73

Harry O. White home

48

71

73

45

Switzerland Lake

WOODSFIELD

18"

18" (Above shoulders)

A

49

YODER Crossover

5" support column

S-curve trestle

A

48

Outer edge of lower-level PRR layout

Abandoned grade to Zanesville

73

STEUBENVILLE

46

VALLONIA

72

69

36
33
22

70

71

2¾-turn helix down to mine at Webb

Wegee Creek

65

Industrial

36

Removable stuctures for hidden-level turnout access

GB

67/63/59

Access area

53½

57

UPPER LEVEL
Ohio River & Western narrow gauge (and hidden portion of PRR dogbone)

47

West dogbone midpoint

LOWER LEVEL
PRR mainlines through Steubenville and branch along the Ohio River

PROFILE/SCHEMATIC

CLOCKWISE   Xenia   Wooster   EAST

Loads
Empties

Yoder

Zearing

OR&W

W&LE

52

Inches above floor

WOODFIELD
Jerusalem
Coat's
Armstrongs Mills
Key
S-curve trestle
Vallonia
Wegee Creek
HELIX
Powhatan Point Loop
Dille Bottom
Webb Mine
Shadyside
BELLAIRE
Bridgeport
Martins Ferry
Yorkville
Tiltonsville
Dogbone-west end
Rayland
Warrenton
Tidd Power Plant
Brilliant
GB Tower
Powhatan Jct.
West Switch
MINGO JUNCTION
Weirton Switch
STEUBENVILLE
Mingo Steel
Dogbone-east end
Weirton

EYE LEVEL

EYE LEVEL

49

48

75
70
65
60
55
50
45

75
70
65
60
55
50
45

60
55
50
45

Loads   Empties   W&LE

W

X   Y   Z

Distance in actual feet

0   10   20   30   40   90   100   110   120   130   140   150   160   170   180

PENNSYLVANIA RR/OHIO RIVER & WESTERN RR

HO / HOn3

Scale of plan: ⅜″ = 1′-0″

TRACK

PRR

Main lines   Other

OR&W narrow gauge (36″)   Dual

Wheeling Transit (5′-2½″, electric)

ELEVATIONS

Railhead elevations above floor in inches — 48

CURVES

PRR dogbone main lines
33″-minimum (eastbound)
30″-minimum (westbound)
30″-minimum, Ohio River branch
18″-minimum, industries-others as marked

OR&W
22″-minimum, helix tracks
18″-minimum, yard/industries

W&LE and Wheeling Transit
As marked

TURNOUTS

Unmarked PRR, no. 6

Standard (straight frog), as marked — 5

Wyes are no. 3 or no. 4, no. 6 or above radius — Y

OR&W narrow gauge, no. 5

Special (curved frog), radii as marked — S 36 / 30

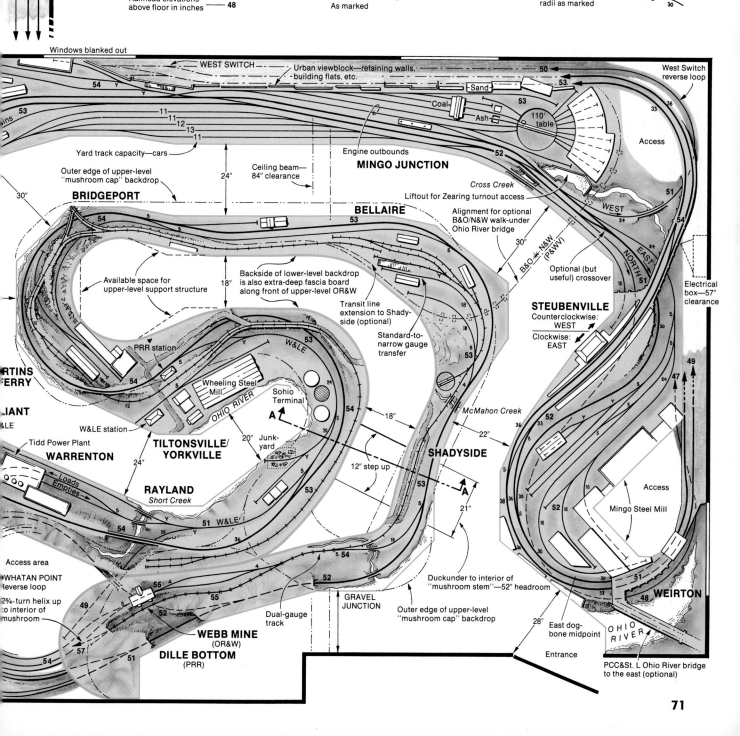

Windows blanked out

WEST SWITCH

Urban viewblock—retaining walls, building flats, etc.

West Switch reverse loop

54   Y

53

50

53

Sand

Coal

Ash

53

110′ table

33   36

Access

Yard track capacity—cars

11   11   12   13   11

52

Engine outbounds

MINGO JUNCTION

51

Outer edge of upper-level "mushroom cap" backdrop

24″

Ceiling beam—84″ clearance

Cross Creek

Liftout for Zearing turnout access

WEST

24

54

BRIDGEPORT

30″

54   5

5

BELLAIRE

53

Alignment for optional B&O/N&W walk-under Ohio River bridge

30″

B&O ※ N&W (P&WV)

Optional (but useful) crossover

NORTH   EAST

51

18

Electrical box—57″ clearance

Available space for upper-level support structure

Backside of lower-level backdrop is also extra-deep fascia board along front of upper-level OR&W

Transit line extension to Shady-side (optional)

Standard-to-narrow gauge transfer

18″

18

STEUBENVILLE

Counterclockwise: WEST

Clockwise: EAST

5

PRR station

53

W&LE

53

MARTINS FERRY

54

W&LE station

RELIANT W&LE

Tidd Power Plant

WARRENTON

12

24″

Wheeling Steel Mill

OHIO RIVER

Sohio Terminal

24

A

Junkyard

20″

Loads   Empties

TILTONSVILLE/ YORKVILLE

54

18″

McMahon Creek

22″

52

53

Mingo Steel Mill

Access

RAYLAND
Short Creek

51   W&LE

Y

54

36

5

12″ step up

53

SHADYSIDE

53

A   A

21″

52

52

49

47

Access area

WHATAN POINT Reverse loop

2¾-turn helix up to interior of mushroom

49

5

52

55

55

5   54

54

52

GRAVEL JUNCTION

Duckunder to interior of "mushroom stem"—52″ headroom

Outer edge of upper-level "mushroom cap" backdrop

28″

East dogbone midpoint

51

WEIRTON

48

57

51

WEBB MINE
(OR&W)

DILLE BOTTOM
(PRR)

Dual-gauge track

Entrance

OHIO RIVER

PCC&St. L Ohio River bridge to the east (optional)

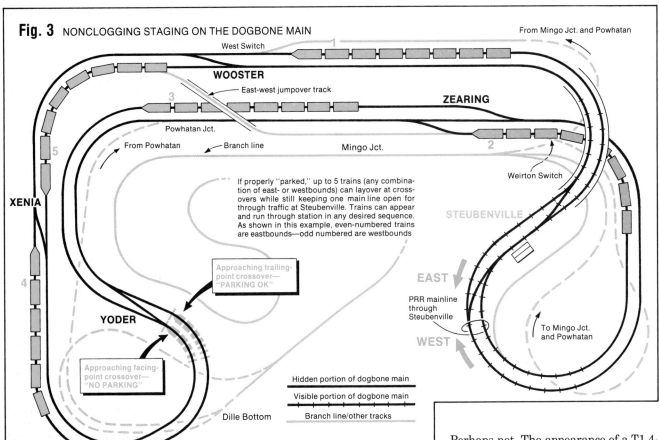

Fig. 3 NONCLOGGING STAGING ON THE DOGBONE MAIN

From Mingo Jct. and Powhatan

West Switch

WOOSTER

East-west jumpover track

ZEARING

Powhatan Jct.

From Powhatan — Branch line

Mingo Jct.

If properly "parked," up to 5 trains (any combination of east- or westbounds) can layover at crossovers while still keeping one main line open for through traffic at Steubenville. Trains can appear and run through station in any desired sequence. As shown in this example, even-numbered trains are eastbounds—odd numbered are westbounds

Approaching trailing-point crossover—"PARKING OK"

XENIA

YODER

Approaching facing-point crossover—"NO PARKING"

Weirton Switch

STEUBENVILLE

EAST

PRR mainline through Steubenville

WEST

To Mingo Jct. and Powhatan

Dille Bottom

Hidden portion of dogbone main

Visible portion of dogbone main

Branch line/other tracks

Pennsy's Panhandle traffic through Steubenville. (The Panhandle Railway, successor to the Pittsburgh & Steubenville, was named for the West Virginia panhandle it crossed. It existed only from December 1867 to March 1868, but its name stuck as the nickname of the Pennsylvania's line west from Pittsburgh—and is doubtless still in use.)

Handling passenger and freight trains of mainline proportions dictates providing continuous-run possibilities on a route of generous curvature with secluded layover tracks. Avoiding the obvious phoniness of visible to-and-fro shuttling means hiding more than half the dogbone, and that gives us a place to stage the trains without having to build and maintain a hidden yard. As shown in Figure 3, any train waiting behind a trailing-point crossover leaves the track alongside clear for through traffic. Also, in this linear style of staging, trains can emerge from hiding in any desired sequence.

The four hidden layover zones have been designated in order as Wooster, Xenia, Yoder, and Zearing—all good Midwestern railroad locations far enough from the territory modeled to avoid confusion with visible topside stations.

To keep the turnouts accessible,

the layover tracks are located under the front edge of the benchwork or at the back of the layout, hidden behind a view block but within easy reach of the aisleway. Train identification can be aided by somewhat wider than minimum track-center spacing and, where convenient, by terracing so that the rear track is a little higher. All you have to do is sneak a peek or hang identifying tags on the control panel—unless developing sophisticated electro-optic or other modern and sexy but expensive and troublesome technology seems more railroadlike and personally appealing.

An east-to-west reversing connection (long enough to serve as an additional layover slot of considerable capacity) avoids forcing trains like the Spirit of St. Louis to run eastbound only, session after session, until someone has the ambition to reassemble its consist pointing the other way. In line with authentic PRR terminology and practice, we can call this track a "jumpover." Converse movements can be made, without backing up, by taking a trip over the branch and around the Powhatan Point loop—all on trackage maintaining the 30-inch mainline radius.

Is a 30-inch minimum radius enough for all Pennsy rolling stock?

Perhaps not. The appearance of a T1 4-4-4-4 duplex seems almost inevitable, even on a pike that a purist would restrict to pre-1931 motive power in synch with the surviving narrow gauge. On a double-track dogbone main line, boosting the minimum radius for operation in one direction needn't take any extra room, so as a "just in case" accommodation the clockwise minimum has been raised to 33 inches.

Railroad No. 2: the branch

Now comes the second railroad, the branch on which more intricate Pennsy-style local freight and passenger operations will take place. The branch—perhaps better called a secondary main line—begins at the Mingo Junction yard complex and represents the line extending down the west side of the Ohio River. The prototype served important steel mills on its way to a coal mining area.

Only moderate use of modeler's license—stealing some schedules from the PRR line to Wheeling, east of the river—allows scheduling fairly extensive passenger service typical of the early 1930s (with through New York sleepers) over the west-bank route. Thirty-inch radius keeps the long cars looking good and the operation of K4 4-6-2s and the more typical G5 4-6-0s and E6 4-4-2s very comfortable. River-line movements in and out of the

Steubenville station are handled by a third track that apparently was not in existence during the era modeled. It keeps local traffic from impeding the main line and involves an interesting back-up movement.

Several large and small industries, sometimes even prototypically named and located, account for the massive freight service on the branch. It is made practical by the out-and-back capability provided by the hidden loop at the Powhatan Point end of the line. To represent the heavy prototype traffic to points north of the east-west main line through Steubenville, there's a continuous run option via Powhatan Junction and Weirton connections.

A disconnected chunk of track representing intertwined W&LE main lines is sneakily configured so it also can be used as a PRR passing track. A Sohio plant "just happens" to line up with a 6-inch column holding up the house, thus allowing the column's first few inches at least to be disguised as one among several storage tanks.

Railroad No. 3: narrow gauge

The first two railroads are wrapped around a walk-in aisleway that is a bit on the narrow side, but adequate for what is basically a "one operator plus visitors" layout. After observing the 27-inch rule (no complex trackwork or scenic feature more than arm's length from the aisle), there's space in the middle of the room for the mushroom, with its narrow gauge railroad hidden inside.

Toward the end of the 19th century the promise of cheap construction led to dreams of a nationwide network of 36-inch gauge track. The Ohio River & Western was one of many such skinny roads that spread over the unlikely topography of Ohio. It got a lot farther than most, from Bellaire on the Ohio River all the way to Zanesville.

Leapfrogging ridges that separated valleys it could follow only briefly, it managed to parlay Ohio's rolling terrain into grades and curves not much easier than those we associate with Colorado or at least the backbone of the Appalachians. Hallmark of its frugal construction—and a "must have" in any model—was its famous S-curve trestle. It was built initially instead of a more costly fill and never supplanted by solid roadbed. It struggled uphill alongside a slope for several hundred feet without even the excuse of a stream to be crossed. The OR&W came under Pennsylvania Railroad control in 1912, and some of its less-than-impressive rolling stock was even let-

tered for the Standard Railroad of the World.

The way to squeeze the OR&W into the mushroom cap is to concentrate on close-to-scale representation of a few characteristic segments, strung out in correct order with only enough space between to keep them reasonably distinct. For photos, articles, and research providing the necessary details to supplement topographic maps showing its route, I am indebted to Dennis White, now of Xenia, whose parental home just east of Key, Ohio, overlooked the OR&W as it writhed over one of its many intermediate summits.

Leaving its minimal interchange and engine service facilities at Bellaire, the narrow gauge main line passed through Shadyside between the unpaved lanes of an early version of a divided-traffic thoroughfare. Not far from there it was joined by a latter-day standard gauge PRR spur. This was tough for the economy of the narrow gauge but handy for this layout—it can include some simple dual-gauge trackwork without messing up an all-standard-gauge empties-in–loads-out pairing with the power plant back at Warrenton. A purely cosmetic third rail continues past the mine to simulate the prototype situation, in which the standard gauge empties were fed into the mine from above.

A 2¾-turn helix at 3 percent suffices to get the OR&W up to second-deck height. Operators ascend to the corresponding platform level by an easy duck-under and a single step. Prior to taking that step up you can catch an upward view calculated to display to best advantage the moderately dizzy heights braved by the little trains negotiating the S-curve trestle. The platform is set at 12 inches due to a desire to deter contact between the owner's scalp and the steel girder overhead.

A separate world

Take that step up and you're in a different, rural world where the narrow gauge is right at home—as in the case of the real OR&W once it climbed out of the the industrialization of the Ohio Valley. Shallow cuts and a short tunnel lead the right-of-way through ridges visually separating individual scenes.

While the topography is somewhat constrained by the fact there's another world below, alternating up and down pitches at 3 percent emphasizes the roller-coaster nature of the narrow gauge. Passing through such compact but recognizable locales as Anderson

Run, Armstrongs (no apostrophe), Mills, and Coat's (with an apostrophe), the line ascends Standingstone Run and curves into Woodsfield. Elementary OR&W facilities in this relatively busy wood-products town are of prototypically catch-as-catch-can nature, with engines crossing one street and ducking under another between enginehouse and turntable!

The mushroom-stem aisleway is a snug 18" wide—ample for one railroader, but requiring that other operators and spectators dispatch themselves so that they meet each other at a wider spot. Space allocated for scenery, on the other hand, is relatively generous. Looking at the mushroom from outside, the cap overhangs the aisleway by 6 inches or so, but the cap's bottom, at about 65 inches above floor level, is well above shoulder height (about 60 inches for a 6-footer).

Engineered solidity

What holds the whole thing up? Some areas, as indicated in the plan views, are available for posts supporting the upper-level grid—primarily during construction. Once the curved lower-level backdrop (presumably ⅛-inch hardboard) is in place, its inherent structural strength and stiffness will be enough to hold up an elephant—assuming the lower-level benchwork is of conventional stoutness (that is, typically overdesigned with 1 × 6s, 2 × 4s, and the like).

Likewise, the upper-level backdrop will contribute so much stiffness that the supporting grid for the upper level can be of shallower-than-normal design. It does take planning, and those backdrops cannot be afterthoughts, but the end result can be more like a bridge than a card table in stability.

Building a pike like this that stacks in an extra 75 percent or so of railroading and scenic authenticity is not a casual, short-term project. Every trick for getting even more enjoyment out of the monster should be welcome. On the basis of experience with similar multilevel schemes, peep holes are an almost-free add-on with startling benefits. During construction of the upper-level trackage—assuming that lower-level operation and some degree of scenery are complete—it will prove impossible to ignore the views of the scenes below. Nothing says you can't leave a few discreet, unobtrusive peep-holes through the upper level scenic treatment (behind rock outcroppings, under removable buildings, or wherever) and keep on enjoying such sights.

The beautiful river valleys of New England provide the scenic theme for the HO scale Atlantic & White Mountains RR. Here, a Maine Central train leaves Canaan, Vt., in May 1955, heading for the Connecticut River bridge that will carry it into New Hampshire.

THE COMPACT ATLANTIC & WHITE MOUNTAINS RAILROAD

A double-deck approach to mainline railroading in a tight space.

WHY DOES a pint of cream cost so much more than a quart of milk?

Back in the home-delivery days before homogenized milk, cholesterol, and plastic containers, the "with-it" third-grader's reply would have been a snappy, "Because it's so much harder for the cow to sit on the little bottle."

Is it reasonable to consider starting a lifetime layout that promises decades of continuing enjoyment even if the space is not ideal? We're talking about many years of exploring operational alternatives, steadily improving the rolling stock, upgrading the scenery, and keeping up with the ever-advanc-

ing state of modeling. To my way of thinking, the right decision is to take the plunge and start building the railroad even if it is in a little bottle. More often than not, the procrastinators who wait for their ultimate space, as well as those who build so-called temporary layouts (anticipating early moves), seldom get much enjoyment. They wind up, after years of lost opportunities, with no trains running at all or with a tabletop system that isn't much fun.

Small space—big push

Some support for my reasoning comes from the small-bottle factor

itself. There is no need to run out of enjoyable things to do. A small yet relatively intricate layout can well absorb at least as much worthwhile thought and effort as a much larger one. With proper planning, the small model railroad offers the same potential for sustained long-term enjoyment as its larger counterpart. How can this be?

Details vary with the individual prototypes involved as well as personal operational and scenic preferences, but successful lifetime model railroads seem to be characterized by some common features. For starters, most have a main line that's long enough and so arranged as to give the impression of a railroad that goes somewhere (go easy on the spaghetti!). The yard, industry, and engine terminal trackage supports activity that is more than continuously running unchanging consists. In addition, most successful lifetime model railroads have a convenient means of cycling the inevitable glut of rolling stock in and out of the operating patterns with an interesting diversity.

Building such lifetime possibilities into a cramped area will almost certainly include one or more of those challenging space-expanding ideas that have surfaced over the years. One major feature worth considering is the double-deck layout with its potential for almost doubling both the main-track mileage and the scenic features possible in the same floor area.

Compared to the typical ideals for lifetime layouts (single deck, wide aisles, and full walk-in design without backtracking), double-decking is far more complicated. However, opening up second-deck territory in an operationally sincere and scenically effective way means one must accept the complication of a helix.

The effectiveness of multidecking has been repeatedly demonstrated over the past decade. Even so, those who have built such railroads agree that it takes considerably more planning, engineering, and patience to overcome the construction challenges. It has also been demonstrated that the gain from a well-chosen feature may be lost if it's bungled in execution. The idea is to pick only the space stretchers suitable for the situation and then carefully incorporate them so their disadvantages are minimized.

Moderate ideas in 10 × 12 feet

The Atlantic & White Mountains is a layout suitable for lifetime ambitions with real railroading in mind. It is confined to a 10 × 12-foot basement alcove that will be enclosed with a partition that contains the room entrance. Favorable squeeze factors include a New England locale and an early late-steam-early-diesel time frame. Of particular interest is the combination of light-tonnage lines, Depression-era poverty, Yankee frugality, and high locomotive prices that resulted in mixtures of slide-valve 2-6-0s, 65-foot open-platform coaches, and early road diesels.

Confining the hypothetical A&WM and its real-life Boston & Maine connections to rolling stock that's compatible in operation and appearance with easemented 20-inch-radius curves is entirely acceptable. For track planning purposes, I used a 24-inch square, giving the space available a rating of 30 square squares.

With adroit track planning, it should be possible to include most of the desirable features of a lifetime layout within this space. An acceptably long main line is possible, requiring little backtracking for operators who follow their trains. There is also sufficient space to provide yard and service facilities in keeping with a 1930s version of what is now called a regional railroad. The A&WM is intended to represent an independent railroad line that just barely meets the Interstate Commerce Commission's old Class 1 requirement of $1 million in annual revenues.

Experience says that a layout fitted into only 30 squares can benefit from every space-expanding trick in the book. That 5 × 5-foot space under the stairs with its 60-inch headroom is not the kind of space one might usually include in an empire, but here those extra squares are worth considering.

Double-deck to start with

New England's generally rugged terrain has always been inhospitable to prototype railroad operations. By the same token, this topography has the verticality that makes it ideal for model railroad purposes. A multiturn helix to a second deck can achieve the track mileage necessary to portray a main line extending from sea level to the summit of the railroad's "big hill."

Sharing the basement with other family activities means the A&WM must be approached from the side—a significant disadvantage. By extending the helix, this mountain-climbing main line might well climb high enough to pass comfortably over the doorway. This would allow a no-stoop, walk-in track plan that makes use of the prime space along all four walls without doubling back at the walk-in point.

Unfortunately, this approach becomes strained on a modestly graded railroad in a tight space such as this. There simply isn't enough room to get back down to a visually attractive and comfortable operational level. In the interest of practicality, the A&WM will have to depict only one side of its mountain crossing.

Point-to-point, up to a point

The main line is long enough, 2 scale miles, for the A&WM to handle a modest and realistic level of point-to-point traffic. The A&WM carries freight and (thanks to a slightly anachronistic steamship connection) a number of passengers between Pilgrim Inlet and an inland resort area at White Mountain Haven. Pilgrim Inlet is a cramped port somewhere north of

Boston, on the lower deck; White Mountain Haven is the upper-deck terminal in a well-forested New Hampshire resort area. Naturally the line passes through a productive territory generating considerable traffic.

At the upper terminal there is room for a partially hidden wye with a long tail track that allows passenger trains to be readily positioned for their return trip. However, a steady diet of turning every consist after every trip gets old in a hurry.

For this reason a pair of return loops are included, one thinly disguised as a coastal B&M connection near the port and the other as a branchline disappearing off toward Vermont near the summit. These loops provide the desirable option of allowing many trains to run, hide a while, and return. The loops also add more track capacity as a hedge against the day when the layout becomes saturated with rolling stock.

Doubling back gracefully

Open aisle arrangements bring the operators into the railroad, but they can't follow the course of their trains without backtracking. Any line that loops back to avoid crossing an entrance ends up paralleling itself somehow. The A&WM dodges the usual choice between two negatives: wastefully hiding one track or leaving both in sight. The latter situation seriously damages the impression that the train is going somewhere, but a display window cut into the family room wall gives visual access to a separate scene along the back side of the loop.

Since this feature is part of a future wall, there is no major construction problem to deal with. However, adding a window to an existing wall might be more difficult. With or without the protection of top-hinged windows, casual visitors can get a peek at an attractive scene. Of course, walking around the peninsula to handle meets at Peeksville may be a nuisance to operators, but almost everything we do in track planning involves a tradeoff.

If the wall location is a political matter that's already been decided, revising the plan would mean swiping most of the space from the aisles. These are already on the narrow side and getting close to a 20-inch limit that's acceptable only as a bottleneck between wider "people-passing" points.

Such constrictions must be compatible with the present and predictable girths of the proprietor and any other railroaders that may share in operating sessions. Since further narrowing of the aisles isn't acceptable, the benefit of fighting for an extra foot or so must be weighed against losing the

Text continued on page 78.

75

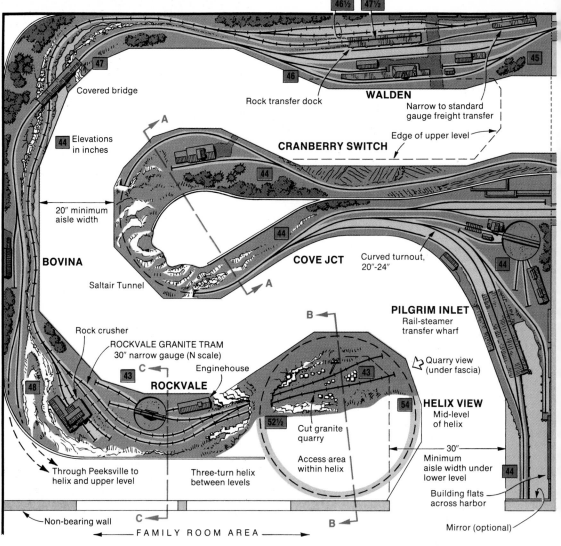

ATLANTIC & WHITE MOUNTAINS RR

HO SCALE

Scale of track plan: ½″ = 1′-0″

HIDDEN FOREST TIMBER CO
Standard gauge branch

ROCKVALE TRAM
30″ gauge quarry tram

CURVES
Minimum radius on A&WM: 20″, with mainline easements
Minimum radius on Hidden Forest Timber Co., Rockvale Granite Tram, and other industrial trackage: 16″

TURNOUTS
Straight frog, unmarked turnouts are no. 5s
Straight frog no. 4s are marked with a ''4''
Wye (Y) turnouts are no. 5 or larger
Curved turnouts are marked with curve diameters
Narrow gauge tram turnouts are approximately no. 4½ to match available N scale track

Labels within main track plan:

46½ 47½
WALDEN
Rock transfer dock
Narrow to standard gauge freight transfer
47
Covered bridge
45
46
Edge of upper level
CRANBERRY SWITCH
44 Elevations in inches
44
20″ minimum aisle width
44
COVE JCT
Curved turnout, 20″-24″
44
BOVINA
Saltair Tunnel
PILGRIM INLET
Rail-steamer transfer wharf
Rock crusher
ROCKVALE GRANITE TRAM
30″ narrow gauge (N scale)
Quarry view (under fascia)
Enginehouse
43
43
HELIX VIEW
Mid-level of helix
48
C
ROCKVALE
52½
54
Cut granite quarry
30″ Minimum aisle width under lower level
Access area within helix
44
Through Peeksville to helix and upper level
Three-turn helix between levels
Building flats across harbor
Non-bearing wall
Mirror (optional)
C
B
FAMILY ROOM AREA

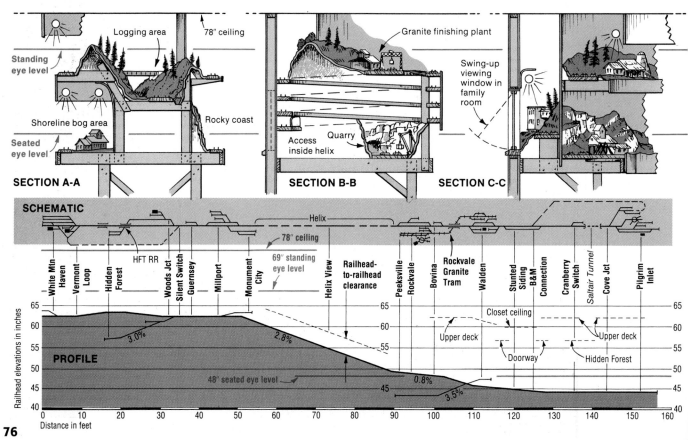

SECTION A-A
78″ ceiling
Logging area
Standing eye level
Shoreline bog area
Rocky coast
Seated eye level

SECTION B-B
Granite finishing plant
Access inside helix
Quarry

SECTION C-C
Swing-up viewing window in family room

SCHEMATIC
Helix
HFT RR
78″ ceiling
69″ standing eye level
Railhead-to-railhead clearance
Closet ceiling
Upper deck
Upper deck
Doorway
Hidden Forest
48″ seated eye level

Stations: White Mtn Haven, Vermont Loop, Hidden Forest, Woods Jct, Silent Switch, Guernsey, Millport, Monument City, Helix View, Peeksville, Rockvale, Bovina, Rockvale Granite Tram, Walden, Stunted Siding, B&M Connection, Cranberry Switch, Saltair Tunnel, Cove Jct, Pilgrim Inlet

PROFILE
Railhead elevations in inches
65 60 55 50 45 40
3.0%
2.8%
0.8%
3.5%
Distance in feet: 0 10 20 30 40 50 60 70 80 90 100 110 120 130 140 150

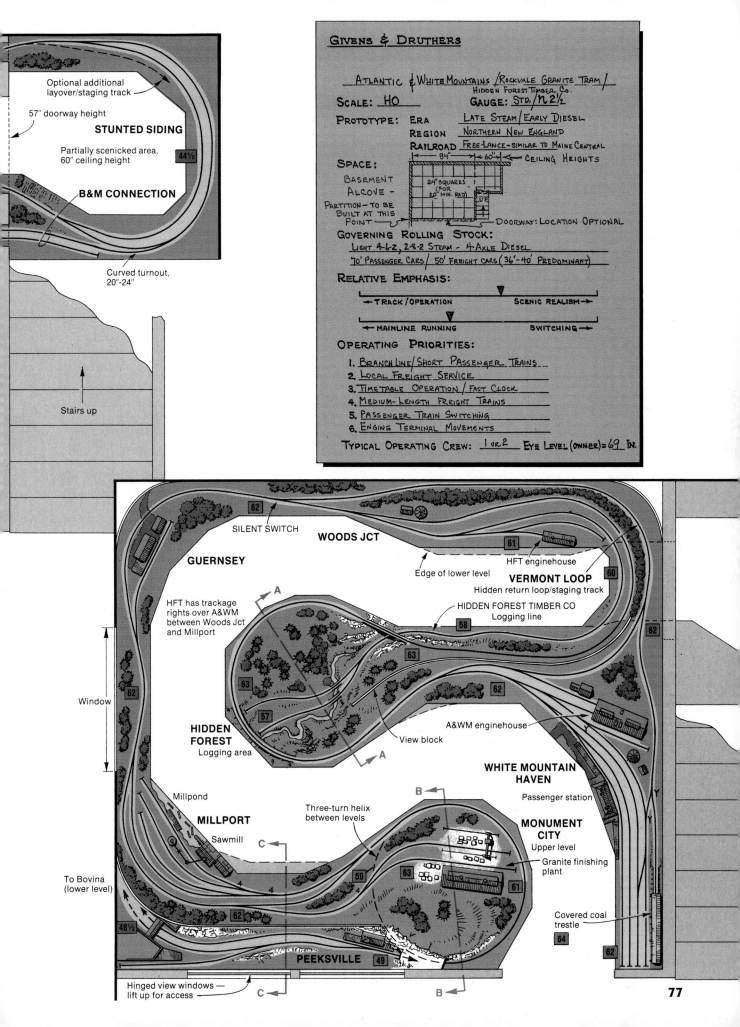

STUNTED SIDING

Optional additional layover/staging track

57" doorway height

Partially scenicked area, 60" ceiling height

B&M CONNECTION

44½

Curved turnout, 20"-24"

Stairs up

GIVENS & DRUTHERS

ATLANTIC & WHITE MOUNTAINS / ROCKVALE GRANITE TRAM / HIDDEN FOREST TIMBER CO.

SCALE: HO   GAUGE: STD./n 2½

PROTOTYPE: ERA   LATE STEAM / EARLY DIESEL

REGION   NORTHERN NEW ENGLAND

RAILROAD   FREE-LANCE-SIMILAR TO MAINE CENTRAL

SPACE: BASEMENT ALCOVE - PARTITION - TO BE BUILT AT THIS POINT

84"   60"   CEILING HEIGHTS

24" SQUARES (FOR 20" MIN. RAD)

UP

DOORWAY: LOCATION OPTIONAL

GOVERNING ROLLING STOCK:

LIGHT 4-6-2, 2-8-2 STEAM - 4 AXLE DIESEL

70' PASSENGER CARS / 50' FREIGHT CARS (36'-40' PREDOMINANT)

RELATIVE EMPHASIS:

TRACK / OPERATION   SCENIC REALISM

MAINLINE RUNNING   SWITCHING

OPERATING PRIORITIES:

1. BRANCH LINE / SHORT PASSENGER TRAINS
2. LOCAL FREIGHT SERVICE
3. TIMETABLE OPERATION / FAST CLOCK
4. MEDIUM-LENGTH FREIGHT TRAINS
5. PASSENGER TRAIN SWITCHING
6. ENGINE TERMINAL MOVEMENTS

TYPICAL OPERATING CREW: 1 OR 2   EYE LEVEL (OWNER) = 69 IN.

62

SILENT SWITCH

WOODS JCT

61

HFT enginehouse

GUERNSEY

Edge of lower level

VERMONT LOOP
Hidden return loop/staging track

60

HFT has trackage rights over A&WM between Woods Jct and Millport

58

HIDDEN FOREST TIMBER CO
Logging line

62

A

63

63

62

Window

62

57

A

HIDDEN FOREST
Logging area

View block

A&WM enginehouse

WHITE MOUNTAIN HAVEN
Passenger station

B

Millpond

MILLPORT

Three-turn helix between levels

MONUMENT CITY
Upper level

Granite finishing plant

Sawmill

C

59

63

61

To Bovina (lower level)

62

48½

49

PEEKSVILLE

Covered coal trestle

64

62

Hinged view windows — lift up for access

C

B

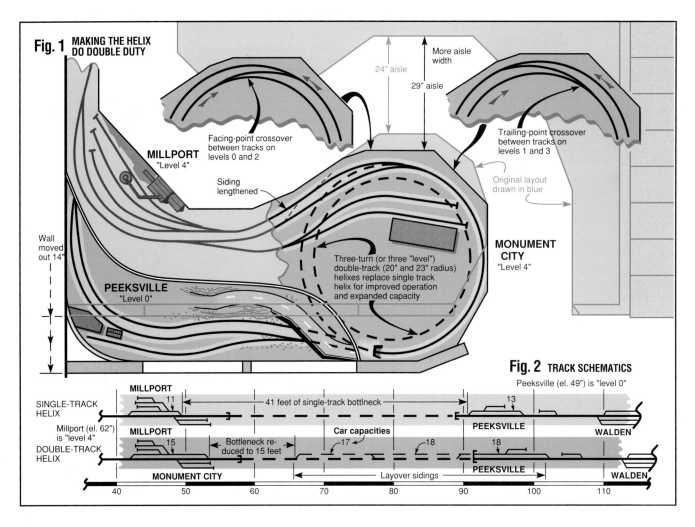

Fig. 1 MAKING THE HELIX DO DOUBLE DUTY

24" aisle

More aisle width

29" aisle

Facing-point crossover between tracks on levels 0 and 2

MILLPORT "Level 4"

Siding lengthened

Trailing-point crossover between tracks on levels 1 and 3

Original layout drawn in blue

MONUMENT CITY "Level 4"

Three-turn (or three "level") double-track (20" and 23" radius) helixes replace single track helix for improved operation and expanded capacity

Wall moved out 14"

PEEKSVILLE "Level 0"

Fig. 2 TRACK SCHEMATICS

Peeksville (el. 49") is "level 0"

SINGLE-TRACK HELIX

MILLPORT

11

41 feet of single-track bottlneck

13

PEEKSVILLE

WALDEN

Millport (el. 62") is "level 4"

DOUBLE-TRACK HELIX

MILLPORT

15

Bottleneck reduced to 15 feet

Car capacities

17

18

18

PEEKSVILLE

WALDEN

MONUMENT CITY

Layover sidings

PEEKSVILLE

WALDEN

40   50   60   70   80   90   100   110

---

already-won space or even the remote possibility of divorce! Depending upon circumstances, reopening the matter may be a worthwhile gamble.

Taming the helix

It takes three turns of minimum-radius main line using a 2.8 percent grade to link Peeksville on the lower deck with Millport on the upper deck. This combination provides enough vertical rise to allow the stacked decks to be scenicked as totally separate segments of the main line.

As those who have 'em have noted, multiturn helixes can have some problems. With the A&WM's tight radius the helix has a grade that is about steep as one can afford on a railroad that likes to handle most of its tonnage without helper locomotives. With only 4 inches between turns (about 29 scale feet in HO), there's plenty of clearance for the rolling stock of the desired era, but there isn't much room for space-wasting engineering or sloppy construction. Be sure to leave enough space between the layers of a helix for a full-size hand to gently retrieve derailed equipment.

Another unfortunate truth is that a lot of good main line is hidden within the helix, especially on a small layout. The helix itself takes up a good chunk of precious space, especially considering that it's an area wide enough to accommodate a circle of mainline radius. This is especially crucial because such spaces exist in only one or two places in the railroad area.

Then there's the potential rocket effect noted by Jim Hediger. Some instrumentation like an easily visible ammeter is needed to maintain an engineer's faith that his quiet-running charge is moving. Otherwise he will keep cranking up the power during the hidden portion of the run with thrilling results when the train emerges at a speed slightly below Mach 1.

The A&WM plan seeks to mitigate these problems in three ways. Since the line from Peeksville is out from under the second deck, it can gain altitude without compromising the scenic independence of the two levels. By starting the grade at Walden and continuing it through Peeksville, a 3¾-turn helix gains sufficient space between decks. With planning, the top three-quarter turn of the helix can be open and scenicked to help extend the

visual run. If the grade started at the base level, it would have taken at least another turn or two in the helix to gain a comfortable 18-inch deck spacing, and much of the enjoyable extra line length would be lost.

Any helix is a subterfuge, so keeping it out of sight is an unavoidable part of the dirty trick. Here, where it forms part of the main line, one of its intermediate segments may be opened up to view from the end without compromising the realism of either deck to give the engineer visual confirmation that the train is still moving.

Even with the specified tight radius, the girth of the hole in the doughnut is still considerably larger than that of the railroader. This makes it possible to add spur tracks at each deck level to simulate the granite traffic between the lower-deck quarry and the finishing mill on the upper deck. The exact width of these areas depends upon how much space must be left for access to the interior of the helix.

Making the helix do double duty

That area beneath the stairs, with its 60-inch ceiling, though far from prime space, is well worth invading to extend the main line. Adding a passing track or two in this secluded location provides additional places to tuck trains away until they are needed for operating purposes. This is all part of the never-ending battle to keep up with the irresistibility of rolling stock (I don't need it, but I've got to have it).

The advent of commercial curved turnouts has made it relatively easy to convert the helix into a good citizen. As Figure 1 shows, it takes only a little more area to make a double-track helix with alternating trailing-point and facing-point crossovers. This track arrangement will do almost unbelievably nice things to the A&WM's operating characteristics. The schematics in Figure 2 show how this change affects the dispatcher, as he now has two additional meeting points to work with. Better still, the longest stretch of single track is reduced from 41 feet to 17 feet so that the clogged-line period, when a train is transiting the helix, becomes far less irksome to operators.

A large part of the compactness within the double-track helix comes from the use of commercial curved turnouts. Examples of different space combinations using more conventional curves of 24- and 26½-inch radius are shown in Figure 3. If room for the straight-turnout oval configuration is available, the extra length and trackage won't be a total loss. Any extra distance gained increases the space between layers. Besides, straight turnouts are less expensive.

The helix as a car sink

Once the helix is double-tracked it is no longer an interruption to the main line and can significantly help the railroad's car capacity. As Figure 2 shows, the monster can keep considerable rolling stock on the job without being conspicuous about it. Such readily available equipment can spice up the variety and length of A&WM consists in day-to-day operations instead of moldering away on shelves. Allowing for the crossovers and a couple of locomotives, the helix can hold almost three dozen 40-foot cars.

After seeing the effectiveness of the double-track helix, it may be worth considering further expansion of its use. As the tables in Figure 4 indicate, each additional turn of a helix represents a major "sink" to absorb excess rolling stock. The quantity of cars involved drastically increases with the curve radius and becomes downright impressive when broad-radius curves are multiplied by numerous layers. It's interesting to consider how many model railroads could benefit from staging capacity capable of squirreling

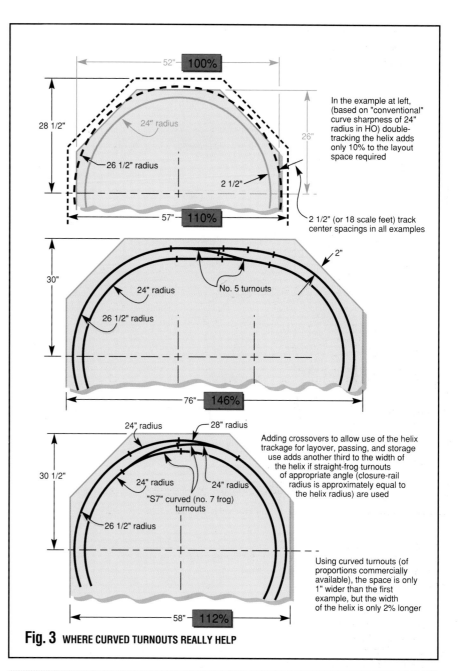

In the example at left, (based on "conventional" curve sharpness of 24" radius in HO) double-tracking the helix adds only 10% to the layout space required

2 1/2" (or 18 scale feet) track center spacings in all examples

Adding crossovers to allow use of the helix trackage for layover, passing, and storage use adds another third to the width of the helix if straight-frog turnouts of appropriate angle (closure-rail radius is approximately equal to the helix radius) are used

Using curved turnouts (of proportions commercially available), the space is only 1" wider than the first example, but the width of the helix is only 2% longer

Fig. 3 WHERE CURVED TURNOUTS REALLY HELP

THE HELIX AS A CAR SINK

CLASS OF CURVATURE	CONVENTIONAL	BROAD	SUPER-BROAD
Minimum radius:			
N scale	13"	16"*	20"
HO scale	24"	30"	36"
O scale	44"	54"	65"
LENGTH OF HELIX TRACK In terms of 40-foot-car capacity**			
Per turn:	24	30	36
Two turns	48	60	72
Three turns	73	91	109
Four turns	97	122	146
Six turns	146	182	219

*Practicality of helix with less than super-broad cuves is questionable in N scale because of limited spacing between turns and thickness of model railroader's fingers

**Coupled length = 45 feet per car; no allowance for lenght of engine or caboose

Fig. 4 HELIX CAR-CAPACITY TABLE

The layout's Rockvale Granite Tram is meant to serve a granite quarry like this Rock of Ages operation near Graniteville, Vt. In this August 1955 photo by John .C. Illman, a Rock of Ages industrial 2-8-0 is about to pick up a flatcar of granite blocks. Researching the quarry business and reproducing its details (guy wires, the retaining wall just below the engine, and various pit working levels) will take a bit of interesting modelwork.

industrial line have taken advantage of the gauge and scale relationships between HO and N and chosen 30-inch gauge. This means that N scale track, locomotive mechanisms, and car trucks can be used in simulating an HO industrial narrow gauge operation.

Developing the RGT may be far more interesting than one might expect because local geography and geology place the quarry far below the only practical mainline connection. As a result, it takes a lot of motive power to work the loads uphill to the transfer point. Short as it is, the tram will need at least one each of all the usual railroad facilities, including a turntable. The geared and tank locomotives envisioned for most of the RGT's work can operate well in either direction, but the master mechanic likes to turn all the engines periodically to equalize flange wear. These little engines are a railfan's delight as they haul outbound cut granite and crushed stone and occasional loads of inbound fuel, machinery, and supplies.

If that isn't enough, the A&WM dispatcher is also faced with the creeping log trains of the Hidden Forest Timber Co. Their Shay drags log cars upgrade from the firm's timberlands to Woods Junction, then operates by trackage rights on the A&WM to reach the log dump at Millport. Naturally, the resulting carloads of outbound lumber traffic help console the A&WM management for this complication.

With the aid of Saltair Tunnel, the Hidden Forest Timber Co. remains just that, so far as lower-level scenicking is concerned. The logging operation is sufficiently depressed in elevation to make the overhead mainline trestle high enough to be worthwhile. Such items are always matters to watch for in double-deck plans to prevent upper level joys from conflicting with necessities down below.

With or without the benefits of a double-track helix, the White Mountain Line demonstrates that railroading in a 10 × 12-foot alcove need not be relegated to "starter set" status.

away another 200 cars. Now, of course, if we had a triple-track helix with suitable crossovers, almost two-thirds of its track would be usable . . .

Back to practicality: In the case of the Atlantic & White Mountains, it would be possible to go to a four-turn helix just by flattening the grade between Stunted Siding and Peeksville. This would add one-third of a mile to the main line and accommodate another long train in the helix, or two short ones if appropriate electrical separation is built in.

Packing in the goodies

What takes longer to build than one model railroad? Two model railroads! Long-term prospects for modeling and operating fun within this alcove should include the promise of a second wind. This could be in the form of a second operation, necessarily more or less parallel to the main line, but different enough to present an entirely new set of construction challenges.

The Rockvale Granite Tram is envisioned as an industrial subsidiary of the A&WM. The builders of the

SOUTHERN NEW ENGLAND RAILROAD

A passenger-oriented early-diesel railroad connecting with the Boston & Albany

THE SOUTHERN NEW ENGLAND is a passenger-oriented road highly reminiscent of the New Haven in the 1950s. Most of its territory in Massachusetts and Connecticut is hilly but not mountainous; with 36 square squares available (after deducting 8 square squares because the space must be entered from the side) it appears that a walk-in, single-deck track plan should be feasible, and so it is. This is double-track territory, which means that we can run the long trains that are a priority without worrying about passing-track length. As a freelance railroad, the SNE isn't tied to any specific prototype trackage, but it should be typical of New England railroading.

Its major passenger terminal doesn't have to resemble Boston or Providence or New Haven, but Springfield, Massachusetts, turns out to be a neat example that will serve as a springboard toward a plausible operating scheme and the trackage to support it—the city is tailor-made for this project's combination of the real and the fictitious. Springfield is the end of the line for the New Haven on its way north from New York, but several pas-

senger trains a day continue to Boston via the Boston & Albany. Adding some commuter traffic and slightly disguising it as Springbush gives this layout a busy railroad junction city somewhere in the Connecticut River valley north of Hartford.

A terraced union station

At the heart of the layout is Springbush Union Station and its associated engine terminal. Passenger traffic is of three principal types:

• Southern New England medium-distance trains between Springbush and New York, with various amounts of shuffling involved in the turnaround process, plus commuter trains terminating at Springbush. These use the upper level of the station. (Passengers reach the platforms via a subway from the station's impressive high-ceilinged waiting room.)

• Boston & Albany through trains (and a commuter train or two) using the lower-level platforms, which are reached by stairways from the waiting room. With destinations as distant as Chicago and St. Louis, some of these trains are long fellows, taxing the

length of the principal platform. Others set out and pick up mail and express cars, and there is a set-out sleeper or two per day that must be accommodated on one of the main tracks for a while, to the irritation of the stationmaster.

• SNE-B&A through trains via West Spring Junction and B&A Junction. These New York-Boston trains must also use the B&A side of the station. Already overloaded, this trackage is relieved a bit by routing the night sleeper-connection train into the upper level stub tracks. A switcher hauls its through cars back past B&A Junction, then pushes them forward onto the B&A train when it arrives.

The station is vaguely reminiscent of the New York Central-Delaware & Hudson station at Albany, with its situation on a sharp curve and track on two levels. The Springbush terminal's two-level trackage helps make the trains somewhat more accessible as well as displaying the SNE's best rolling stock much better than a single-level station with that many tracks. As snowy as the weather is here, the umbrella sheds are rather short—the

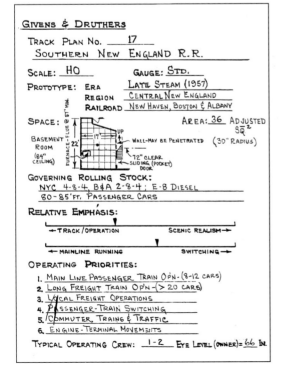

The church steeple visible over the locomotive adds a confirming New England flavor to this scene of New Haven 4-6-2 No. 1311 leading a Boston-Waterbury train out of Hartford, Connecticut. Photo by Kent W. Cochrane.

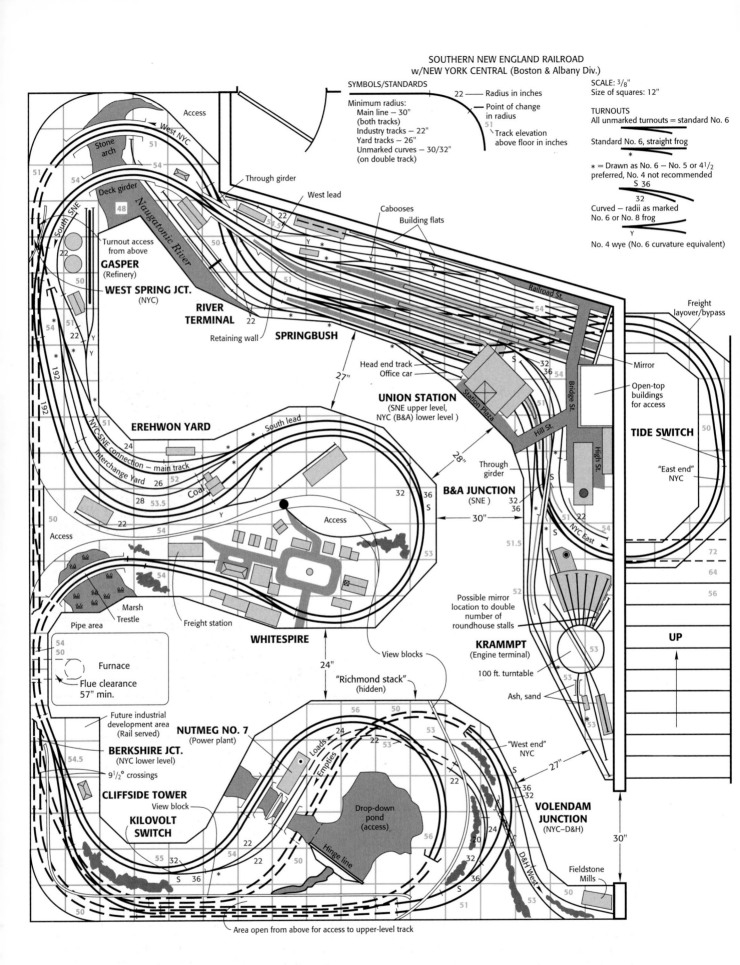

SOUTHERN NEW ENGLAND RAILROAD
w/NEW YORK CENTRAL (Boston & Albany Div.)

SYMBOLS/STANDARDS

22 — Radius in inches

Minimum radius:
Main line — 30"
(both tracks)
Industry tracks — 22"
Yard tracks — 26"
Unmarked curves — 30/32"
(on double track)

— Point of change
in radius

51 — Track elevation
above floor in inches

SCALE: ³/₈"
Size of squares: 12"

TURNOUTS
All unmarked turnouts = standard No. 6

Standard No. 6, straight frog

* = Drawn as No. 6 — No. 5 or 4¹/₂
preferred, No. 4 not recommended

S 36

32

Curved — radii as marked
No. 6 or No. 8 frog

Y

No. 4 wye (No. 6 curvature equivalent)

Access

West NYC

Stone arch

Deck girder

Naugatonic River

48

South SNE

22

GASPER
(Refinery)

WEST SPRING JCT.
(NYC)

RIVER
TERMINAL

Turnout access
from above

50

51

54

22

Y

Y

192

192

NYC-SNE connection — main track

Interchange Yard

24

26

52

28

53.5

Coal

Y

50

Access

22

54

Retaining wall

Through girder

West lead

Cabooses

Building flats

SPRINGBUSH

Head end track

Office car

UNION STATION
(SNE upper level,
NYC (B&A) lower level)

Station Plaza

Railroad St.

Bridge St.

Hill St.

High St.

54

51

S

32
36

54

Mirror

Open-top
buildings
for access

Freight
layover/bypass

TIDE SWITCH

"East end"
NYC

50

27"

EREHWON YARD

South lead

32

36

S

B&A JUNCTION
(SNE)

Through
girder

28"

30"

32
36

S

51

22

54

NYC East

51.5

53

Access

Possible mirror
location to double
number of
roundhouse stalls

52

72

64

56

WHITESPIRE

View blocks

"Richmond stack"
(hidden)

24"

KRAMMPT
(Engine terminal)

100 ft. turntable

Ash, sand

53

53

53

UP

Marsh

Trestle

Pipe area

Freight station

54

50

Furnace

Flue clearance
57" min.

Future industrial
development area
(Rail served)

BERKSHIRE JCT.
(NYC lower level)

9¹/₂° crossings

CLIFFSIDE TOWER

View block

KILOVOLT
SWITCH

54.5

NUTMEG NO. 7
(Power plant)

Loads

Empties

Drop-down
pond
(access)

Hinge line

56

24

22

53

53

22

22

"West end"
NYC

22

27"

S

36
32

36
32

VOLENDAM
JUNCTION
(NYC–D&H)

D&H West

30"

Fieldstone
Mills

55

32

S   36

54

22

50

56

20

24

32

36

S

50

53

50

51

Area open from above for access to upper-level track

82

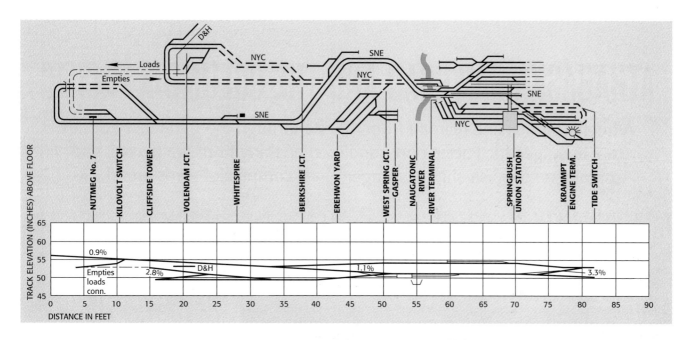

station tracks serve as the coach yard, and you want as much of the array to be as visible as you can get away with.

Bridge traffic coal from nowhere

B&A freight traffic consists primarily of long through trains, Berkshire-hauled over a continuous-run route that's mostly out of sight. Too bad, but the hidden segments also serve as staging tracks. Some trains make set-outs and pickups for the SNE out in the middle of nowhere at the Erewhon interchange yard.

Southern New England's freight traffic into the area is primarily local, worked out of a yard behind Union Station that's considerably stretched out—in appearance if not in capacity—by an artfully placed mirror, its top concealed by the Bridge Street overpass. Most critical is the building-front-concealed access area. Overall width of the terminal trackage strains the 27-inch arm's-length rule for proximity to the aisle.

A major function of SNE's local freight is shoving long cuts of coal hoppers into the Nutmeg No. 7 power plant and retrieving yesterday's empties. The loads don't come from a mine anywhere on the layout but rather from a B&A or NYC interchange with the Delaware & Hudson somewhere to the west near Albany—New England has never been noted for its production of anthracite and bituminous.

All that is represented of the D&H is a short fake section of main line on a bridge at Volendam Junction and two interchange tracks surreptitiously connected to the power plant in standard empties-in–loads-out fashion. The skewed through-truss bridge that carries the D&H is also a nice piece of

Boston & Albany train 33, the *Wolverine* for Detroit and Chicago, prepares to depart Worcester, Massachusetts, behind a smoke-deflectored 4-8-2. Behind the tender are stainless-steel-sheathed New Haven parlor cars that will return to their home rails at Springfield to complete their Boston-New York run. Photo by Philip R. Hastings.

scenery that helps the B&A exit gracefully into its reverse loop.

The scenic highlight of the nonurban parts of the layout is a 125 percent typical New England town, with a Congregational church at the head of the village green. Whitespire's attractive station is on a 16-foot-radius cosmetic curve, and somehow enough Yuppies 25 years ahead of their time have settled in town to make it an important SNE commuter stop as well as a tourist attraction. (Whitespire is the only visible commuter station on

the layout, though there is room for one or two more.)

Krammpt engine terminal is the scene of interesting back-and-forth moves getting SNE and occasional B&A locomotives in and out. Its situation insures that the most interesting facilities are up front and visible. To relieve the Krammpt area (and spread out the points of railfan interest) SNE located its coaling station on the main line out by Erewhon yard. This location results in train delays coaling up, but it is closer to the source of the fuel.

ATHABASKA RAILROAD AND THE COLUMBIA PACIFIC

A freelance mainline railroad from Alberta through the Canadian Rockies to a busy, generic Pacific port handles everything from grain, coal, and containers to cruise-ship passengers via a complex of yards and docks

IN THE EARLY PART of this century the Athabaska Railroad was built from Grand Rivière, Alberta, to a port on the Pacific coast. It overcame all the obstacles to a new rail route: the Canadian Rockies, rugged winters, the Grand Trunk Railway, Vancouver and Prince Rupert politicians, and early-day environmentalists!

Now it's 1965 and the "prototype" Athabaska has matured into a prosperous line handling vast tonnages of export coal and grain, a substantial number of those marine intermodal containers just now coming into favor, and even a fair number of passengers, including trainloads of eager tourists connecting with cruise ships to Alaska.

An invitation to helixes

The obstacles overcome in finding a place for this N-scale representation of the Athabaska are at least in proportion to those the prototype faced. A cavity had to be carved out of the rocky ground under an existing house, its sides shored up, and finished walls installed—and all this in an area where basements are a rarity. This pristine space is uncluttered and windowless, but entry is by doors from the outside that can only be arranged to swing inward.

Faced with the same mountain ranges as those the Canadian Pacific tamed with such engineering feats as the spiral tunnels, the Athabaska plan need have no hesitation in employing helixes to attain altitudes allowing walk-in or at least comfortable walk-under access to fully walk-around aisleways. Therefore no entrance-from-the-side deduction is called for, and the space amounts to some 63 square squares with a super-broad radius of 20 inches.

Because somewhat shallower shelves are appropriate in N scale, and because the closer spacing between decks sufficient for the smaller trains still keeps the stacked scenes visually separate, the Athabaska is double-decked to such an extent that its main line from Grand Rivière to Prince Arthur is more than seven scale miles long. Considering the relatively slow average speeds appropriate for this mountain railroading, that's more than long enough to make a point-to-point track plan appropriate for the Athabaska itself.

Keeping that main line supplied with traffic depends mostly on its connection with one of Canada's transcontinental railways. Here it has been dubbed the Columbia Pacific rather than the Canadian Pacific to retain the initials and wine-red livery of the real CP while allowing somewhat more freedom in adapting the big road to the needs of this layout. As shown by the schematic, the CP is basically a continuous-run affair with reversing connections, dedicated to out-of-sight staging of several long consists.

Surfacing at Grand Rivière, CP trains bring in and haul away the interline traffic that is the basis of the

A Canadian Pacific freight heads into the night east of Crowsnest Pass, Alberta, as the sun sets behind the mountains. Kalmbach Books photo by Mike Schafer.

GIVENS & DRUTHERS

TRACK PLAN NO. __18__
ATHABASCA R.R. / COLUMBIA PACIFIC

SCALE: __N__   GAUGE: STANDARD

PROTOTYPE: ERA   1965-70
           REGION   BRITISH COLUMBIA / ALBERTA
           RAILROAD FREE-LANCE / CANADIAN PACIFIC

SPACE: AREA: __63__ ADJUSTED
OUTSIDE-   SQ²
ENTRANCE   (20" RADIUS)
BASEMENT
(90" CEILING)   WORKBENCH
                                        DOORS MUST OPEN
                                        INWARD
GOVERNING ROLLING STOCK:
SIX-AXLE DIESELS, 85' DOME PASSENGER CARS,
2-10-4 LOCOMOTIVE (EXCURSION)

RELATIVE EMPHASIS:

←TRACK/OPERATION   SCENIC REALISM→

←MAINLINE RUNNING   SWITCHING→

OPERATING PRIORITIES:
 1. LONG FREIGHT TRAIN OPERATION (>20 CARS)
 2. MAIN-LINE PASSENGER TRAIN OP'N (8-12 CARS)
 3. ENGINE TERMINAL MOVEMENTS
 4. HELPER DISTRICT OPERATIONS
 5. LOCAL FREIGHT OPERATIONS
 6. PASSENGER-TRAIN SWITCHING

TYPICAL OPERATING CREW: __1-3__   EYE LEVEL (OWNER) = 65 IN.

Before the advent of the stainless-steel, domed *Canadian*, CP's premier train was the *Dominion*, a mix of lightweight and heavyweight wine-red cars. CP photo.

Athabaska's prosperity, much of it in large blocks of cars or even solid train-loads to or from southwest or east. This interchange is designed to provide a nice mix of varied switching moves—changing motive power, switching vans (there's no such thing as a "caboose" in the Dominion!), and car-by-car classification, also fun but potentially tedious in the amount necessary to assemble the number of trains it takes to keep the main line busy all day.

Both roads are essentially dieselized at this point but still servicing the new power in adapted (and inherently more interesting) steam-era facilities. Grand Rivière's yard tracks, though far from prototypical in length or number, do include all 17 types of assignment likely to be found in such a division-point and junction complex.

A taste of the prairies

Coming up from its hideaway at Occident Switch—where an eastbound Athabaska run-through train can take off for a quick turnaround if westbounds are in short supply—the Columbia Pacific main line passes through the last fairly level terrain east of the mountains. Wide open except for that "prairie skyscraper" grain elevator, it provides a nice contrast with what lies ahead.

West of Grand Rivière the two railroads parallel each other on opposite sides of the milky, glacier-fed Archer

River before going separate ways. From there on the Athabaska main line is as curvy as any other railroad route winding its way through the Rockies, Monashees, Selkirks, or Coast Ranges to reach tidewater. With passing tracks spaced as far as a scale mile apart, dispatching trains efficiently is challenging. To help the engineer keep up with his train despite its disappearances into tunnels, helixes, and loops, west is always to the left—sunny side toward the aisle—and nothing more uncomfortable than a 64-inch walk-under impedes the trip all the way to the Pacific.

Aside from various spurs serving important sources of timber and minerals, and a steam-era wye near the summit—now a handy turnaround point for local freights—the most important intermediate trackage is the branch from Chilanko Forks down to a major resort area at Banff-like Chilko Lake. In season, the branchline mixed that brings coal to the hotel power plant may also haul sleeping cars in and out several times a week.

The port's the thing

Reaching sea level at Foothill, the Athabaska continues past a major lumber mill to the start of double track and the first of several specialized subports making up the Prince Arthur complex. Coves, inlets, and even a sound provide sheltered docking for

mineral, grain, break-bulk, container, and cruise ships to receive the wealth of the interior brought by the railroad.

First comes the elevator-serving yard at Glenwood Cove, full of the 40-foot narrow-door boxcars typically carrying grain in this era. Farther along is sufficient trackage for getting incoming cars to their proper sidings and assembling eastbound trains to relieve the glut of empties, but not much more than that. Terminal yardmasters and switch crews must know what they're doing or things will quickly congeal into a mess. The principal traffic that arrives in open-top cars is coal from the Alberta mine on the CP just west of Archer Split. The Gilford Island bulk export terminal has some subterranean trackage allowing it to absorb long cuts of loads and disgorge empties ready for the trip back east.

Unloading of the daily transcontinental CP/Athabaska passenger train takes place only after a switcher has pushed the rear cars into the second platform track. The number and ingenuity of moves required to splice the cars of its eastbound counterpart together in the right order and facing in the right direction after servicing in the coach yard makes this trackage the most effective on the whole railroad in providing fun per foot. It's a good thing there's a lot of main line between here and the loop east of Grand Rivière.

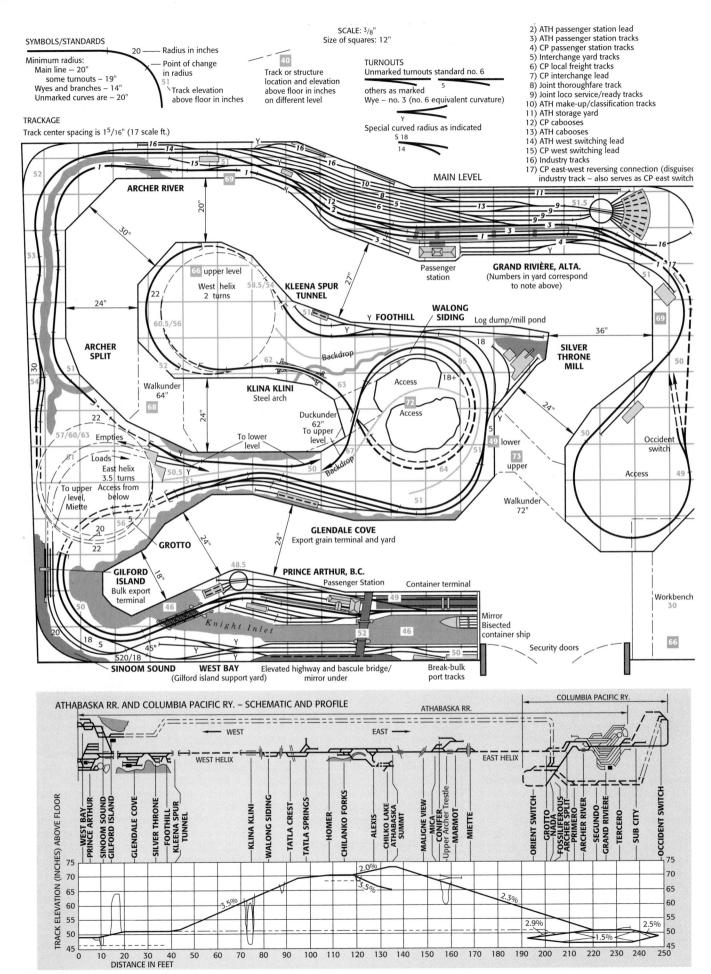

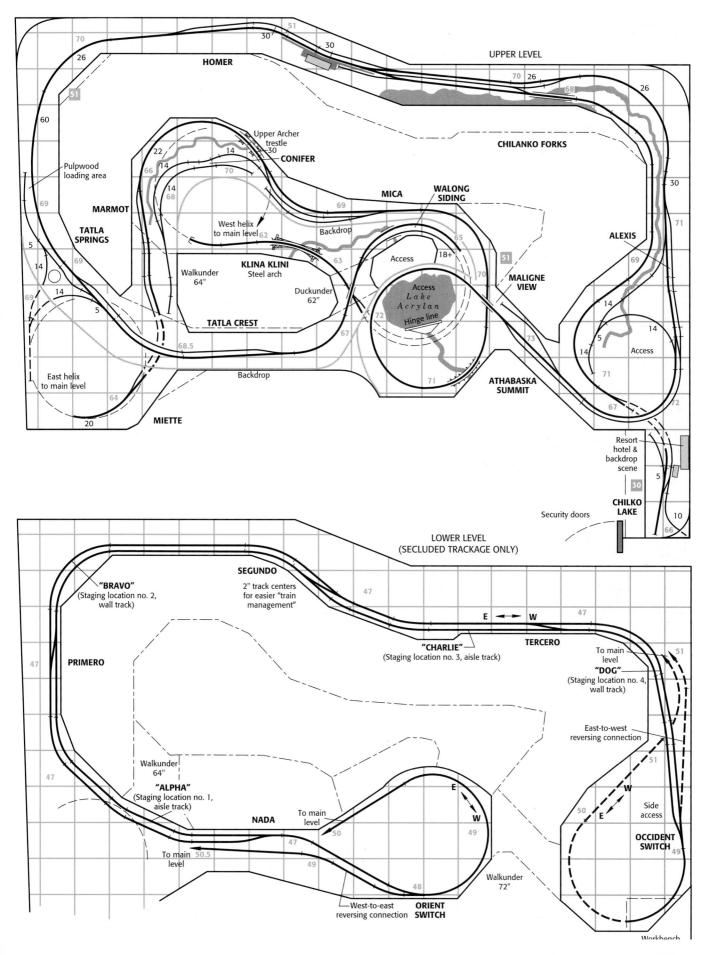

UPPER LEVEL

HOMER

CHILANKO FORKS

Pulpwood
loading area

Upper Archer
trestle

CONIFER

MICA

WALONG
SIDING

ALEXIS

MARMOT

West helix
to main level

Backdrop

MALIGNE
VIEW

TATLA
SPRINGS

KLINA KLINI
Steel arch

Access

18+

51

Access
Lake
Acrylan
Hinge line

Walkunder
64"

Duckunder
62"

Access

East helix
to main level

TATLA CREST

68.5

Backdrop

ATHABASKA
SUMMIT

MIETTE

Resort
hotel &
backdrop
scene

30

CHILKO
LAKE

Security doors

LOWER LEVEL
(SECLUDED TRACKAGE ONLY)

"BRAVO"
(Staging location no. 2,
wall track)

SEGUNDO

2" track centers
for easier "train
management"

E ⟷ W

47

TERCERO

To main
level

"CHARLIE"
(Staging location no. 3, aisle track)

"DOG"
(Staging location no. 4,
wall track)

PRIMERO

East-to-west
reversing connection

51

Walkunder
64"

"ALPHA"
(Staging location no. 1,
aisle track)

NADA

To main
level

E

W

W

Side
access

OCCIDENT
SWITCH

To main
level

West-to-east
reversing connection

ORIENT
SWITCH

Walkunder
72"

Workbench

A brand-new three-unit FT works as a mid-train helper to assist a 2-8-8-2 in the Montana Rockies. GN photo.

GREAT NORTHERN RAILWAY — JOHNSON PASS DIVISION

An HO paraphrase of Big G's crossing of the Cascades during the final years before diesels and tunnel ventilation doomed the electrification

OF ALL THE MOUNTAIN crossings of North American railroads, few are more scenic than the Great Northern's line from the Columbia River valley up and over the Cascades to Puget Sound, and few have had as varied an engineering history. Stevens Pass was first climbed by a series of 4 percent switchbacks while a 2.5 mile tunnel was being hacked through the granite. Conditions in this tunnel under steam operation were so bad that one of the first mainline electrifications, 4 miles of cumbersome double-trolley, three-phase overhead, was put in service in 1909. The slow, constant-speed AC electrics were a major improvement. They hauled trains through the bore, steam locomotive and all; the fires were banked to keep smoke down through the tunnel.

The line was located in one of the heaviest snow belts in the country, and it suffered blockages despite the protection of more and more snowsheds. In 1927 a modern single-phase electrification was put into operation over a reasonably long engine district—the 73 miles from Wenatchee to Skykomish—and in 1929 the new 7.79 mile Cascade Tunnel, longest in the hemisphere, was opened. The new line was 500 feet lower at its crest and much less vulnerable to snow. In 1947 it was further enhanced by the addition of a pair of immense streamlined B-D+D-B locomotives. The electrified district suffered only from the complication of those two extra engine-changes per trip, and it remained in service until a new ventilation system allowed diesel operation through the tunnel. The wires came down in 1956.

Although it is obviously patterned on the Great Northern during the final years of steam and electric operation in the Cascades, the Johnson Pass Division has been fictionalized by locating it in an equally rugged and scenic Montana area a few hundred miles east. Why? Attempting to re-create the scenes and towns—in compressed form, of course—along a specific segment of railroad also means copying its track and structures. If the spur takes off to the left at East Bullwhip, that's the way it has to go on the model, or anybody familiar with the town can yell "foul!" Unfortunately, the ways of the prototype often don't work out well in the model. The siding may have to be on the aisle side, so the train in the hole blocks a nice view of the Limited roaring by, for example. This alternative approach—creating a typical but generic chunk of Great Northern mountain-scaling main line—may actually result in squeezing more authentic GN railroading into the layout area. At the top of the generic pass you can cavalierly plan a summit tunnel that's only long enough to cross over a doorway, without worrying about how much longer you would have to make it to keep it from being ludicrous if labeled Cascade Tunnel.

A second, more whimsical reason for a fictional location is to indulge a second hobby—baseball history—by naming towns and other locations on this version of the Great Northern for players on the only team of Washington Senators to win a World Series.

The railroad is pure G.N.

While the pass is named for the most famous star of the 1924 team, "Big Train" Walter Johnson, and the division point at the east end of the electrified zone is named McNeely, the rolling stock is strictly GN, and its operations are patterned directly on those in the late 1940s and early 1950s, when steam and electric locomotives teamed up with a few diesels to get 'em over the hump.

The 19 × 24-foot L-shaped basement has both good and unfortunate points. Entry is by a stairway from above, and it's permissible for a track along the wall to penetrate a riser. There is an alcove-like space beside the stair landing. On the basis of the 30-inch radius that the modeler's largest locomotives can be trained to accept, the alcove is wider than 2 squares and therefore is usable.

The bad news is that there are two outside entrances. The doorway to the garden is little-used, particularly during the railroading season, so a drop-leaf crossing should not be too serious an inconvenience. The door to the alley leads to the garage, however, and passage can't be seriously impeded. With the steep grades that will test the mettle of the mighty electrics, there is little doubt that the main line can rise high enough to provide walk-in entry. The key will be in routing it so the summit occurs there.

Adjusting for the space lost around the stairway, the count comes out an expansive 67. It should be possible to have a walk-in, walkaround arrangement with a non-backtracking main line long enough to represent an electrified district going up and back down the mountain without double-decking the layout. It may even be possible to do that without the hidden trackage of a multi-turn helix.

Doing it with only two blobs

As the schematic shows, the main line meeting these goals is 250 feet long (about 4 scale miles). The plan is an around-the-walls loop connecting to a single serpentine peninsula fully utilizing the center of the room, Allowing for the fact that trackage above shoulder height can overhang a bit without impeding passage, aisle widths of 24 inches or better are maintained except in two low-traffic cul-de-sacs.

What accounts for this generally blissful result? Basically it's because this plan, despite its size, does the job with only two space-consuming blobs. One is in that alcove, where the only plausible scheme to fit in some extra, visible main line is a Tehachapi-style loop, filled in neatly with an almost-full-size minor league baseball park. Making the flat surface of Tate Field a drop leaf also solves the access problem associated with loops of this size.

The other blob is the return bend that is inevitable at the end of any peninsula. This one pays for the 4 square squares it occupies by doing triple duty. As shown in the supplementary diagrams, both ends of the loop-to-loop main line are stacked below. The bottom level is a conventional loop with three staging sidings, and the middle level is a reverted loop leading to four tail tracks extending under the main lines.

Living with a loop-to-loop

Coal or other mineral traffic in open-top cars on the GN main is limited, so eastbound and westbound freights don't look much different—most lumber was loaded in boxcars in this era. That sneaky connection between Leibold and Mt. Zachary to permit continuous-run routing may see only occasional use. Most trains leaving the scene westbound will return as eastbounds and vice versa, since the end-loop routings provide access to the staging tracks so important in accommodating the hundreds of cars such a large layout will inevitably attract. Even with one track clear for incoming traffic, these tracks can stash away some 180 car-lengths of train.

A significant amount of traffic in other forest products—logs, pulpwood, wood chips—does travel in or on cars that reveal their empty or loaded status. There are conventional empties-in, loads-out industry connections for this traffic at Mt. Zachary and Wingfield.

The bread-and-butter through traffic, freight and passenger, comes off a staging track, pauses to change motive power, crosses the divide, and again changes engines at the end of catenary. That works smoothly westbound, where there's a turntable to send the steam locomotives, properly pointed, back to the east, but what about all those eastbound locomotives accumulating at Mogridge with no way to turn around? Well, there was a turntable at that end of the electric territory, but it was taken out when that end of the railroad was dieselized—strictly with double-ended locomotive combinations—last year. There's still room to put it back if you ever want to turn back the clock. Meanwhile, Mogridge's two-stall motor barn is the sole servic-

One of the 1-C+C-1 motors later sold to the Pennsylvania Railroad stands at Skykomish, Washington, in 1956 while the eastbound *Cascadian* pauses at the station before continuing east into the electrified district behind its two-unit FT. Photo by Richard Steinheimer.

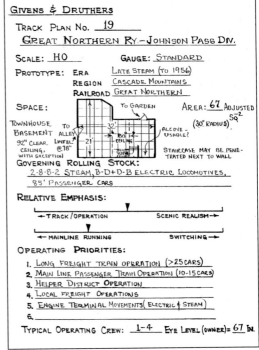

GIVENS & DRUTHERS

TRACK PLAN NO. 19
GREAT NORTHERN RY.—JOHNSON PASS DIV.

SCALE: HO   GAUGE: STANDARD
PROTOTYPE: ERA   LATE STEAM (TO 1956)
           REGION   CASCADE MOUNTAINS
           RAILROAD GREAT NORTHERN

SPACE: AREA: 67 ADJUSTED
                        TO GARDEN   SQ²
TOWNHOUSE   TO   (30" RADIUS)
BASEMENT   ALLEY
92" CLEAR LINTEL   ALCOVE—
CEILING,   @ 78'   USABLE?
WITH EXCEPTION   STAIRCASE MAY BE PENE-
                         TRATED NEXT TO WALL
GOVERNING ROLLING STOCK:
2-8-8-2 STEAM, B-D+D-B ELECTRIC LOCOMOTIVES,
85' PASSENGER CARS

RELATIVE EMPHASIS:
    ◄—TRACK/OPERATION   SCENIC REALISM—►
    ◄—MAINLINE RUNNING   SWITCHING—►

OPERATING PRIORITIES:
1. LONG FREIGHT TRAIN OPERATION (>25 CARS)
2. MAIN LINE PASSENGER TRAIN OPERATION (10-15 CARS)
3. HELPER DISTRICT OPERATION
4. LOCAL FREIGHT OPERATIONS
5. ENGINE TERMINAL MOVEMENTS (ELECTRIC & STEAM)
6.

TYPICAL OPERATING CREW: 1-4   EYE LEVEL (OWNER) = 67 IN.

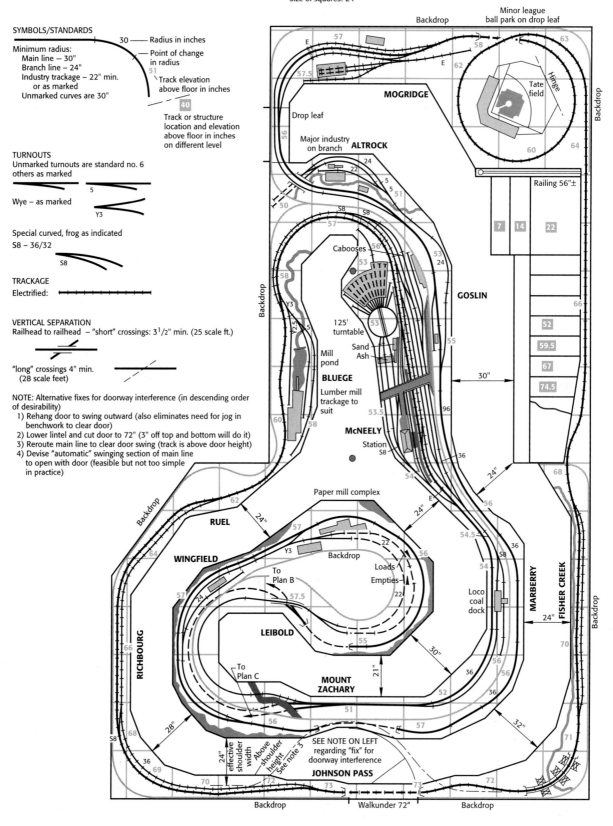

ing point for those reliable juice hogs. Room enough? Amazing as it may seem, the GN made do through World War II with only 13 electrics!

How much wire?

Electrified track is indicated on the plans with cross-ticks; their spacing does not indicate catenary-pole locations. On electrified railroads, no more wire was strung than necessary—it was too expensive to install and maintain. When it was necessary to turn an electric locomotive, to equalize wheel wear or whatever, the steam or diesel shop goat would haul it to the turntable.

What about live catenary on a model railroad? The Johnson Pass plan avoids the stickiest problem in accommodating catenary and two-rail operation on the same track, since there are no reversing loops in the electrified district. It is possible, if tricky, for electrics drawing power from catenary to coexist with two-rail steam and diesel locomotives. The electrics must have wheels insulated on one side and arranged to pick up current from the overhead wire and one rail. The easy out, electrically if not mechanically, may be to settle for dummy catenary so that current distribution is a straight two-rail proposition throughout.

Have the non-electric locomotives been short-changed in this version of the Great Northern? Eastbound steam- and diesel-powered trains leave McNeely and disappear into the Dakota loops after only a short run through visible territory.

Well, when heavy traffic pressured GN to get trains over the line more quickly than the available electric horsepower could manage, a common practice was to insert four FTs as a mid-train helper and end things with a 2-8-8-2 pushing on the rear under the wire all the way to the tunnel.

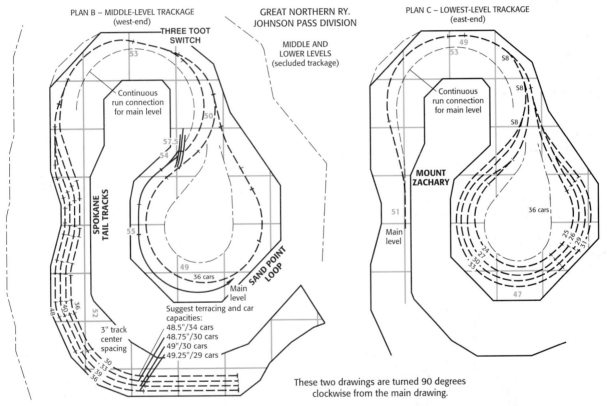

These two drawings are turned 90 degrees clockwise from the main drawing.

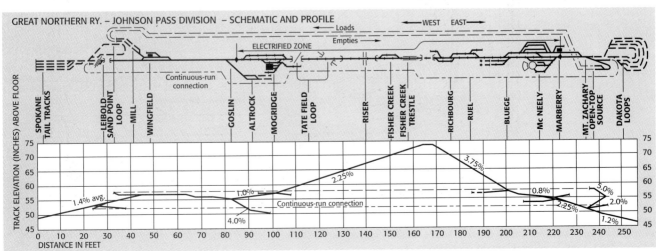

LAWRELYN OVERLAND RAILROAD

A busy, scenic, freelance main line through the Piedmont and Blue Ridge in North Carolina and Virginia, to be built in a 24 × 50-foot room over a garage, with staging to accommodate for no fewer than 175 locomotives and 750 cars

WHEN THE NUMBER of passenger cars on hand passes 100, the locomotive roster approaches 200 units, and the freight car count wouldn't look puny for a Class 2 railroad if it showed up in *The Official Railway Equipment Register*, it's time to provide suitable exercise facilities for all that investment. The Lawrelyn Overland is just that—a double-track railroad to show how trains from several Class 1 railroads in the Southern and Pocahontas districts might operate over a jointly owned but fiercely independent mainline railroad between eastern North Carolina and central Virginia. It's a sort of Richmond, Fredericksburg & Potomac crossing the Blue Ridge. A cogent reason for modeling such a "free-lance prototype" railroad is the chance to create a line that is better than the real thing from the standpoint of operational, scenic, and railfan interest. It can be authentic if you do your homework in learning and adapting 12" = 1' practices.

The setting is a 24 × 50-foot room enclosed in vertical 8-foot walls over a four-car garage. There is a 4 × 8-foot trap door for bringing plywood sheets

and the like up from below, located so it will probably line up with an aisle and not mess up the track plan. Access from the house is by a stairway at one end, adjoining the logical location for a workshop. For a walk-in plan the main line will have to rise above head height, but since the route is to surmount the Blue Ridge, that should be no problem. In the absence of obstacles, and in anticipation of a generous 36-inch radius to accommodate Big Boys and the like (should the Lawrelyn decide it needs the ultimate), the adjusted square-squares figure is a whopping 120.

A no-excuse plan

With an area like that, there should be no excuse for planning anything less than a convincing pike that's commodious and comfortable to build, operate, and maintain. An around-the-wall loop feeding into and out of a single, spiral peninsula makes efficient use of the space for a long, once-around, no-backtracking main line. The main difference in a design this large is that the layout can be four comfortable

aisles wide at the critical point, allowing an extra turn in the spiral.

It would be entirely possible, with a little squeezing, to have a five-aisle, one-blob plan with a main line close to 10 scale miles long. However, such a string bean would not provide for much operation until the whole route was in place and would less readily accommodate the enormous staging-track capacity desired.

Dedicating about 7 percent (8 square squares) of the space to two end-loop blobs makes possible a main line more than seven miles long, connecting two seven-track yards with almost 600 boxcar-lengths of staging trackage. Holding the yards to arm's reach and spacing tracks a generous 3 inches apart does cost some capacity. But it makes identifying trains far easier (also tinkering and, on rare occasions, rerailing). It also means that the supports for the upper layers of track can be located anywhere—even between tracks.

Through Alexandria, Virginia, Richmond, Fredericksburg & Potomac has four tracks. In this November 1984 scene a southbound piggyback train departs behind two GP40s and a GP35 while a northbound RF&P piggyback train disappears in the distance toward Potomac Yard and a short Southern Railway passenger train with an office car on the rear heads for Washington on the track nearest the station building. Photo by Alex Mayes.

GIVENS & DRUTHERS

TRACK PLAN No. __20__

LAURELYN OVERLAND R.R.

SCALE: __HO__   GAUGE: __STANDARD__

PROTOTYPE: ERA   LATE STEAM TO PRESENT
            REGION   N.C./VA PIEDMONT/BLUE RIDGE
            RAILROAD N&W; SOUTHERN; ACL; SAL

SPACE: AREA: __120__ ADJUSTED
TRAIN ROOM   SQ²
OVER 4-CAP   (36" RADIUS)
GARAGE.
(96" CEILING)

GOVERNING ROLLING STOCK:
4-8-8-4 STEAM, 8-AXLE DIESEL LOCOS; 85' DOME,
DBL. DECK PSGR CARS; 89' HI CUBE BOX; DOUBLE-STACKS

RELATIVE EMPHASIS:
←TRACK/OPERATION   SCENIC REALISM→

←MAINLINE RUNNING   SWITCHING→

OPERATING PRIORITIES:
1. LONG FREIGHT-TRAIN OPERATIONS (> 25 CARS)
2. MAIN-LINE PASSENGER TRAIN OPNS (8-12 CARS)
3. TIMETABLE OPERATION (FAST CLOCK)
4. HELPER-DISTRICT OPERATIONS
5. ENGINE TERMINAL MOVEMENTS
6. LOCAL FREIGHT OPERATIONS

TYPICAL OPERATING CREW: __1 TO 5__ EYE LEVEL (OWNER) = __66__ IN.

How practical are yards this large located 8 inches apart vertically? To be sure that they are practical, they are staggered lengthwise, so that turnouts at both ends are readily accessible from the aisle.

Yards within reach

Lawrelyn was destined to become a big city. That's why the owning railroads set up the jointly-owned line with a suitably big station, and schedule through and terminating trains to tap its passenger-traffic potential. As the division point on the Lawrelyn Overland, it also has a large freight yard and busy engine service facilities. Locating the freight facilities out in the boondocks not only gets them out of the high-cost city but solves the HO-scale fact that convenient stations and yards can only be so wide—side by side along a wall they would be either too small or hopelessly unreachable.

How about all those locomotives? A roundhouse that has more than a half-circle of stalls keeps too many engines out of sight and makes the reach too long, especially for a place where even experienced hands will sometimes put a wheel on the ground. With separate passenger and freight engine terminals, the Overland can keep 75 or more locomotives ready to go and in view.

Alternate routes

Several alternate routes are incorporated in the plan, generally connected with inconspicuous junctions. They include a continuous-run connection so that loaded and empty coal trains can traverse the line in appropriate directions, a route that bypasses the mountain for the operation of long trains without the necessity for helpers, and a bypass that allows the mountaineers to run a few trains without bothering the crews busy switching the Lawrelyn station and yards.

Construction by stages

These bypass routes aren't part of the Overland's basic route structure, although they provide some welcome variety in connecting with some of its owner roads at different junction points. Although construction can be relatively rapid, since all the trackwork in this plan is commercially available, no railroad this large has to await the driving of the golden spike to accommodate meaningful operations. Some of these connections allow extensive stage-by-stage train running with a minimum of temporary connections as the monster takes shape.

Construction must start from the bottom, of course. Fortunately, that lower staging yard can go down quickly, and out-and-back running from whatever trackage is in place in the Lawrelyn passenger station will serve to check it out before the second level is added. A temporary connection between the east end of the Lawrelyn freight yard area and the upper staging yard will result in a vast increase in traffic over the loop-to-loop route now available.

The final trackage, apart from its extensiveness, follows the pattern you'd expect to find on a busy, efficient railroad built through tough territory. A few points:

• As a double-track line, it comfortably accommodates long trains. Since they can meet each other anywhere, it's the distance between crossovers rather than the length of passing tracks that determines just how long a consist can be overtaken by a faster train. The important consideration is that facing-point crossovers (right track to left track) alternate with their trailing-point counterparts.

• A third track with a set of mid-grade crossovers, extending just past the wye for turning steam helpers at the summit, expedites traffic up the steeper side of the mountain.

• The wye also serves a branch more than a scale mile long which takes off at right angles to the main line. As a practical point, in a fully walk-around plan the summit is the only point where this can be done. For the first 40 feet or so it is on a second deck 20 inches above the scene below. Otherwise the Overland is single-deck.

• Trains serving the branch are based at a small yard down the mountain at Lakeside where there is room. The mine that generates much of the significant traffic on the branch is connected with its coal-consuming power plant by a more nearly adequate four-track version of the usual loads-in—empties-out scheme.

• The Overland has its passenger-car shops and locomotive backshop facilities at Lawrelyn; the latter provide inconspicuous access within a knot of trackage over seven feet wide. In addition, the road assembles much of its rolling stock at its sprawling Mt. Airy shops within buildings that hide even more spread-out trackage holding another 100 cars or so.

• Sweeping cosmetic curves and No. 8 crossovers enhance the appearance of the long trains. At Hawks Nest the Overland has borrowed a scene from the Chesapeake & Ohio line through the New River Gorge, crossing the river in two stages with single lines on each bank between the two bridges. Elsewhere the scenery is what you would expect to find in the Appalachians on the Southern or Norfolk & Western, only better.

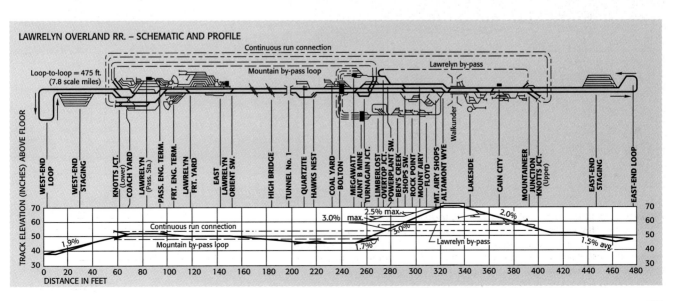

LAWRELYN OVERLAND RR. – SCHEMATIC AND PROFILE

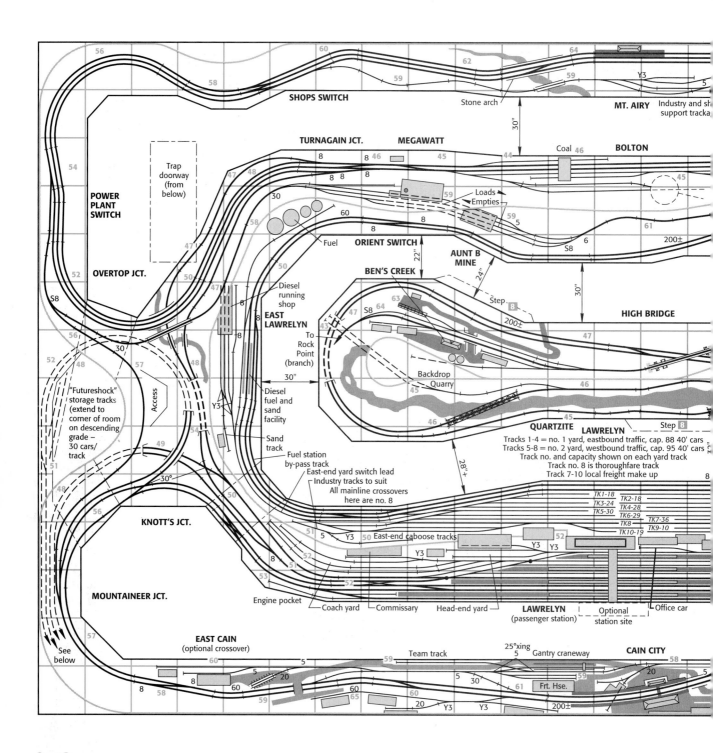

SHOPS SWITCH

Stone arch

MT. AIRY Industry and sh
support tracka

BOLTON

Coal 46

TURNAGAIN JCT.   MEGAWATT

POWER
PLANT
SWITCH

Trap
doorway
(from
below)

Loads
Empties

OVERTOP JCT.

S8

Fuel

ORIENT SWITCH

AUNT B
MINE

HIGH BRIDGE

Diesel
running
shop

BEN'S CREEK

EAST
LAWRELYN

S8

To
Rock
Point
(branch)

30"

Backdrop
Quarry

"Futureshock"
storage tracks
(extend to
corner of room
on descending
grade –
30 cars/
track

Access

Diesel
fuel and
sand
facility

QUARTZITE LAWRELYN
Tracks 1-4 = no. 1 yard, eastbound traffic, cap. 88 40' cars
Tracks 5-8 = no. 2 yard, westbound traffic, cap. 95 40' cars
Track no. and capacity shown on each yard track
Track no. 8 is thoroughfare track
Track 7-10 local freight make up

Sand
track

Fuel station
by-pass track
East-end yard switch lead
Industry tracks to suit
All mainline crossovers
here are no. 8

TK1-18
TK3-24   TK2-18
TK5-30   TK4-28
         TK6-29
         TK8   TK7-36
         TK10-19 TK9-10

KNOTT'S JCT.

East-end caboose tracks

Y3 Y3

MOUNTAINEER JCT.

Engine pocket
Coach yard Commissary Head-end yard

LAWRELYN
(passenger station)

Optional
station site

Office car

EAST CAIN
(optional crossover)

Team track

25°xing
Gantry craneway

CAIN CITY

See
below

Frt. Hse.

200±

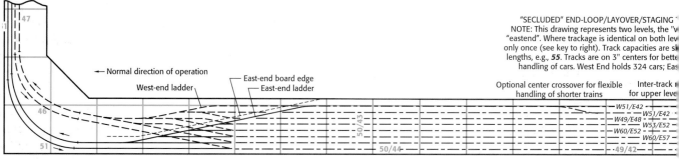

← Normal direction of operation

West-end ladder

East-end board edge
East-end ladder

"SECLUDED" END-LOOP/LAYOVER/STAGING
NOTE: This drawing represents two levels, the "w
"eastend". Where trackage is identical on both lev
only once (see key to right). Track capacities are s
lengths, e.g., **55**. Tracks are on 3" centers for bette
handling of cars. West End holds 324 cars; Eas

Optional center crossover for flexible
handling of shorter trains

Inter-track
for upper leve

W51/E42
W49/E48   W51/E42
W53/E52   W53/E52
W60/E52
          W60/E57
50/44   49/42

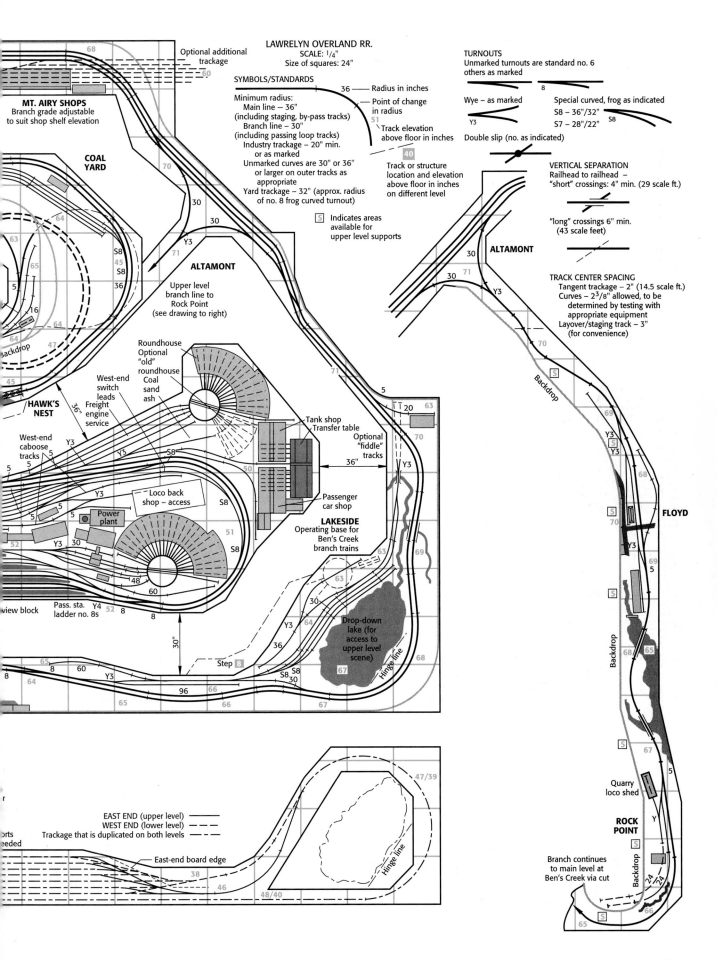

LAWRELYN OVERLAND RR.
SCALE: ¼"
Size of squares: 24"

MT. AIRY SHOPS
Branch grade adjustable
to suit shop shelf elevation

COAL YARD

Optional additional trackage

SYMBOLS/STANDARDS
Minimum radius:
Main line – 36"
(including staging, by-pass tracks)
Branch line – 30"
(including passing loop tracks)
Industry trackage – 20" min.
or as marked
Unmarked curves are 30" or 36"
or larger on outer tracks as
appropriate
Yard trackage – 32" (approx. radius
of no. 8 frog curved turnout)

36 — Radius in inches
— Point of change
in radius
Track elevation
above floor in inches

Track or structure
location and elevation
above floor in inches
on different level

S Indicates areas
available for
upper level supports

TURNOUTS
Unmarked turnouts are standard no. 6
others as marked

8

Wye – as marked
Y3

Double slip (no. as indicated)

Special curved, frog as indicated
S8 – 36"/32"
S7 – 28"/22"
S8

VERTICAL SEPARATION
Railhead to railhead –
"short" crossings: 4" min. (29 scale ft.)

"long" crossings 6" min.
(43 scale feet)

TRACK CENTER SPACING
Tangent trackage – 2" (14.5 scale ft.)
Curves – 2³⁄₈" allowed, to be
determined by testing with
appropriate equipment
Layover/staging track – 3"
(for convenience)

ALTAMONT
Upper level
branch line to
Rock Point
(see drawing to right)

ALTAMONT

HAWK'S NEST

West-end switch
leads
Freight
engine
service

West-end
caboose
tracks

Roundhouse
Optional
"old"
roundhouse
Coal
sand
ash

Tank shop
Transfer table

Optional
"fiddle"
tracks

Loco back
shop – access

Power plant

LAKESIDE
Operating base for
Ben's Creek
branch trains

Passenger
car shop

Pass. sta. Y4
ladder no. 8s

view block

Step 8

Drop-down
lake (for
access to
upper level
scene)

Hinge line

Hinge line

FLOYD

Backdrop

Backdrop

Quarry
loco shed

ROCK POINT

Branch continues
to main level at
Ben's Creek via cut

Backdrop

EAST END (upper level) ————
WEST END (lower level) – – – –
Trackage that is duplicated on both levels – ·· – ·· –

East-end board edge

Index and box score

The layout itself

Name	Page	Location	Size	Gauge	Radius	Square squares	Walk along entire main route	Sincerity— only once through scene	Entry and access
CN/CP in New Brunswick	9	Basement	20 x 31	O	68	13	Backtrack	No	Walk- and duck-under
Santa Fe—West Texas	15	Room	11 x 11	HO	30/24	15	No	Yes	Duck-under
Boston & Albany	20	Garage	16 x 30	O	50	15.5	Yes	Yes	Walk-under
Western Colorado	24	Room	11 x 14	Sn3	30	16	Backtrack	Yes	Walk-in
NKP—Conneaut Terminal	30	Garage	11 x 20 + 7 x 9	HO	33	24	Yes	Yes	Walk-in
WM—Thomas Subdivision	34	Attic	21 x 29	O	52	25	Backtrack	Yes	Walk-in
Santa Fe—Altus District	38	Room	11.5 x 19.5	HO	24	28	Backtrack	No	Walk-in
SP—Shasta Route	41	Room	11.5 x 19	HO	30	29	Yes	Yes	Walk-under
Eclectic Electric Lines	46	Basement	34 x 41	O	54	41	Yes	Yes	Walk-in
PRR—Middle and Pittsburgh Divs.	51	Building	24 x 32	S	48	41	Yes	Yes	Duck-under
San Joaquin Southwestern	54	Building	17 x 29	S	36	43	Yes	Yes	Walk-in
Erie-Lackawanna	57	Basement	14 x 15	N	20	43	Yes	No	Walk-in
Upper Mississippi Railroad	61	Basement	13 x 22	HO	26	50	Yes	Yes	Walk-in
San Juan Southern	64	Basement	25 x 42	On3	42	60	Yes	Yes	Walk-in
PRR and Ohio River & Western	68	Basement	18 x 23	HO, HOn3	30/22	40	Yes	Yes	Walk-in, duck-under
Atlantic & White Mountains	74	Basement	11 x 12 + 5 x 5	HO	20	29	Backtrack	No	Walk-in
Southern New England	81	Basement	17 x 22	HO	30	36	Yes	Yes	Walk-in
Athabaska and Columbia Pacific	84	Basement	14 x 19	N	20	63	Yes	Yes	Walk-in
GN—Johnson Pass Division	88	Basement	19 x 24	HO	30	67	Yes	Yes	Walk-in, duck-under
Lawrelyn Overland Railroad	92	Room	24 x 50	HO	36	120	Yes	Yes	Walk-in

Main routes

Name	Page	Compression ratio	Extent in train lengths	No. of main tracks	No. of passing points	Operating configuration	Continuous run option	Staging tracks No.	Capacity in car lengths
CN/CP in New Brunswick	9	30:1	12	1, 1	4	Wye to loop	Yes	3	75
Santa Fe—West Texas	15	60:1	3 and 7	2, 1	2	Loop to wye	Yes	3	75
Boston & Albany	20	25:1	7	2	4	Continuous and loop	Yes	6	145
Western Colorado	24	15:1	19	1	4	Point to point	No	3	33
NKP—Conneaut Terminal	30	6:1	4	1	2	Loop to loop	Yes	6	165
WM—Thomas Subdivision	34	60:1	9	1	4	Continuous and loop	Yes	4	80
Santa Fe—Altus District	38	34:1	15	1	4	Continuous and loop	Yes	4	64
SP—Shasta Route	41	55:1	13	1	5	Loop to loop	No	10	180
Eclectic Electric Lines	46	NA	7, 14	1, 2	3, 4	Wye/loop to loop	Yes	6	165
PRR—Middle and Pittsburgh Divs.	51	10:1	11	2, 4	7	Loop to loop	Yes	2	45
San Joaquin Southwestern	54	24:1	20	1	5	Loop to wye	No	7	90
Erie-Lackawanna	57	30:1	7, 7	2	7, 7	Stub/loop to loop	Yes	7	200
Upper Mississippi Railroad	61	NA	11	2	6	Continuous and loops	Yes	10	220
San Juan Southern	64	17:1	18	1	4	Point to point and loops	No	4	100
PRR and Ohio River & Western	68	25:1	12	2, 1	4	Continuous and point to loop	Yes	5	150
Atlantic & White Mountains	74	NA	27	1	4	Point to point and loops	No	3	20
Southern New England	81	12:1	3, 5	2	2	Loop to stub, loop	Yes	3	70
Athabaska and Columbia Pacific	84	40:1	30	1	9	Point to point and loops	No	4	96
GN—Johnson Pass Division	88	15:1	14	1	7	Loop to reverted loop	Yes	7	215
Lawrelyn Overland Railroad	92	17:1	16	2, 3	10	Loop to loop	Yes	12	640

Other features

Name	Page	Branch or subsidiary lines No.	Separation from main route	Gimmicks Double-decking % of layout area	Helixes No.	No. of concealed turns
CN/CP in New Brunswick	9	1	Vertical	20	0	
Santa Fe—West Texas	15	2	Horizontal, vertical	0	1	1
Boston & Albany	20	1	Horizontal	12*	1	2
Western Colorado	24	0		45	1	1.5
NKP—Conneaut Terminal	30	2	Horizontal, vertical	85	2	4
WM—Thomas Subdivision	34	1	Horizontal	35*	1	0.5
Santa Fe—Altus District	38	1	Vertical	0	0	
SP—Shasta Route	41	2	Both vertical	60	0	
Eclectic Electric Lines	46	3	2 horizontal, 1 vertical	40*	0	
PRR—Middle and Pittsburgh Divs.	51	0		2	2	4.5
San Joaquin Southwestern	54	2	Both vertical	4	0	
Erie-Lackawanna	57	1	Horizontal	40	2	4.5
Upper Mississippi Railroad	61	1	Vertical	0	0	
San Juan Southern	64	1	Horizontal	0	0	
PRR and Ohio River & Western	68	1	Vertical and horizontal	27*	1	
Atlantic & White Mountains	74	2	Both vertical	90	1	2.5
Southern New England	81	0		0	0	
Athabaska and Columbia Pacific	84	3	2 horizontal, 1 vertical	80	2	5.5
GN—Johnson Pass Division	88	0		0	0	
Lawrelyn Overland Railroad	92	1	Horizontal	7	0	

* Mushroom configuration with raised floor